I0882118

Intellectual Property Law in Switzerland

Intellectual Property Law in Switzerland

Fifth Edition

François Dessemontet

This book was originally published as a monograph in the International Encyclopaedia of Laws/Intellectual Property Law.

Founding Editor: Roger Blanpain
General Editor: Frank Hendrickx
Volume Editor: Hendrik Vanhees

Wolters Kluwer

Published by:
Kluwer Law International B.V.
PO Box 316
2400 AH Alphen aan den Rijn
The Netherlands
E-mail: lrs-sales@wolterskluwer.com
Website: www.wolterskluwer.com/en/solutions/kluwerlawinternational

Sold and distributed by:
Wolters Kluwer Legal & Regulatory U.S.
7201 McKinney Circle
Frederick, MD 21704
United States of America
E-mail: customer.service@wolterskluwer.com

DISCLAIMER: The material in this volume is in the nature of general comment only. It is not offered as advice on any particular matter and should not be taken as such. The editor and the contributing authors expressly disclaim all liability to any person with regard to anything done or omitted to be done, and with respect to the consequences of anything done or omitted to be done wholly or partly in reliance upon the whole or any part of the contents of this volume. No reader should act or refrain from acting on the basis of any matter contained in this volume without first obtaining professional advice regarding the particular facts and circumstances at issue. Any and all opinions expressed herein are those of the particular author and are not necessarily those of the editor or publisher of this volume.

ISBN 978-94-035-4923-1

e-Book: ISBN 978-94-035-4794-7
web-PDF: ISBN 978-94-035-4804-3
Stämpfli: ISBN 978-3-7272-3568-9

© 2022 Kluwer Law International BV, The Netherlands

All rights reserved. No part of this publication may be reproduced, stored in a retrieval system, or transmitted in any form or by any means, electronic, mechanical, photocopying, recording, or otherwise, without the prior written permission of the publisher.

Permission to use this content must be obtained from the copyright owner. More information can be found at: www.wolterskluwer.com/en/solutions/legal-regulatory/permissions-reprints-and-licensing

The Author

Of Counsel, Dessemontet & Ghosn, Avocats, Lausanne, Switzerland.

Prof. François Dessemontet studied at Lausanne University (*docteur en droit*, 1974), in Montreal and at the Max-Planck Institute of Munich. Admitted to the Bar of Lausanne (1975), he was a Professor at the School of Law of the University of Lausanne between 1976 and 2006, of which he is now professor emeritus. He also served as a Permanent Guest Professor for Intellectual Property at the University of Freiburg between 1977 and 2006 and a guest professor at the University of Nantes for eight years. Professor Dessemontet served as Chairman of the Third-Expert Committee on the Revision of Copyright Law, as well as a member of the Three-Expert Committee on the Revision of the Swiss Company Law. He has been Chairman of the Board of the CEDIDAC – Centre for Business Law of the University of Lausanne, which he founded in 1985, and has edited 70 treatises and monographs published by CEDIDAC, a series with 115 books published as of 2021. He is the author of over 270 publications on *Intellectual Property, Law of Obligations, International Private Law, Corporate Law and Arbitration Law*. Active in international arbitration, he has served as a member of approximately ninety international arbitration panels, two World Trade Organization (WTO) Dispute Resolution Board proceedings, and as an expert in approximately hundred World Intellectual Property Organization (WIPO) Uniform Domain Name Dispute Resolution Policy litigations as well as a mediator. Further, Prof. Dessemontet has been a director of two financial companies for twelve years and a member of a banking institution for twenty years. (*See* www.dessemontet.ch/biography.php).

The Author

Table of Contents

Table of Contents

List of Abbreviations

Courts

Appeal Comm.	*Rekurskommission, Commission fédérale de recours en matière de propriété intellectuelle*
Appel. Ct	*Cour de cassation, Chambre des recours, Appellationshof,* (Appellate Court)
Arbit. Trib.	*Tribunal arbitral, Schiedsgericht* (Arbitral Tribunal)
Cant. Ct	*Tribunal cantonal, Kantonsgericht* (Cantonal Court)
Civ. Ct	*Cour de Justice civile, Obergericht* (Civil Court)
Com. Ct	*Tribunal de commerce, Handelsgericht* (Commercial Court)
Dist. Ct	*Tribunal de district, Bezirksgericht* (District Court)
Fed. Pat. Trib.	*Federal Patent Trib.* (in existence since 2012), *Bundespatentgericht, Tribunal fédéral des brevets*; *cases to be found* on www.bundespatentgericht.ch
Fed. Trib. Adm.	*Federal Administrative Tribunal, Tribunal administratif fédéral, Bundesverwaltungsgericht.*
Just. Ct	*Cour de Justice, Obergericht* (Civil Court)
Trib. Fed.	*Tribunal fédéral, Bundesgericht* (Federal Tribunal)

References Sources

ACTA	Anti-Counterfeiting Trade Agreement of 15 April 2011 (not ratified)
ATF	*Arrêts du Tribunal fédéral suisse* (Official Compilation of Judgments of the Swiss Federal Tribunal) (until 1994, including Vol. 120: I: administrative and constitutional cases; II: civil cases; III: debt and bankruptcy cases; IV: criminal cases; V: social assurances. Since 1994, starting from Vol. 121: I: constitutional cases; II: administrative and international public law cases; III: civil and bankruptcy cases; IV: criminal cases; V: social assurances)

List of Abbreviations

BJM	*Basler juristische Mitteilungen* (Judicial Communications of Basle)
EPO	European Patent Office
EU	European Union
ECJ	European Court of Justice
FF	*Feuille fédérale* (Federal Bulletin) (published weekly by the Chancery of the Swiss Confederation, Berne)
GATT	General Agreement on Tariffs and Trade
GUI	Graphical User Interface
JdT	*Journal des Tribunaux* (Reporter of the Courts) (Lausanne)
OJ	Official Journal of the European Community
OR	Official Reporter of Swiss Federal Laws
PCT	Patent Cooperation Treaty
PMM Bl	*Patent-, Muster- und Markenblatt* (Patents, Trademarks, and Design Bulletin) (Federal Intellectual Property Office, Berne)
RDS	*Revue de droit suisse* (Review of Swiss Law) (Basle)
RIDA	*Revue internationale de droit d'auteur* (International Review of Author's Right) (Paris)
RO	Recueil Officiel des Lois Fédérales (Official Reporter of the Federal Laws)(same as OR above, French edition)
RS	*Recueil systématique du droit fédéral* (also: *Systematische Sammlung des Bundesrechts*) (Systematic Compilation of Federal Laws and Decrees) (Federal Chancery, Berne)
RSJ	*Revue suisse de jurisprudence* (also: *Schweizerische Juristenzeitung*) (Swiss Review of Case Law) (Zurich)
RSJB	*Revue de la Société des juristes bernois* (Review of the Society of Jurists of Berne)
RSPI	*Revue suisse de la propriété intellectuelle* (Swiss Review of Intellectual Property) (Zurich) (until 1996)
RSPIDA	*Revue suisse de la propriété industrielle et du droit d'auteur* (Swiss Review of Industrial Property and Copyright) (Zurich) (Note that this is the same review as mentioned in the preceding entry, but as published before 1985)

SIC	*Revue du droit de la propriété intellectuelle, de l'information et de la concurrence* (also: *Zeitschrift für Immaterialgüter-, Informations- und Wettbewerbsrecht*) (Review of Intellectual Property, Informations' and Competitions' Law) (Note that this review succeeds to the one mentioned as RSPI above, but as published from 1997); starting 2021 the Publisher is Helbing & Lichtenhahn, Basle. The Review can be accessed through www. legalis for cases and articles.
SJ	*Semaine judiciaire* (Weekly Judicial Report) (Geneva)
SR	Systematic Recueil of the Swiss Legislation (*see* above RS)
TRIPS	Trade-Related Aspects of Intellectual Property
UCA	Unfair Competition Act
UNO	United Nations Organization
US	United States
WPPT	WIPO Performances and Phonograms Treaty
WTO	World Trade Organization
ZR	*Blätter für zürcherische Rechtsprechung* (Zurich Case Reports)

List of Abbreviations

General Introduction

§1. GENERAL BACKGROUND

I. Geography and History

1. Switzerland is a country poor in national resources, but for water and wood. Economic development started later in the seventeenth century. The banking industry and ceramic manufacturing were spurred by the immigration of French Huguenots after the revocation of the *Edit de Nantes* by the King of France in 1685. For the eighteenth and the first half of the nineteenth century, however, emigration of the labour force and mercenaries was the only effective way of fighting against unemployment and poverty in the Swiss countryside.

II. Political System

2. When the new Confederation emerged in the middle of the nineteenth century, the constitutional apportionment of jurisdiction between the Swiss States (cantons) and the central authorities divided public opinion. In 1866, the people rejected the concept that the Central State could edict a Copyright Act. In 1882, it rejected as well the central competence regarding patent legislation.

The Swiss electorate is, therefore, the only population in the world that could express twice an opinion on the suitability of intellectual property legislation, and the opinion was each time negative.

3. Later on, the Confederation as such received legislative powers for the whole area of intellectual property. Still, the first patent statute was noticeably narrow, and Switzerland has been cited as the paramount example of industrialization taking place without national patents.[1] Then, it was under the pressure of our big neighbours, France for copyright and Germany for patents, that our federal legislature passed enactments on intellectual property. Nowadays, the pressure to harmonize our law with that of the European Union (EU) certainly remains the moving force behind our legislative programmes, as will be seen, for example, with the Law on Designs and Models of 2001 and the revision of the Copyright Act in 2019.

1. E. Schiff, *Industrialization Without National Patents*, The Netherlands (1869–1912), Switzerland (1850–1907) (Princeton, 1970).

III. Population Statistics

4. Switzerland is a small country, with 8,830,283 inhabitants at the end of 2021 and an estimated 8,927,007 at the end of 2022.[2] Roughly two-thirds of the residents speak German, one-fifth French, 10% Italian and 1% *Rheto-Romanche*.[3] The residents of foreign citizenship account for more than one-fourth of the Swiss citizens. It is rumoured that the economic importance of Switzerland might be proportionally superior to the figure of its population.[4] For new or modified brands especially, Switzerland is a test market, which explains that many litigations are reported in the area of trademarks and tradenames.

5. This might explain why industrialists and pharmaceutical laboratories pushed towards a strong intellectual property protection during the second half of the twentieth century. Switzerland played, for example, a leading role in the negotiations towards a General Agreement on Tariffs and Trade (GATT)/Agreement on Trade-Related Aspects of Intellectual Property (TRIPS), as well as in the Western-nations reluctance to suspend patent protection during the COVID-19 pandemic.

§2. Historical Background

I. Before the 1798 Revolution

6. Modern Intellectual property derives from the privileges of old. In 1531, Basle edited the first law against the copying of books, a monopoly valid for three years being granted to the local printers.[5]

The old Federal Diet gave privileges in 1659, 1676, 1680, 1703, 1760 and 1786, for example, for musical works or a Greek-Latin dictionary. The States gave privileges for inventions, for example, in 1534 (Graubünden), 1577 (Berne), 1730 and 1741 (Zurich). The city of St-Gall imposed in 1537 on textile producers and traders the use of a sign of identification, what would be called nowadays a 'collective' trademark or a 'certification' mark.

2. *See* www.countrymeters.info/fr/. Swiss territory measures approximately 41,000 square kilometres.
3. *See* F. Dessemontet, *Le droit des langues en Suisse* (Law of Languages in Switzerland) 19 et seq. (Québec, 1984), (population).
4. Swiss imports totalled CHF 265 billion in 2017. Swiss exports amounted to CHF 294 billion. In 2020 imports diminished 11.2%, and the exports 7.1%, due to the COVID-19 pandemic. However, both imports and exports are on the rise again in 2021 and 2022. The Swiss finance and insurance industries are very active in foreign markets. According to the Global Innovation Index prepared by Cornell University, INSEAD and the World Intellectual Property Organization, Switzerland has been from 2010 through 2021 at least world leader or second-best ranking in innovation, according among other factors to the number of patents filed and the number of companies established.
5. Text cited by A. Troller, 39, n. 82. Most historical notes in Swiss literature are taken from the standard work of A. Troller, *Immaterialgüterrecht* (Intellectual Property), vol. 1, 39 et seq. (3d ed., Basle & Francfort-on-the-Main, 1983).

II. After the 1798 Revolution

7. The first Swiss Patent Act was enacted on 25 April 1799 and lasted three years. Then some cantons passed Copyright and/or Patent Acts, for example, Geneva in 1827, or Ticino 1835. A Treaty between the cantons on copyright was open to ratification in 1854, and only six cantons did not adhere.

8. International bilateral treaties were entered into with France (1864), Belgium (1867), Italy (1868) and various German states (1869, consolidated in 1882). Then came the memberships in the Paris Union (1883) on Industrial Property and in the Berne Union (1886) on Copyright.

9. The main enactments and revisions were as follows:

- 1879, 1891, 1992, 2013 and 2021: Law on Trademarks;
- 1883, 1922, 1992, 2007 and 2019: Law on Copyright;
- 1887, 1907 and 1954: Law on Patents (revised on substance in 1976, 1999, 2007 and 2016);
- 1900, 2001 and 2007: Law on Designs and Models, now Law on Designs.

The end of the twentieth century has brought an overhaul of most ancient statutes. Minor changes have been made pursuant to the entry into force of the TRIPS Agreement and the WIPO Internet Treaties. Further changes may be expected in the future to keep in line with the development of the European law in the field of intellectual property as well as in other areas. Yet it should be noted that in 2021 the European Commission failed in its endeavour to oblige Switzerland to a constant adaptation of its legislation to keep it in conformity with developments of European law in all areas through the conclusion of a so-called Framework Agreement replacing the existing bilateral treaties. Most notably, Switzerland did object to the European Court of Justice having the last word on the conformity of Swiss law with European law. As a consequence, Switzerland is now dealt with as a 'Third Party' and cannot participate for the moment on an equal footing in common European promising enterprises, such as scientific research within the Horizon programme.

Chapter 1. Copyright and Neighbouring Rights

§1. Sources of Legislation

I. The Law on Copyright and Neighbouring Rights of 9 October 1992

10. The New Copyright Act of 1992, as amended in 2019 for the last time, replaced the Law of 1922, which was amended in 1955 following the ratification of the Brussels Act of the Berne Convention.[6] Three-expert committees and two Bills (1984 and 1989) were necessary to prepare for the enactment of the 1992 Law. The Copyright Act was modified in 2002 through the addition of Article 12*bis* providing for the national exhaustion of copyrights on audio-visual works in derogation of the principle of the international exhaustion for copyrighted works in general. Article 12*bis* was subsequently amended by the law of 20 June 2003 (RS 443.1). Further, the revision of 5 October 2007 introduced the following major changes, some to comply with the WIPO Internet Treaties of 1996 and some going beyond those requirements:

- A right to make available to members of the public.
- Expanded legal remedies against the circumvention of technological safeguards, subject to the exception of consumers' private uses.
- Modified exceptions in favour, among others, of Internet users and service providers, public libraries and other archives, broadcasting organizations and the disabled.
- The performers' moral right to attribution.

The signature and later implementation of the Anti-Counterfeiting Trade Agreement (ACTA) Treaty of 15 April 2011 by Switzerland should not have required any legislative change, at least according to the opinion of the Swiss Government as advised by the Federal Intellectual Property Institute. However, after the rejection of ACTA by the European Parliament on 4 July 2012, the Swiss Government decided not to ratify ACTA.

In 2012, a governmentally appointed Working Party with representatives of interested circles prepared minor modifications of the Copyright Act; a Bill to this effect was presented to Parliament in November 2017 and the Parliament adopted the revised Copyright Act on 27 September 2019.[7] The former state of the law as regards downloading (allowed for private use) and uploading such in P2P torrents (illegal) is not be changed, contrary to the legislation HADOPI in France and the practice in Germany, to name two of Switzerland's neighbours.

Concerning internet infringement, the main amendments to the former Act are as follows:

6. RS 231.1. An English translation is of the original 1992 Copyright Act is to be found in WIPO, Copyright 1993, No. 9, September 1993, Geneva. Current texts of Swiss laws and ordinances can be found at www.wipolex.wipo.int
7. The revised Act entered into force on 1 Apr. 2020.

- a provision exonerates hosts from liability if they install a system of notice of a suspected violation of copyright, and then enforce takedown of the infringing material and *stay down* (new);
- a civil action is made available to enforce the obligations of hosting services under Article 39d CA in serious cases of infringement by users;
- copyright owners may have access to the IP addresses of individual net users, but only whenever the copyright owner intends to file a criminal complaint against the infringer.

The Swiss legislature did not wish for Swiss law to reach out to foreign hosting or other piracy sites, and the system is limited to Swiss hosting services.

In other areas, the following modifications should be noted:

- non-original photographs receive a protection for fifty years after execution;
- the term of protection of neighbouring rights is extended to seventy years since the first publication; if it has not been published, the term is seventy years since the right started to exist; for broadcasts, the term remains fifty years from their first broadcasting;
- authors and performers receive an untransferable right of remuneration on the making available of audio-visual works on demand ('video on demand') (streaming);
- the collective licensing schemes apply in more areas than under the former Act;
- the procedure for adopting and reviewing the tariffs of the collecting right societies (sometimes called collective right management organizations) are streamlined;
- further exceptions allow for data mining and texts mining, as well as for libraries and archival purposes;
- the use of so-called orphan works is allowed against the payment of a fee to a collecting right society.

– an extended collective licensing framework enables the collecting right societies to grant licensing arrangements for right owners who are not represented in the societies, yet do not expressly opt-out of the arrangement.

11. The present legislation does not confer a public lending right when the lending is free of charge. No *droit de suite* has been introduced. No complete alignment on the European Directive on Copyright in the Digital Single Market of 2019 was intended. That might be the topic of a further effort towards revision, as is suggested by the collecting right societies. For the moment, the new European Digital Services Act and related European developments do not necessarily entail the revision of Swiss law on internet platforms.

II. Ordinance on Copyright and Neighbouring Rights of 26 April 1993

12. The ordinance mainly regulates the Federal Arbitral Commission which oversees the tariffs applied by collecting right societies. One further provision deals with the interoperability exception for software, and four other articles with the intervention of customs authorities.[8]

III. Case Law

13. Approximately 320 cases have been published since 1923 in the area of copyright. Some of them are outdated because of amendments to the Law, but most of them are still of persuasive authority. They are to be found mainly in the two following reports:

(1) *Bundesgerichtsentscheide* [BGE] = *Arrêts du Tribunal fédéral suisse* (Official Reporter of the Judgments of the Federal Tribunal) [ATF], Lausanne, since 1876.
(2) Schweizerische Mitteilungen über Immaterialgüterrecht (Swiss Review of Intellectual Property) [SMI] = Revue suisse de la propriété intellectuelle [RSPI and RSPISDA] Zurich, now SIC (Zeitschrift für Immaterialgüter-, Informations- und Wettbewerbsrecht = Revue du droit de la propriété intellectuelle, de l'information et de la concurrence) (Review of Swiss Intellectual Property Law, Information Law and Competition Law) since 1997, to be accessed at www.legalis.ch. Some unpublished decisions can also be found at *www.bger.ch.*

§2. Subject Matter of Protection

I. Different Categories of Protected Works

A. *According to Statute*

14. While some statutes in the British tradition attempt exhaustively to classify works, the French and Germanic traditions in copyright law undertake to protect any and all works of 'art or literature' in the broadest meaning of these terms. Swiss Copyright Law follows this latter approach.

The Copyright Act does not condition legal protection on the fact that a work may be subsumed within a given class of works. Article 2(2) of the 1992 Act merely lists examples of protected works, but it does not preclude the protection of subject matter which might not be mentioned in that list or not included in one of the categories which it enumerates. But for minor differences of a terminological nature, the

8. RS 231.11, modified e.g., on 21 May 2008 (RO 2008, 24227), 7 Oct. 2015 and 29 Sep. 2017 (RO 2017, 6213 and RO 2021 589).

list in Article 2(2) coincides with that set forth in Article 2(1) of the Paris Act of the Berne Convention for the Protection of Literary and Artistic Works,[9] although it is less detailed.

15. For example, Article 2(2) of the 1992 Act uses the general term 'literary, scientific and other works that make use of language', but does not mention 'books, pamphlets, ... lectures, addresses, sermons' which nonetheless fall under the term 'language'. After listing 'works of music and other acoustic works', it distinguishes between 'works of fine art, particularly painting, sculpture and graphic works' and 'works with scientific or technical content, such as drawings, plans, maps or three-dimensional representations'. It then lists the following: 'works of architecture' and 'of applied art'; 'photographic, cinematographic and other visual or audio-visual works'; 'works of dance or mime'. Article 2(3) of the 1992 Act states that 'computer programs shall also be deemed works', but without specifying what kind of works they belong to. Sports events are not considered to be works of art, nor are the rules for practising a sport or organizing a competition. Of course, choreography, even on ice, is considered to be 'artistic' within the meaning of the Copyright Act. Perfumes or recipes are excluded from the copyright protection in Switzerland, but the law against unfair competition might apply. Further, photos of meals e.g., in cooking manuals or on Internet can be protected under the new quasi-copyright regime for photographs even devoid of individuality.

16. Works 'with scientific or technical content' merit a special remark.[10] As copyright does not protect ideas or technology, it is not possible to protect a scientific or technical work on the strength of its underlying notions: the judge has to ask whether to protect it on the basis of its expression or form.[11] As has been expressed in a case decided by the Federal Tribunal:

> In order to know if copyright has been infringed, the sole test is whether the author's thoughts have been stated in a personal, original manner. This may be the case even for empty thoughts.[12]

Now, on the one hand, it sometimes happens that a given idea can be correctly expressed only with one definite statement: for example, since logarithms are not

9. RS 0.231.15.
10. *See* in general M. Altenpohl, *Der urheberrechtliche Schutz von Forschungsresultaten* (The Copyright Protection for Results of Scientific Research), thesis (Zurich, 1987).
11. *See* ATF 113 II 306 (no protection afforded to the idea that the role of a famous Viennese psychiatrist for children should be appraised on the background of the controversy opposing S. Freud and C. Jung); ATF 120 II 65 (no protection afforded to the concept of space between buildings on a university campus and their planned environment). *See also* Civ. Ct Schwyz, 31 Dec. 1996, SIC 1997, 143 (denying copyright protection to tables showing correct air pressures for tires because there was no room for creative freedom in the presentation of such data); Cant. Ct Vaud, 16 Jan. 2009, SIC 2010, 428 (protection denied to simple sketches of a roundabout and a bridge to redirect road traffic).
12. ATF 88 IV 123, esp. 129.

subject to variations of form, the courts have not protected logarithmic tables or stationery for logarithmic computations;[13] nor have accounting charts and papers, or systems of musical notation, been protected.[14] On the other hand, it is often the case that the same concept may be expressed in a variety of ways; thus, each of these expressions is protected to the extent it is individual.[15] It should also be noted that prior case law tended to raise the standard of protection when the special statute protecting industrial designs also applied to the work at issue, but the special design protection was not available because of formalities not being complied with, or if the protection had expired. The reluctance of the Swiss courts to afford copyright protection in such a situation led to enforce a heightened standard of individuality; the recent developments of the German case law in this respect now brings us back to a less stringent Swiss judicial requirement of individuality for the copyright protection of designs in the future (*see* footnote 73 below).

17. In including 'photographic works' with 'cinematographic and other visual or audio-visual works', the legislature endeavoured to clarify that all sorts of visual works are protectable, be they video clips, holograms, video samplings, multimedia works,[16] etc. Nonetheless, some courts had previously taken a rigorous approach to the requirement of creativity as applied to photographs, and the 1985–1986 Third-Expert Committee explicitly rejected a proposal to overturn the current case law.[17] Except for the Unfair Competition Act (UCA), there is no other law available to protect photographs.[18] Thus, the 1992 Act had left many press photographs lacking individuality without protection. The 2019 revision of the Copyright Act has now provided for protection similar to the German protection for all photographs, even

13. ATF 64 II 162; Appel. Ct Berne, *in* RSJB 1942, 37.
14. ATF 70 II 57. *See also* Fed. Trib. *in* ZR 1932, 109 (an advertising method); Appel. Ct Solothurn *in* RSJ 1951, 59 (denying protection to an educational game); Fed. Trib. *in* RSPI 1995, 101 (protection denied to scientific researches conducted at the Swiss Institute of Technology).
15. *See*, e.g., ATF 69 II 53 (booklet on mental arithmetic); Justice Commission Lucerne *in* RSPI 1994, 292 (illustrated catalogue for art exhibition).
16. *See* J. de Werra, *Le multimédia en droit d'auteur* (Multimedia and Copyright Law), RSPI 237 (1995); *see also* W. Egloff, *MultimediaProdukte und Urheberrecht* (Multimedia Products and Copyright Law), 4 *Plädoyer* (1995) 38.
17. *See* ATF 130 III 714 (denying for want of individuality the protection of a photograph of Christoph Meili (known for violating the banking secrecy in connection with orphaned bank accounts). But *see*, e.g., ATF 130 III 168 (protecting a photograph of Bob Marley in concert, by virtue of the individuality of the image which uniquely captured the musician's energy, playing with his hair flying); *see also* Judgment Bob Marley II, 25 Nov. 2010, Federal Tribunal Case 4A_522/2010, confirming the decision of the Cantonal Court of Zurich not to allow any damages for the reproduction of that photograph on posters; *see also* SIC 2011, 227/Bob Marley Case II, Sup. Ct of Zurich; further, denying protection, *see* Appel. Ct Zurich *in* RSJ 1972, 308; Appel. Ct Zurich *in* RSPI 1985, 221; But *see* Just. Ct Geneva *in* SJ 1964, 171; ATF 54 II 52. A certain dissatisfaction with the *Meili* and *Marley* cases may explain why the Parliament following the Government, both listening to the advice of Dr. W. Egloff, decided to enact a protection for photographs independently from their individuality. Cf. Ch. Schütz, Schutz der Pressephotographie, SIC 2016, 53; R. Oertli, Neues Urheberrecht für Fotografien, SIC 2020, 600; G. Walter, Der neue Art. 2 Abs. 3*bis* URG, SIC 2021, 377.
18. The UCA of 19 Dec. 1986, as revised for the last time on 13 Jun. 2013 [RS 241].

those devoid of any originality. The occasional photograph showing enough individuality will be protected for the usual period of protection of all works, while the photographs devoid of individuality will be protected fifty years from their production.

B. According to the Courts

18. Thus, the 1992 Act, as revised, continues the large scope of Swiss copyright protection, which a summary perusal of the cases will serve to illustrate. No general conclusion should be drawn from these examples since the facts of each case play an essential role in all copyright litigations.[19]

1. Federal Tribunal

19. The Supreme Court has affirmed the possibility of protecting the following types of works that might not be obviously covered by copyright as a matter of course: a building[20] or the layout of a sales outlet;[21] maps and plans such as a map of cliffs;[22] a catalogue shaped like a silhouette;[23] clothing designs;[24] the title of a newspaper;[25] mathematical forms and technical charts;[26] a design for embroideries;[27] the character of Mickey Mouse,[28] but not of Sherlock Holmes or Watson;[29] a treatise on typewriting[30] and an article on the psychological effects of colours;[31] stenographic transcriptions of an interview.[32]

---

19. For further analysis, *see* para. 56.
20. ATF 56 II 413; ATF 58 II 290. The Fed. Trib. denied the protection of copyright to a highway tunnel devoid of originality, but envisaged the protection of technical data relating to it under Arts 5a and 5b UCA against the piracy of technical data that have been delivered within the framework of a contract or a procurement competition; *see* SIC 2013, 445.
21. ATF 100 II 167.
22. ATF 59 II 401; ATF 103 Ib 324; Fed. Trib. *in* JAAC 1981, 330.
23. ATF 57 I 62.
24. ATF 60 II 62.
25. ATF 64 II 109.
26. ATF 64 II 162.
27. ATF 76 II 97.
28. ATF 77 II 377.
29. ATF 85 II 120. For further details, *see* para. 44.
30. ATF 88 IV 123. Affirming the protection of a handbook on chemical substances for firemen, ATF 136 III 225. For cases denying protection to sheer meteorological or pharmaceutical data, *see* Fed. Trib. *in* SIC 2006, 260 & SIC 2008, 482. Denying protection to a company logo, for want of originality: Fed. Trib. *in* SIC 2001, 729.
31. ATF 101 II 102.
32. Fed. Trib. *in* RSPI 1994, 64.

2. Cantonal Tribunals

20. Swiss courts have considered, *inter alia*, the following types of works as protected by copyright: choreographic works;[33] architectural works and pieces of furniture;[34] advertising posters;[35] geographic works such as city or tourist maps;[36] automobile guides;[37] catalogues, even of items in the public domain;[38] a petition before a court of law;[39] the coat of arms of a city;[40] the cabaret character of a listless college professor;[41] the Oscar statue;[42] a firm's logo;[43] computer software.[44] It is interesting to note that Swiss courts have rejected protection for logarithmic tables,[45] banal advertising letters,[46] advertising methods[47] and a game for children.[48]

II. Works Excluded from Protection

21. According to Article 5 Copyright Act excluded from protection are the following sorts of works.

33. Arbit. Trib. Zurich *in* RSPI 1990, 338.
34. Sup. Ct Zurich, RSPI 1991, 88; Sup. Ct Zug, SIC 2010, 721; Canton. Trib., St. Gallen, SIC 2001, 491; Civ. Ct, Zurich, SIC 2001, 504; Civ. Ct Schwytz in *Entscheide Schwytz* (Decisions' Compilation of Schwytz), 1973/1974, 24. *See also* Appel. Ct Zurich *in* RSJ 1972, 202 (exhibition stall). But *see* Appel. Ct Aargau in RSPIDA 1975, 153 (protection denied to a house for lack of creativity).
35. Fed. Trib. *in* ZR 1932, 109 et seq.; *See* Appel. Ct Zurich *in* ZR 1932, 290 (billboards). But *see* Appel. Ct Zurich *in* RSJ 1971, 277 (protection denied).
36. *See*, e.g., Appel. Ct Berne, SIC 2009, 244 (affirming protection of the maps 'Expo-02'); Com. Ct Berne *in* RSPIDA 1978, 272; Com. Ct Berne *in* RSJB 1978, 282; Cant. Ct Graubünden *in* RSPIDA 1982, 184; Cant. Ct Neuchâtel *in* RSJ 1926/1927, 206 (map of Mt. Olympus). In an unpublished decision of 17 Nov. 2006, the Geneva Ct of Justice denied the protection of sheer free hand sketches showing the best ways to climb mountains and cliffs as they were necessarily dictated by the information they conveyed, and as such not individual enough to be protected by copyright.
37. Just. Ct Geneva *in* SJ 1977, 433; Just. Ct Geneva *in* RSPIDA 1978, 108. For the protection of a teaching handbook, *see* Dist. Ct Horgen, SIC 2002, 589.
38. Fed. Trib. *in* ZR 1926, 368. For a Berne Appel. Ct decision granting protection to articles in the press *see* SIC 2001, 613.
39. Appel. Ct Zurich *in* RSJ 1933/1934, 266.
40. Cant. Ct St-Gall *in* RSJ 1963, 169.
41. Appel. Ct Zurich *in* RSJ 1949, 204.
42. Cant. Ct Zug *in* RSPI 1992, 53. For the tattoo reproducing the Mexican skull well-known all over the world as the symbol of All Saints Day, see Com. Ct. Aarau, SIC 2015, 449.
43. In re J.P.S., Appel. Ct Berne *in* RSJ 1981, 65; Appel. Ct Berne *in* RSPIDA 1980, 83; Appel. Ct Berne *in* RSJB 1981, 171 (protection denied).
44. Cant. Ct Zug *in* RSPI 1989, 58; Civ. Ct Aargau *in* RSPI 1991, 79; Just. Ct Zurich *in* RSPI 1992, 199; Cant. Ct Zurich, SIC 2011, 230.
45. Appel. Ct Berne *in* RSJB 1942, 37.
46. Appel. Ct Zurich *in* ZR 1979, 194; Appel. Ct Zurich *in* RSPIDA 1980, 189. Sup. Ct Berne, SIC 2000, 500 (rejecting the protection under copyright of the domain name 'beam.to'); Sup. Ct BL SIC 2000, 285 (rejecting the protection of the design of a bicycle under the Copyright Act); Sup. Ct Berne, SIC 2016, 56 (rejecting the protection of a questionnaire and replies for the driving licence examination).
47. Fed. Trib. *in* ZR 1932, 109.
48. Appel. Ct Solothurn *in* RSJ 1951, 59.

A. Laws, Ordinances, International Treaties and Other Official Acts

22. This exception encompasses all regulatory acts of a general nature, such as the Acts of Parliament (be it the Federal or the State Parliaments), the Federal or State Ordinances, the regulatory by-laws of state or city corporations, the Ordinances and Decrees entered by the Federal or the State governments and the Judiciary.

23. The Collective Agreements in the area of employment and the renting of premises are also excepted from the protection, at least when a Government (be it State or Federal) has extended their validity throughout the industry.

24. No exception from protection applies to the comments and explanatory notes, when they are of individual character, but official guidelines, reports on the bills pending before Parliament and Legislative programmes should partake of the same uncopyrightability as the statutory Acts, although maybe under the heading of 'reports' mentioned in Article 5(c). The exception does not apply to privately drafted General Terms and Conditions, nor to Standard Forms of Agreements, nor to Industry Standards and Technical Regulations issued by other entities than the State.

B. Means of Payment

25. Banknotes and coins, as well as other official means of payment, if any, are excepted from copyrightability. There is some controversy about whether this exception encompasses all means of payment, as was intended by the Third-Expert Committee. For example, the drawing or scenery to be found on private checks formerly emitted by banks were not excluded from copyright, in this writer's view,[49] because the main purpose behind that provision was to exclude any unjust claim by the Swiss National Bank against cartoonists who might want to use the reproduction of the banknote.[50] There is also a mounting controversy about postage stamps that may or may not qualify as 'means of payment' under Article 5(b).

C. Decisions, Minutes and Reports of Public Authorities

26. As Article 5(a) excepts from copyright general Acts and Ordinances, Article 5(c) excepts particular decisions that are handed down in the Executive or the Judiciary, as well as reports and minutes of State agencies and all branches of Government.

27. Arbitral awards are not covered by this exception, nor are the expert opinions, depositions, technical reports, etc., that may have been filed by persons other

49. For a differing view, *see* Barrelet & Egloff, No. 5 *ad* Art. 5 Copyright Act.
50. *See* Fed. Trib. *in* RSPI 1986, 124 (*'L'Illustré'* case); ATF 99 IV 50.

than state agencies and public offices in the course of a public enquiry or litigation. The issue of the confidentiality of arbitral awards is a different question; unlike in some other jurisdictions, arbitration awards are usually confidential when the seat of the arbitral tribunal is in Switzerland. This does not interfere with the regulations applying, for example, to the institutional arbitration proceedings, WIPO and WTC arbitrations and other similar arbitration proceedings[51].[52]

28. The exception of Article 5(c) combines qualifications relating to the source of the work and to its nature, so that many books, reviews or other material published by the State or Federal authorities still enjoy the protection of copyright; such is the case, for instance, of geographic maps, information notices, school books, etc.

29. As there is no rule on works made for hire or on employed authors within the Copyright Act itself, the Copyright Act does not regulate the ownership of copyrights of public works either.[53] It entirely depends upon the applicable public regulations. For instance, this writer has advocated that the Swiss Universities enjoy no title to the copyright covering works made by professors, candidates to the doctorate and other students, while the copyright of works made by assistants should in many cases be deemed to have been conveyed by implication to professors – but never to the University.[54]

D. Letters Patent for Inventions and Published Patent Applications

30. As with most patent systems nowadays, the Swiss Patent Act provides for publication not only of the patents that have been granted but also of patent applications.[55] There is no copyright protection on the patents, nor on applications which have been published. As the very idea of the patent system is to contribute to the technological development by way of generalizing the knowledge of the invention to the public, the uncopyrightability of patents and applications is understandable.

31. Nonetheless, the same reasoning might lead to denying the copyrightability of all sorts of technical reviews, scientific books and other sources of knowledge. The difference is, of course, that the patent owner has received a monopoly in

51. See F. Dessemontet, Arbitration and Confidentiality, 7 The American Review of International Arbitration, 1996, 299-318.
52. *See* for the non-copyrightability of notices for medical drugs Decision by the President Civ. Ct. BS, SIC 2004, 490.
53. *See* for the Federal Polytechnical Schools in Zurich and Lausanne Art. 36 of the Law on the Federal Polytechnicals Schools (RS 414.110) (title onto software is conveyed as of right to the Schools; for all other copyrighted matters the title remains with the authors).
54. *See* F. Dessemontet, *Les droits d'auteur à l'Université* (Copyrights in University), in *Droit cantonal et droit fédéral* (Cantonal and Federal Law) 13 et seq. (Lausanne, 1991). For cantonal universities cantonal statutes usually allow the authors to keep their copyrights while all other intellectual property rights are assigned *ex lege* to the State.
55. *See* paras 224 and 233 et seq. For the importance of determining who is the author of a non-copyrightable official report as concerns the Freedom of Information Act (Law on the Transparency, RS 152.3) see Fed. Trib. SIC 2020, 620.

exchange for his disclosing to the world the technical information that is mentioned in the patent, whereas the publisher of reviews and books did not.

Nobody ever argued that the Copyright Act, which protects the form or the expression rather than the substance or the idea, hinders the generalization of knowledge that is to be found in technical or scientific publications. On the contrary, marketing is helped by copyright protection. The same might well hold true for patents and applications. At least the data banks on patents and applications should, therefore, escape the exception to copyright under Article 5(d).

E. Translations (of the Aforementioned Works) as Are Required by Law

32. The exception of Article 5(2) is self-explanatory. If there is no copyright, there is also no possibility that one and only one publisher would hold the rights to the translation of a state work – as one publisher once tried to obtain them for the draft of a new Constitution then published under a publishing contract with the Swiss Confederation.

33. Private translations of judicial decisions, or minutes, or reports are not subject to the exception, as long as they are not mandated by law.

III. Special Categories of Works

A. Computer Software

34. Until the end of the 1980s, the dominant opinion in Switzerland was favourable to a *sui generis* protection for software. The Third-Expert Committee still opined in favour of a wholly separate set of rules on software within the general framework of the Copyright Bill of 1987. Nevertheless, the Government's Bill of 1989 just provided for total assimilation of software and other works of art or literature. Article 2(3) of the 1992 Act, therefore, states that 'software is deemed to be a work' within the meaning of the law.[56]

There are a few remnants of the separate chapter regulating software differently from other works.

56. ATF 125 III 263 ss, esp. 269. As a consequence of the assimilation between software and copyrighted literary works, the source code and the object code must be shown to the court in order to obtain protection; apparent similarities on the screen do not suffice to prove the infringement; *see* Sup. Ct Zurich, SIC 2006, 851. A Zurich case maintains the view that the protection of software should be the rule, and the non-protection the exception; the burden of proving that the software is devoid of individuality is on the party denying individuality; sequences are protected to the extent that they are recognized in the counterfeiting software; Sup. Ct Zurich, SIC 2013, 697. For a software allowing to see the breathing of a patient in a mechanical ventilator the Fed. Trib. has decided that the legal protection if any will depend on the patent law and not the copyright law; case 4A_609/2019, judgment of 16 Jul. 2020, www.bger.ch.

1. Article 12(2) Copyright Act

35. The exhaustion of right – which is known in the United States (US) as the first-sale doctrine – is restated with slightly different wording: software copies that have been sold by the author or with his consent can be *used* or resold. The international exhaustion doctrine prevails for software rather than the specific national exhaustion that Article 12 paragraph 1*bis* CA provides for movies and other audiovisual works.[57]

The meaning of that wording is to make clear that as against the buyer of a software the author has fewer rights than other authors against the buyers of a copy of any other work of art, as the author cannot claim any protection against the use of the software, that often entails reproducing the software. Nevertheless, the right of lending is not exhausted by the first sale as it concerns software, although it is for other copies of protected works.

Article 17(1) of the Ordinance expounds in more detail on what is meant by legitimate ‘use’.

2. Article 13(4) Copyright Act

36. An exclusive right of lending or renting is conferred upon the author of the software, although Swiss Law does not confer that right to the author of other works, but only a right to remuneration in case of renting copies of the work for a charge.

3. Article 17 Copyright Act

37. The employer of an author of software made for hire has the exclusive rights to use the software. There is no general provision on the works made for hire in the Swiss Copyright Act. This had been a controversial topic during the 1989 revision of the Copyright Act. Finally, Parliament provided for software only a regulation that devolves to the employer the rights of use, thus taking up the principle laid down in the EC Directive 91/250.[58] This transfer of rights is limited to the rights mentioned in Articles 10 and 11(1) of the Copyright Act. In other words, the *droit moral* is not totally transferred to the employer. The author still retains the right to be acknowledged as author. Besides, third parties have to receive authorization from the employer in order to use the software or modify it.

---

57. ATF 133 III 273 (Enter the Matrix). For the case of the *Graphical User Interface see* Report of the AIPPI Swiss Group, Protection of GUI under Swiss-IP Law, SIC 2017, 763: GUI are excluded from patent protection both under Swiss Law and the Munich Convention. As under the law on industrial designs only screenshots could possibly be protected, not animated GUI’s. Therefore, Art. 2 (2)(g) Copyright Act is the main source of protection.
58. EC Directive 91/250 of 14 May 1991 on the Legal Protection of Computer Programs, OJ No. L122/42 of 17 May 1991. There is no employment contract when the partner of a company with limited responsibility brings in his programme as partner contribution; Cant. Ct St-Gallen, SIC 1999, 248.

4. Article 19(4) Copyright Act

38. There is no exception for private use of software. The only copy which may be made lawfully is the copy for archival purposes.

5. Article 21 Law and Article 17(2) Ordinance

39. Decompilation of programmes is authorized to the extent needed in order to assure the interface between the original programme and the new one. The exception aims at a solution identical to Article 6 of the EC Directive 91/250; however, some drafting dissimilarities may be noted between the Swiss and the European regulations:

(1) Whereas Article 6 of the Directive allows decompilation for information which is not 'readily available', Article 17(2) of the Copyright Ordinance of 26 April 1993 speaks of information 'immediately available' ('*librement accessibles*', '*ohne weiteres zugänglich*'). That difference might mean that the offer of a licence by the owner of the original software may preclude the application of the decompilation defence under Article 6 of the Directive, but not under Article 21 of the Law and Article 17(2) of the Ordinance in Switzerland.[59]
(2) Whereas Article 6 of the Directive requests that the decompilation be absolutely *necessary*, the Swiss law does not request it, but only that the information so obtained be used for development or maintenance, and operation of compatible programmes. Article 17(2) of the Ordinance then requests the necessity of that information, but that provision is of doubtful validity in this regard, for want of legal basis.
(3) Finally, whereas Article 6 of the Directive limits the decompilation defence to compatible programmes, which implies that the defence applies only to the extent that an independent programme has been established by the defendant, Article 21 Swiss law is broader since it mentions as well development and maintenance (that often involves smaller or larger adaptations).

B. Databases

40. At present, Swiss law does not know of specific protection of *databases*, as foreseen in the EC Directive 96/9 on databases of 11 March 1996.

59. *See* a case denying the violation of trade secrets of the original software developer when an intermediary has to decompile the original software in order to remedy a bug, Ct Just. Geneva, SIC 2010, 23 ff. The same case does stress that the Swiss provisions should be construed in light of European law as far as possible. The differences mentioned in the text above are not discussed by the Court, which mainly considers the contract between parties in order to allow for the decompilation. The judgment repeats the rule of Art. 17 Ordinance on Copyright without examining whether the Ordinance does not exceed the legal basis on which it is premised, namely Art. 21 LDA.

This does not mean that no protection at all would be afforded to compilations and databases.

41. First, databases may evidence sufficient *originality* to be protected as a variety of the 'compilation' (Article 4). Originality may be found, *inter alia,* in the classification, the architecture or the research tools of the databases.[60] Then the Swiss Copyright Act shall apply, the rights of the copyright owners, if any, on works included in the database being protected by Article 4(2). The idea to make a database is not in itself sufficiently original to be deserving of protection. For example, the sheer renumbering of pages for books or materials recorded in the database, or the arrangement of stock exchange listings in purely alphabetical order would not entail a sufficient originality.

42. Further, the Unfair Competition Law of 19 December 1986[61] might apply against the pirating of the whole or an important segment of databases. The unauthorized downloading of data is not addressed by a specific rule of the Act against Unfair Competition but might fall under the general provision prohibiting any and all acts that are contrary to good faith and influence the relationship between competitors or suppliers of goods or services and customers. In a very special case, it might fall under Article 5 (c) of the same Act whenever there would be a misuse of someone else's technical achievements through some mechanical means. This protection would stop as soon as the principal could recoup her investment, so that it is limited in time. Courts are usually averse to applying this provision.

43. For example, Article 5 (c) UCA has been considered by Swiss courts but rejected because the Unfair Competition Law does not purport to strengthen a monopoly (already existing in the particular case for the importation and distribution of spare parts of cars).[62]

60. Sup. Ct Zurich, RSPI 1993, 331 (rejecting protection under the Copyright Act for a compilation of data); data of telephone listings are not protected, according to Dist. Ct Winterthur, SIC 2000, 98.
61. RS 241. An English translation is to be found in Industrial Property, September 1988.
62. *See* Dist. Ct Affoltern *in* ZR 1989, 187. *See* also ATF 131 III 384, 388–396 (under Art. 5 (c) UCA—hereinafter 'UCA') & 397 (Art. 2 UCA) (to prohibit the copying under Art. 5 (c), it is necessary that the copy did not entail extensive costs for the respondent in comparison with the costs that have been incurred by the plaintiff). *See also* decision of the District Attorney Winterthur, SIC 2000, 98 (Twix Tel); unpublished judgment of the Cant. Ct Schwyz, 24 May 2005, cited in Rehbinder & Vigano, URG, No. 2 *ad* Art. 21 CA; Ct Aargau *in* RSPI 1991, 79; Just. Ct Zurich *in* RSPI 1992, 199. For the limitation in time see ATF 134 III 166.

C. Others

1. Titles

44. Titles may be protected if, by themselves, they constitute an individual work. They have to evidence all the characteristics of copyrightable subject matter in general.[63]

The originality is difficult to accept when newspaper or magazine titles are at stake. It may be present in titles of novels or plays, as well as in cinematographic works.

2. Characters

45. The Swiss law is not very firm on the protection of characters, although Swiss practice fully knows of merchandizing agreements. The character of *Mickey Mouse* has been protected against misappropriation by a cafeteria owner who had decorated his rooms and plates with the Walt Disney creature.[64] The name of the character was deemed to belong to the public domain for want of originality.

46. The character of *Sherlock Holmes* has not been protected for want of originality and because new authors should be free to conceive novels or plays in which the characters of other writers appear, which is a noteworthy if questionable tenet.[65] The character of a senile professor with the name 'Professor Cekadete' (the phonetic equivalent of the key terminal letters of a well-known Basle family) has been protected, on the ground that this character was deemed to be a work, 'the embodiment of which is a fictive personality as real as any person we could meet on the street';[66] furthermore, the public and the critics attributed that character to the cabaret performer who had invented it, regardless of the somewhat similar character imagined by a German satirist and of the speeches that the stammering, fictive professor tried to utter.

3. Works of Applied Art

47. A work of applied art is protected under the Swiss Copyright Act to the extent that it is individual enough. This has been decided, for example, as concerns

63. *See* ATF 64 II 109; ATF 77 II 377. Rejecting the protection of '*Rivista del Mendrisiotto*', Appel. Ct Ticino, RSPI 1996, 290; rejecting the protection of '*Swatchissimo*', Just. Ct Geneva, RSPI 1993, 299.
64. ATF 77 II 377. In a given case trademark protection might be obtained, if for ex. the figure of an animated cartoon is not to be deemed part of the public domain for the products for which protection is claimed; *see* fn 402 below.
65. ATF 85 II 120.
66. Appel. Ct Zurich *in* RSJ 1949, 204.

pieces of furniture designed by Le Corbusier,[67] the 'Oscar' statue,[68] a table lamp[69] and the figures on a wristwatch.[70] A separate law, the Federal Law on Designs of 2001,[71] provides for the registration of ornamental designs and models (by contrast with the industrial models, protected, e.g., in Germany). Under the 2001 Act, the protection lasts up to twenty-five years. The requirement of novelty is relative: the design or model need not be novel worldwide, as a patent for an invention should be, but only within Switzerland. Therefore, Swiss courts are rather demanding on the requirement of originality under the Design Act. When a design or model has been denied protection under that Act, then it is understandable that the court shall be wary of granting under the Copyright Act protection limited in time to all but the most original creations. As a result, it is often stated that the protection of copyright shall lie for designs and models only in an exceptional case,[72] and that a higher degree of originality is required for the protection under Copyright Law than under the Law on Designs,[73] which is not based on the text of these laws, but only on the questionable practice of the courts.

48. There is some controversy as to the copyrightability of functional works; that is, works aiming at practical use. The correct view is that this should not hinder the protection under copyright, as is shown by the case law relating to architectural works,[74] geographic maps[75] and pieces of furniture.[76] Some dicta hold to the contrary.[77] Functionality did not impede the protection of a petition filed with a court of law[78] or of a gravestone.[79]

67. ATF 113 II 190. *See also* Sup. Ct Zug, SIC 2010, 721; Canton. Trib. St. Gallen, SIC 2001, 491; Civ. Ct Zurich, SIC 2001, 504 (reference was made to the former 1900 Law on Designs and Models). For Max Bill stools *see* Fed. Trib. ATF 143 III 373, SIC 2017, 723.
68. Cant. Ct Zug *in* RSPI 1992, 53; Appel. Ct Berne, SIC 2009, 244 (affirming protection of the maps 'Expo-02'); Com. Ct Berne *in* RSPIDA 1978, 272; Com. Ct Berne *in* RSJB 1978, 282; Cant. Ct Graubünden *in* RSPIDA 1982, 184; Cant. Ct Neuchâtel *in* RSJ 1926/1927, 206 (map of Mt. Olympus).
69. Appel. Ct Zurich *in* RSPI 1991, 88.
70. Appel. Ct Zurich *in* RSPI 1989, 208. *See* however Just. Ct Geneva SIC 1999, 247 (rejecting protection of a watch showing the main Church in Sienna for want of originality).
71. RS 232.12. *See* hereinafter 'paras 546' et seq.
72. ATF 106 II 71.
73. Dist. Ct Horgen *in* RSPI 1989, 51. Following a change in the legal practice of Germany, this opinion seems to have been reversed in the Max Bill case, Fed. Trib. SIC 2017, 723 c. 2.6.1.
74. ATF 100 II 167; *see* ATF 117 II 466; Appel. Ct Aargau *in* RSPIDA 1975, 153; Appel. Ct Zurich *in* RSPI 1991, 88.
75. ATF 101 II 366, esp. 369–370; ATF 103 Ib 324; Cant. Ct Graubünden *in* RSPIDA 1982, 184; Appel. Ct Zurich *in* RSPIDA 1983, 108.
76. ATF 113 II 190; Fed. Trib., SIC 2011, 504 (Le Corbusier III); Zurich Sup. Ct, SIC 2012, 378 (Le Corbusier IV).
77. Appel. Ct Zurich *in* RSPI 1985, 110; Dist. Ct Horgen *in* RSPI 1989, 51 (protection of directions for use).
78. Appel. Ct Zurich *in* RSJ 1933/34, 266.
79. Appel. Ct Berne *in* RSJ 1940/41, 70 (protection denied *in casu* for want of originality); Sup. Ct Zurich, SIC 2002, 342 (rejecting protection for want of individuality); Sup. Ct Zurich SIC 2001, 504 (admitting individuality).

4. Letters, Diaries

49. A few cases deal with advertising letters, mainly from the viewpoint of originality. Protection has been denied at times for want of individuality.[80] However, there is no doubt that private letters and entries into diaries as well as e-mails are protectable if individual enough.

50. If protected, the right of first publication belongs to the author or his heirs and not to the addressee. The physical ownership of the text does not change the copyright situation. The author wishing to publish letters of which he kept no copies will be entitled to access to the original letters, in view of making a copy thereof. The ownership of the original letter will remain with the addressee.

5. Photographs

51. According to Article 2(2)(g), photographic work is copyrightable. This is not a special regime, but in order to get the full protection of copyright, the normal requirements of individuality as enacted in the Copyright Act apply to photographs as well. If deserving of protection, they will enjoy it for the full period of duration of any protected work. If, however, the photograph is not original enough, it will now receive the weaker protection deriving from the revision of 2019, as commented above (paragraph 17).

The case law is stringent enough for originality.[81] The new Law of 1992 did not alleviate the legal requirements but introduced the notion of 'visual work', which covers video clips, holograms, combinations, etc. As for all other works, the style of a photograph is not protected.[82]

80. ATF 88 IV 123; Appel. Ct Zurich *in* RSPIDA 1980, 189.
81. Protection denied: ATF 130 III 714 (denying for want of individuality the protection of a photograph of Christoph Meili, a convict known for violating bank secrecy laws in connection with orphaned bank accounts). *But see*, e.g., ATF 130 III 168 (protecting a photograph of Bob Marley in concert, by virtue of the individuality of the image which uniquely captured the musician's energy, playing with his hair flying); further, denying protection: Appel. Ct Zurich *in* RSJ 1972, 308; Appel. Ct Zurich *in* RSPI 1985, 221; Com. Ct Aargau, SIC 2013, 344 (denying protection for one photo, protection awarded for the other one, however without granting remedies); less demanding: Just. Ct Geneva *in* SJ 1964, 171; Dist. Ct Zurich, SIC 2006, 23 (finding that in a photograph, the configuration and processing of the image, the choice of theme, the lighting, etc. may individualize a photographic work and warrant to give it protection); *see also* Cant. Ct St-Gallen, SIC 2000, 188; X-rays images are not protected: Appel. Ct Zurich *in* RSPI 1986, 313; the fact that the panorama has changed along the years cannot lead to the conclusion that the photograph is individual when there is no originality otherwise: App. Ct BS, SIC 2016, 594. However, photos that are not protected as works of art may still be subject to restrictions in their use and the obligation to cite the source, e.g., by reason of the special legislation on meteorological data; Fed. Trib., SIC 2006, 260.
82. *See* Fed. Trib. *in* RSPI 1992, 58, esp. 60. As pointed out above para. 17, the revised Copr. Act now grants a specific protection to photographs devoid of individuality.

6. Audio-visual Works

52. The Swiss Law on Copyright does not provide a specific status to films and other audio-visual works.

For the televisual retransmission of sports events, no protection is granted as such, since there is no work of art. However, the broadcasting organization enjoys neighbouring rights for the whole of its broadcasts (Article 37). Documentary films are protectable to the extent that they show individuality.

53. Rights on interviews belong to the interviewer and to the interviewee to the extent he or she says something in an individual fashion. They may be transferred to the organization hiring the interviewer, as per the contract between them.

§3. Conditions of Protection

I. Formal Requirements

54. Swiss Law does not know of any formal requirement for the protection of copyrighted works. Deposit is neither necessary nor possible. Indeed, there is even no compulsory deposit of printed books with the National Library in Berne.

55. There is no general requirement of *fixation* for the protection of works of art and literature. Nevertheless, sheer ideas could not be protected under the Copyright Act, since only the *form* of a work is protectable. Certain works cannot really exist without fixation, among them paintings, sculptural works, films and photographs. However, poems and musical works (improvisations) are protected without any necessity of an embodiment in a record or a book.

56. The Swiss Law on Copyright explicitly protects draft works and parts of work (Article 2(4)), so that no requirement of achievement may be read into the law.

II. Substantive Requirements

57. The Law of 1992 requires the *individuality* of a creation in order for it to be protected (Article 2(1)). This criterion takes up the former notion of *originality*, which is still common in case law and commentary. The new wording has been chosen to make clear that the requirement is addressed to the work itself, whereas the case law on originality sometimes requires that the *personality* of the author be mirrored in the work. Thus, individuality shall be deemed to exist independently of any 'personal stamp' which the author would print on his creation.

58. In any case, the ethical or aesthetical or economic *value* of a work is irrelevant to its protection. Protection may be afforded even if the contents are *contra bonos mores.*[83]

Three notions of individuality seem rooted in Swiss Law.

59. According to a clever and uniquely Swiss doctrine, the *statistical uniqueness of the work* to be protected is the test. In an ideal world, *uniqueness* would be enough, for it is the very signpost of individuality. Nevertheless, the courts very seldom have the opportunity to verify that no duplicate work exists. In practice, even if they do find that a very similar creation parallels the work at stake, they will not deny protection.[84] Thus, it is only possible to require a *statistical probability* that no other work could be identical to the one at issue.[85]

60. Although this theory never received the full endorsement of the Federal Tribunal, it certainly helped the Swiss commentary away from the more obscure formulation of the European tradition asking whether the work somehow reflects the personality of the author. The statistical uniqueness doctrine somehow dissociates the judgment on copyrightability from the more or less marked intervention of a particular author. It accounts for 'ready-made' works of art, that actually are no longer so fashionable as fifty years ago. The criterion of statistical uniqueness is more *objective* than any other test. It explains why protection should be afforded to the many products of the media. They often bear a striking similarity to each other, and yet, they are undoubtedly protected. This test allows for the extension of the protection to every creation which is not likely to be found elsewhere in exactly the same shape.

Nevertheless, the main weakness of the statistical uniqueness test is precise that no merit, no connection to toil, virtue or genius need be evidenced for the protection to be granted. However, automatic legal protection is a meaningless concept, even though the legislature endorsed it in 2019 for banal photographs. For all other products, either the author or the work has to show some merits, even though the merits are not judged from an ethical nor from an aesthetical point of view, but rather from a social point of view, which is best served when bestowing exclusive rights on works having a quantum of originality.

---

83. Map of the City of Zurich for Men: Appel. Ct Zurich *in* RSPIDA 1983, 108, correctly allowing no claim in damages for the violation of copyright on immoral works (maps indicating occasions to sin in the City of Zurich). The SUISA collecting right Society may petition the criminal courts to get protection for the pornographic videos authored by authors that it represents, according to two cases decided by the Fed. Trib.: SIC 2002, 841 and 1998, 388.

84. For an architectural work, *see* ATF 142 III 387 c. 3.1; ATF 117 II 466; for a character, *see* Appel. Ct Zurich *in* RSJ 1949, 204.

85. *See* M. Kummer, *Das Urheberrechtlich schützbare Werk* (Work Protectable by Copyright) (Berne, 1968).

61. The judicial practice, therefore, defines the necessary individuality as the *distinctiveness* vis-à-vis other creations of the same kind, due to characteristics of the work itself or to the personal stamp of its author.[86]

If the author's personal stamp is recognizable, originality is certainly present.[87] In the absence of such a personal stamp, individual features of the work itself will suffice. Those features may be individual because of expression or because of the ideas.

62. In this regard, it will not go unnoticed that no protection is afforded to the ideas as such. Nonetheless, the individualism of scientific writers is mainly apparent through their substantive ideas, more than through some fancy expressions that may wrap them. On the whole, Swiss case law is right, therefore, to take into account the novelty of ideas when appraising the individuality of the work.

63. Individuality may finally be seen as the result of skill or inventiveness above the ordinary level of skill or inventiveness, especially in the fields where there is little room for personal variations; however, if there is a simple combination or adaptation of known shapes, lines and colours, there would be no individuality, unless there is shown to be an independent intellectual activity leading to the work.[88] Now, this test of the independent creative act is the safest one, in the sense that it limits the arbitrariness of the court in dealing with the question of individuality. The judge may look at the facts surrounding the conception of the work. He may see to which extent the would-be author just copied something that was already conceived by another one, or independently recombined shapes and solutions that were known. Individuality tends to be relative.

86. *See*, e.g., ATF 136 III 225; Fed. Trib., SIC 2008, 462 (this judgment argues that statistical unity should be tested at the level of the creation of the work (*Modus operandi* of the artist or author), which neglects a basic tenet of Kummer's theory, to wit the protection of ready-mades that are not necessarily the result of 'personal decision of the author', nor 'of a combination both surprising and unusual', and yet can be 'statistically unique'); the better view is expressed in App. Ct BS, SIC 2016, 594: the process of creation is not the test for individuality, but the result of the creative process, the work itself. *See* further Fed. Trib., SIC 2001, 729 (stating that the 'individuality' requirement under the 1992 Copyright Act is identical to the 'originality' requirement as read by the courts in the 1922 Act) (*see*, e.g., ATF 106 II 71; ATF 101 II 102). For a detailed endorsement of the test of distinctiveness through comparison with the work of the other party to the litigation, *see*, e.g., Appel. Ct Ticino, SIC 2002, 509–510 (citing F. Dessemontet, *Le droit d'auteur*, 119, by whom this doctrine was first proposed; adopted for example by R. Stutz, *Das originelle Design* (The Original Design), SIC 2004, 3 at 11 & n. 69); Com. Ct St-Gallen, SIC 2003, 796. Further Fed. Trib. cases: e.g., ATF 125 III 328; SIC 2003, 28. *See* further commentary M. Senn, *Die urheberrechtliche Individualität – eine methodische Annäherung* (The Individuality in Copyright – Closing the Gap), SIC 2017, 521.

87. ATF 117 II 466. However, the 1992 Act supplants any criterion of a 'personal stamp'; *see* Just. Ct Geneva *in* RSPI 1994, 183; Just. Ct Geneva *in* RSPI 1996, 263; ATF 120 II 65. According to Sup. Ct Luzern, SIC 2003, 699 (*aff'd* on other grounds in ATF 129 III 545), the opinion of the professional circles as expressed, e.g., through a prize given to a certain project should not be taken into account by the courts when passing judgment on the individuality.

88. ATF 117 II 466. *See also* hereabove para. 16 at fn. 12.

64. This last assertion is twofold. Primarily, individuality shall exist with regard to the prior works that existed at the time of creation. This is the traditional meaning of *distinctiveness*. In some circumstances, however, the originality of the work the author which claims protection, will be compared to the second work produced later by the defendant. This entails that individuality is not an absolute value, but that the level required rather depends on the circumstances of the case.

In case of outright piracy, no high level of the individuality of the pirated work should be shown. In case of the reuse of some elements of the first work in a second, highly brilliant creation, the level of originality required from the first work is higher.

65. Finally, no confusion between the test of individuality under the Copyright Act and the test of *non-obviousness* under the Patent Act should be entertained. The Patent Act has to guarantee that a vast area of minute industrial progress be left unfettered by patents for the daily technological progress of industry. Hence, a rather stringent level of non-obviousness is requested from an invention in order for it to be patentable – besides a worldwide novelty. By contrast, almost all productions of the media industry and most creations by any other author whomsoever are protected under Copyright Law. The area in which freedom to copy is preserved is very limited because it is usually easy to find other expressions for the same functionality. Therefore, the standard of individuality is rather low.

§4. Ownership

I. The Author

A. The Creator Principle

66. According to Article 6 of the Copyright Act, the author is always the physical person who reduces the work to form or expression. Swiss Law is premised on the idea that only the *creative* contribution by an individual entitles that person to hold a copyright. The investment consented by a legal entity is not considered as creative, as giving birth to copyright, as it were. Thus, Swiss Law does not know of copyright bestowed on legal entities from the start. This is known as the 'creator's principle' (*Schöpferprinzip*): only a transfer by contract could give the legal entity the whole or part of the copyright.

67. In so doing, the new Law of 1992 is even more absolute than the French Law of 1985, for example, since Article L. 113-5 of the French Code of Intellectual Property admits to an originary acquisition of copyright by legal entities on collective works, that are the sort of works for which the question is most acute (movie industry, encyclopaedias, etc.).

B. The Work Made by a Machine, a Computer, an Animal

68. When a computer or a machine, or possibly an animal such as a monkey, is at work to create the subject matter of copyright, the title to copyright shall be vested in the person who selects the materials so produced. This might be the case for Artificial Intelligence when a real person selects the material; otherwise, Article 393 CO might sometimes apply, when the machine is working according to a task that has been decided by an Editor, who will then obtain the copyright.

In a bizarre case, a medium contended to hear voices from spirits; the Federal Tribunal rightly decided that only the medium was the author, and not as claimed by some clever lawyer the spirits – who cannot appear in court, of course, but whose creativity was involved just to deprive the medium of his rights.[89]

69. The creator's principle is important only to the extent that some inalienable components of the moral rights remain vested in the physical creator. Further, the interested parties have to enter into an agreement in order for a legal entity to use the work. As no form is mandated for this contract, however, and no minimal requirements are imposed by law as to the remuneration or other particulars, the protective effects of requiring an agreement to use are limited. Recent commentators often argue in favour of legislating detailed rules on the contracts binding authors, as is the case, e.g., in Germany. This would be deeply illiberal and contrary to our Swiss free-market tradition.

II. Joint Works

70. The works that are created by several persons belong jointly and severally to all co-authors (Article 7(1)).

71. Of course, when a person does not participate in a creative way in the joint work, as is the case of a technician, he or she shall not be deemed to be a co-author. The financial support is not deemed to be a creative contribution. In the case of audio-visual works, especially, Swiss practice distinguishes between the main authors (art director, scriptwriter, scenario writer, composer of the music) and the ancillary contributors (cameraman, cutter, hair stylist, dress and set designers); after

89. ATF 116 II 351. In ATF 136 III 225, the Federal Tribunal correctly follows the *Creator principle* to restate that when there are two or several persons involved in the creation of the work, a co-author is only the physical person who actually *makes decisions towards the formatting of the work.* To share the financial risks and burden of the creation is not a creative contribution, as noted in Sup. Ct Zurich, RSPI 1988, 117 concerning advertisements. Where the respective contributions of the authors of a work can be clearly distinguished and that each contribution is exploitable in an independent manner, such as the music of a movie, the status will not be that of joint work but of work of collaboration (*see* below para. 73). The exploitation can then be simplified if one or several of the authors give up their copyrights or transfer them to a sole individual or legal entity (*see* Dist. Ct St-Gallen, SIC 2002, 589, 595). For decisions rendered under the general principle that an action for damages must be brought in the name of all authors of a joint work, *see* ATF 129 III 715; Appel. Ct Ticino 2004, 20, 22.

initial reluctance and a litigation, the rights of the ancillary authors are now acknowledged by the collecting right societies (*Suissimage* and *Société suisse des auteurs*).

72. The joint authors have to authorize any and all sorts of use of the joint work unless a differing provision has been agreed upon by all of them at the outset (Article 7(2)). However, Article 7(2) (last sentence) of the Copyright Act specifically restates a general principle which is already mentioned in Article 2 Swiss Civil Code, to wit: Everyone has to follow the rules of *good faith* when invoking his rights and performing his obligations. The law does not admit the obvious misuse of a person's rights. The legislature thought it was important to restate here the principle of good faith for the authors of joint works so that the exploitation of these works would not be unduly hindered by the common ownership of copyright. The alternative solution might have been to order the compulsory designation of a co-author or third party who would act as the legal representative of all co-authors. As the law stands, only a contractual agreement to that effect can lead to a smooth procedure for granting such authorization as the working of the joint work may necessitate. In my view, Article 7(2) (last sentence) entails four main consequences:

(1) The co-author who rejects an application to use the joint work has to indicate the grounds of his decision, so that the co-authors or the court may appreciate whether his rejection is abusive.
(2) The co-author who already authorized the use of the joint work cannot abusively withdraw his approval. Withdrawal would be abusive if estoppel by conduct could be found to lie in the first authorization.
(3) The co-author must show which interest is pursued by his refusal. This interest must be a legitimate one. The court shall strike a balance between his interests and the interests of the other co-authors. The source of this real limitation to the exclusive right of the rejecting author is the fact that he consented to a community of sorts between all co-authors. Of course, if the community is a partnership regulated by law (as the *Société simple* according to Articles 530 et seq. Code of Obligations, which give the legal status applicable to most joint ventures), then the increased duty of faithfulness shall apply. The same may be said if one of the co-authors is linked to the other one(s) by way of a labour contract.
(4) If the circumstances change, the author who rejected the proposed utilization of the joint work has to re-examine a new application. For example, if he opposed a performance of a play by an amateur ensemble, he shall reconsider his position if some professionals are hired to strengthen the show.

73. For parts of joint works that admit separate exploitation, such as musical accompaniment of visual work, etc., the law vests each of the authors with the right to authorize the use of his part of the joint work, provided no other agreement has been executed and if the use of the joint work itself is not jeopardized.

74. Vis-à-vis third parties, all co-authors have to act jointly in order to authorize the use of the copyrighted work. Each of them can, however, act alone to file a suit against unauthorized use of the work, but he has to request relief on account of all the authors (Article 7(3)).

III. Works Made for Hire

A. *Theory of the Finality*

75. The Parliament did not follow the provision proposed in the 1989 Bill on works made for hire, according to which, in the absence of a covenant to the contrary, the copyright on works made for hire by an employee during his activities for the employer and in performance of his contractual obligations would be transferred to the employer to the extent required by the employment contract.

76. This provision was advocated as a restatement in the particular setting of employee-employer relationships of the prevailing legal theory of the *finality* valid for all contracts in the area of copyright (*Zweckübertragungstheorie*). Therefore, even in the absence of a provision in the law for employees' works, that theory applies. In Germany, the said theory aims at protecting the author against too broad a transfer of his rights: only the transfer of those rights necessary to obtain the purpose of the contract is deemed to have taken place.[90]

In Switzerland, the theory of finality is not conceived as a limitation to the transfer of rights, but as its very justification: the purpose of the contract may imply that a transfer has taken place.

77. In the case of an employment relationship, the theory of the finality leads most of the time to the conclusion that the employer can use the copyrighted work as usual, and that the employee retains only moral rights, as well as residual rights to use the work that fall in the ordinary exploitation of the work by the employer. New, unexpected uses belong to the employee. For example, the use of a video or a film shot by an employee of the Frères Lumière could not have been envisioned before World War I, so the copyright on this use could not have been transferred to the employer.

78. In the case of the commissioning of a work of art, the artist does not give away any copyright, with the possible exception of the right to display.

79. For advertisements, it has been judged that the advertising agency keeps all copyrights on the materials and ideas of the campaign; the client can only use it

90. Compare A. Dietz, *The Reform of Copyright Law: Experiences Abroad*, Lausanne, 3 Nov. 1989, 18 et seq. & 34 (Zurich, 1990) and Fed. Trib., SIC 2013, 605.

once.[91] The same opinion could prevail for the layout of a magazine unless the commissioning party made clear that the magazine was to be published for a long time thereafter with the same layout.

B. Software

80. Article 17 of the Copyright Act states that the employer has the exclusive right to use the software made by his employee within the framework of his activities for the employer and in conformity with his contractual obligations.

There is some discussion about whether that provision entails a transfer of the copyright or only an exclusive licence.[92]

§5. TRANSFER

I. Assignment of Copyright

81. According to Article 16(1) of the Copyright Act, assignment of copyright and its conveyance to heirs is possible. This settles a long-drawn controversy between the admirers of the German and Austrian solution, in which no assignment of copyright as such is accepted, and the practitioners who were inclined to accept the full conveyance of title to the copyright, thus allowing for smooth marketing of the protected work. Whereas the 1984 Bill provided for the non-assignability of copyright between living persons, the 1989 Bill followed the 1986 Draft Bill and recognized a full assignment of copyright as possible.

82. The assignment of copyright and the conveyance of the title through inheritance do bring up some delicate questions on the moral right which is a component of the copyright. In this writer's view, Article 9(1) of the Copyright Act is based on the so-called *monist* concept of copyright.[93] Therefore, an assignment or conveyance of title means that the entire right may be transferred to the heir – or to the assignee, if such is the common intent of the parties to the assignment contract. Of course, Article 16(2) qualifies that principle to the extent that the transfer of one particular privilege conferred upon the author does not imply the transfer of other particular privileges, absent an agreement to the contrary. Nevertheless, it precisely follows therefrom that the transfer of the whole right is possible. Now, in this case, what is to become of the moral rights?

---

91. Civ. Ct BS *in* BJM 1995, 248, RSPI 1996, 67. For the case of a handbook on aviation, *see* Dist. Ct St-Gallen, SIC 2002, 389. For the special case of software developed by a hired employee, *see* ATF 125 III 263, 266; for the case of software developed under a commissioning contract *see* Cant. Ct St-Gallen, SIC 1999, 248. For the case of a photograph, *see* Sup. Ct Zurich, SIC 2011, 227.
92. *See* von Büren, *Der Werkbegriff* (The Notion of Work), in *SIWR II/1*, 235, n. 3 (2d ed., Helbing, 2013); Barrelet & Egloff, No. 6 *ad* Art. 17 Copyright Act.
93. *See* paras 101 et seq.

83. For this writer, sharing a minority view, the general answer is that moral rights are assignable and susceptible to be conveyed to the heirs, inasmuch as they derive from the Copyright Act. Article 11(2) on the right to authorize modifications is based on this premise when it states: 'Even if a third party is authorized by contract (…) to modify the work, the author may oppose any distortion of the work that is damaging to his personality.' However, the right to prohibit mutilations that may endanger his personal interests, *as they are protected under Article 28 Swiss Civil Code*, cannot be transferred to the assignee because highly personal interests are not transferable at all. Henceforth, there is a 'hard kernel' of moral rights, based on the Swiss Civil Code, that shall remain at the disposal of the author assignor. However, the assignee can invoke the right to prohibit modifications and the right to be named as author in the case of ghostwriting (if such was the common intent of the parties when entering into the assignment agreement).[94]

84. The Copyright Law mentions some rights vis-à-vis the collecting right societies that appear in a part of the commentary as not assignable,[95] *inter alia,* the right of the 'author' to participate in an appropriate manner in the decisions of the societies (Article 42(d)) and the right to receive proceeds and royalties (Article 49(3)). Nonetheless, the point is debatable whether these rules that lay down the organic framework of the collecting societies should be seen as having a bearing on the assignment of copyright. Further, one of the provisions explicitly allows for private agreements to differ and to take precedence over the legal rule (Article 49(4)). Nevertheless, if a third party, for example, a video library, has acquired some author's rights, it cannot invoke this as a defence against the collecting right societies.[96] On a quite different point, it may be interesting to note that the collecting right societies usually receive approximately 10% of their revenues from abroad.

85. The Swiss Copyright Law does not contain rules on the rights of heirs. They certainly inherit the copyright as a whole, and their heirs after them until the seventy years delay elapses. To some extent, the author may bind them through his last will, for example, if he wants to forbid the publication of intimate diaries, letters or

94. *See* already ATF 69 II 53. However, ATF 136 III 225 cons. 3.3 carelessly asserts that the moral right is not transferable, without giving much justification for this view. The controversy in the commentary is summed up by J. de Werra, in *Urheberrechtsgesetz* (Copyright Act) (Müller & Oertli ed., 2006), No. 17 ff *ad* Art. 16 Copyright Act. On a different point, Cant. Ct Graubünden, SIC 2007, 364, recalls that the transfer of intellectual property rights does not always follow the rules of civil property on material goods, e.g., as to the protection of the bona fide purchaser of goods and wares (Art. 933 ff Civil Code). *See* generally B. Bieler, *Die Übertragung des Urheberrechts* (Transfer of Copyright), Basle 2014; C. Bötschi, *Bestimmung der Art und des Umfanges der Rechtseinräumung im Urheberrechtsvertrag* (Determination of the Type and Extent of Transfer of Copyright), Zurich 2021 (comparing Swiss and German conceptions). In administrative proceedings concerning public tender for a building, the moral right of the architect should not interfere except in as far as the protection of the personality of the author under Art. 27 and 28 CC would prevent it; see Fed. Adm. Trib., SIC 2019, 422.
95. *See* Barrelet & Egloff, No. 8 *ad* Art. 16 Copyright Act.
96. *See* Fed. Trib. in SIC 1999, 26–28.

draft works. An executor may be appointed to ensure the respect of the will. Otherwise, the rules of the Civil Code on the community among the heirs should give the answer to any practical problem about the authorization of publication or of performance, etc.[97]

There are no requirements of form for the agreement on assignment. The last will and the appointment of an executor must comply with the forms set up in the Civil Code to this end.

II. Licences

86. Licences are not regulated either by the Copyright Law or by a specific chapter of the Swiss Code of Obligations. Therefore, copyright licences are a contract sui generis, to which only the general provisions of the Swiss Code of Obligations (Articles 1–183 Code of Obligations) need to apply. Licence agreements are not subject to any requirement of form.[98] 'Open source' or 'creative commons' so-called licences might be characterized most often as a unilateral renunciation to file an action for infringement of copyright if the terms and conditions of the licence are respected. In case those terms and conditions are not respected, there may not lie a contractual action with contractual rules on the venue, cautionary notice and damages applying, but only an action against infringement. There is a dearth of precedents as the courts seldom adjudicate claims relating to licensing agreements, since those contracts usually refer any dispute to arbitration.

A. *Definition*

87. The licence agreement gives the licensee the authorization to use the copyrighted work within the provisions of that contract. It should not be confused with the publishing agreement, regulated at some length in Articles 380–393 Code of Obligations.

88. The publishing agreement entails for the publisher the duty[99] to print the book or to manufacture other supports as may seem appropriate for the marketing of the work: audiotape, videotape, CD or CD-ROM. The copyright is transferred to

97. *See* ATF 121 III 118. *See* generally J. Guinand, *Law of Inheritance*, in *Introduction to Swiss Law* 86 (F. Dessemontet & T. Ansay ed., 3d ed., Kluwer, 2004).
98. ATF 125 III 26 (Software License); Fed. Trib., case 4A_643/2012, citing Fed. Trib., case 4A_104/2008 (available at www.bger.ch). *See also* Fed. Trib., SIC 2013, 605: Swiss law would follow the maxim *in dubio pro auctore* ('in doubt favour the author') in the sense that if the nature of the transaction is not certain, the court shall admit a license rather than an outright transfer. If for some reason the written form is required, just clicking on a button is not equivalent to the 'signature' under Art. 14 CO; see Fed. Adm. Trib., SIC 2019, 554 ('*Helsana*').
99. Art. 380 Code of Obligations.

the publisher to the extent and as long as necessary for the performance of the publishing agreement,[100] whereas the licence agreement does not transfer any copyright to the licence. Under Swiss Law, unlike under German law, there is only a contractual claim of the licensee vis-à-vis the licensor, and no property interest (*dingliches Recht* or *quasi-dingliches Recht*) is vested in the licensee vis-à-vis third parties. As a consequence, the licensee was not in a position to bring a suit against counterfeiting or other violations of the copyright, unless he had been especially empowered to do so by the licensor.[101] The Copyright Act was amended in 2007 by the introduction of Article 62, paragraph 3, setting a presumption that the exclusive licensee may sue for infringement, and that all licensees are able to join any action for infringement in order to claim damages for their own harm. Before that amendment, some commentators had been influenced by the German tradition according to which the *exclusive* licensee should be able as of right to sue third parties who endanger his exclusivity through violation of the copyright.[102] For criminal actions, the assignee (but not presumably the licensee) of the copyright may bring them into court.[103]

B. Obligations of the Licensor

89. The licensing agreement grants the authorization to use the work. Therefore, the licensor is under the obligation to tolerate that use; in other words, he must not introduce any action against the licensee that would be based on copyright law. Now, this obligation of the licensor is valid only to the extent that the contract is still in force. When the contract is validly terminated, the actions under the Copyright Law may be brought against the former contractual partner.[104]

90. The authorization may bear upon all kinds of use of the copyrighted work. For instance, it shall cover the use of software on a computer or at the site where the licence is active (*site-licence*), or on several sites. Licence of the Object Code

100. Art. 381(1) Code of Obligations. *See* ATF 101 II 102; Just. Ct Geneva *in* RSPIDA 1980, 87. Under Art. 383(1) Code of Obligations, the transfer is valid for one edition or use only; further under Art. 384 Code of Obligations, any transfer to a third party for publishing needs the authorization of the author.
101. *See* ATF 113 II 190; Fed. Trib., SIC 2008, 209 (non-exclusive licensees may sue to have the court state that a third-party retransmitting broadcasts of television is acting unlawfully); Cant. Ct BS, SIC 2003, 217 (the reporters assign their right of publication to the publisher of the newspaper, so that the publisher may file actions against third-party infringers).
102. R. Ramseyer, *Le contrat de licence des brevets d'invention* (License Contract of Invention Patents), thesis, 24 (Geneva, 1948); A. Meier-Hayoz, *Berner Kommentar* (Berne Commentary), Bd. IV/1/1, *Systematischer Teil und allgemeine Bestimmungen* (Systematic Part and General Provisions) (Berne, 1981), 1958, *Syst. Teil* No. 127.
103. *See* ATF 99 IV 50; Appel. Ct Thurgau *in* RSPI 1986, 123.
104. Just. Ct Geneva *in* RSPIDA 1980, 87 (publishing contract).

does not entail licence of the Source Code.[105] It may cover the distribution of a film in movie theatres or the sale of videotapes; it may allow for a novel to be filmed, etc.[106]

91. The licence may be an exclusive licence, a sole licence or a non-exclusive licence.

92. The licensor may undertake some further obligations, for example, to adapt his novel in view of the elaboration of the script for shooting the film, or to cooperate with a scriptwriter to this end. The software licensor may be under the obligation to provide the latest versions of a given programme to all his licensees. Accompanying documents may have to be provided by the licensor, as well as documents and statements for tax authorities or insurance purposes.

93. Under Swiss Law, the licensing agreements may be concluded for a very long period of time, for example, twenty years or more.[107] If such is the case, the only way to terminate the agreement is to show either that the other party does not properly discharge his obligations, or that there is a 'just cause' for termination, which concept is applied with restraint. Unless repeated, the violation of a minor obligation may not constitute a breach of contract allowing for the termination of the agreement even if the breach is not stopped upon notice. By the way, the same is true for the violation of a licensee's obligation, for example, to send inventories and accounts of sales, unless there is a gross understatement. Only the repetition of minor breaches may culminate in a just cause, and it is in all events necessary, first to serve upon the other party a notice asking him to fulfil the specific obligations whose breach shall be invoked, later on, to terminate the agreement.[108]

94. There are no implied warranties as to the quality, the merchantability or the return upon investment afforded by the goods under licence. There may be express undertakings, for example, to the effect that a given TV series shall be ready and shown at about the same time as the merchandising starts with goods adorned with a given character. Swiss law admits liquidated damages or penalties if such an undertaking is not respected. The court can always reduce excessive penalties.

---

105. ATF 125 III 263 et seq. *See also* Fed. Trib., SIC 2009, 159.
106. *See* R. Muttenzer, *Der urheberrechtliche Lizenzvertrag* (Intellectual Property License Agreement), thesis, esp. 51 et seq. (Basle, 1970). *See also* von Büren, *Lizenzvertrag* (License Agreement), in *SIWR I/1*, 338 (2d ed.); U. Zenhäusern, *Der internationale Lizenzvertrag* (The International License Agreement), thesis, 16 et seq. (Freiburg, 1991).
107. Fed. Trib. *in* RSPIDA 1978, 279 (contract valid as long as there is commercial interest in the distribution of a film).
108. *See* an interesting arbitral award in ICC No. 4496, resumed in S. Jarvin, *Arbitrating International Disputes*, 23 LES Nouvelles (1988), 23 (a trademark case). *See also* Sup. Ct Luzern, SIC 1997, 458: recurrent cash flow bottlenecks of the licensee may justify the early termination of the licensing agreement for cause. *See* however Fed. Trib., SIC 2013, 600 under citation of ATF 138 III 304: the repetition of minor violations of the contract does not necessarily entail a just cause to terminate the contract but may justify it.

95. In case of a publishing contract, the law provides for a warranty of title. The author is *ex lege* responsible on two accounts: he is entitled to transfer the copyright at the time of executing the contract; the copyright really exists, if the work is protected[109] (Article 381(2) Code of Obligations).

96. No such legal warranty exists in the case of a licence. Nevertheless, a contractual warranty with the same contents will often be implied in the wording of the contract because it would be contradictory in most circumstances to purport to 'authorize' the use of work which is in the public domain or on which the 'licensor' has no valid title. Good faith may prevent the would-be licensor from denying his responsibility if, after all, he was not entitled to authorize the use of a work and he knew it. If there is uncertainty on entitlement because of litigation, good faith in the negotiation would entail, or so it seems, that the would-be licensor informs the other party about the litigation (*see* Article 382(3) Code of Obligations *per analogiam*).

C. *Obligations of the Licensee*

97. The first and foremost obligation shall be to pay royalties.

98. The licensee also has to safeguard the integrity of the work to the extent feasible. For example, software programs are at times in need of modification to run smoothly in a given environment, and the licensee would appear to be entitled to modify them. The same may be said, for example, of an architectural design which is licensed to a contractor in order to build several houses, minor adjustments being required from case to case.

99. The information requirements from licensee to licensor, for example, to compute the royalties due according to the sales, are a frequent source of misunderstanding. As has been mentioned, the continued or repeated violation of such information duties by the licensee, or one gross misstatement about the sales may suffice for the licensor rightfully to terminate the agreement.

100. The licensee may undertake to use the copyrighted work to a minimal extent determined in the contract.

101. While respecting antitrust laws, the licensee may undertake not to embark on competing with the licensor. Under the present Law on Cartels (RS 251, last amended on 19 March 2021), the parties to intellectual property agreements are no longer dispensed of complying with the antitrust law of Switzerland.

109. By which it is meant that no warranty for the copyright exists as to works that are already in the public domain, which is obvious [*see* Art. 381(1) Code of Obligations in French, providing for a warranty if the work is *protected*. Another interpretation might be based on the German and Italian texts of Art. 381(2) Code of Obligations, whereby there is a warranty that the author has the copyright when the work is *protectable*. *See* R.M. Hilty, *Kommentar zum schweizerischen Privatrecht* (Commentary of the Swiss Private Law), *Obligationenrecht I* (Code of Obligations) (Basle and Francfort-on-the-Main, 1992), No. 9 *ad* Art. 381 Code of Obligations].

§6. SCOPE OF EXCLUSIVE RIGHTS

102. The Swiss Law on Copyright first provides the author with an encompassing exclusive right. Article 9(1) states:

> *The author has the exclusive right on his work.*
>
> The use of the singular 'right' and the lack of any qualification really means that the Swiss legislature adopted the idea of a sole right, the so-called monist or unitary theory. According to that theory, the copyright cannot be split in its various components as stated later in the Law, the enumeration of which does not exhaust therefore all the powers and privileges of the copyright owner.

103. The principal consequences of the monist theory as adopted in the 1992 Law are not the same as in Germany or Austria because the Swiss legislature did not prohibit the transfer of the copyright as a whole. Therefore, five features of the monist concept are of significance in Switzerland:

(a) The copyright encompasses both economic and moral rights. No categorization of particular power or privilege is needed in one or the other sort of rights, since there are no differences in legal status.
(b) The copyright is endowed with *elasticity*, which means that, if a particular right is licensed or assigned to a third party, as soon as the license is terminated or the assignment is invalidated for some reason, the author's copyright revives to the prior extent.
(c) The copyright does not exhaust itself in the listed powers and privileges mentioned later on in the Law so that in case of the appearance of a new method of using the work, the copyright owner can claim his exclusive right to it.
(d) The copyright is an exclusive right, it is *a right of property*. As such, it enjoys the constitutional guarantee of property.
(e) It pertains to these absolute rights that the constitutional guarantee of property rights applies to them, so that the State cannot encroach upon, even for some reason of social justice or for the user's convenience.

I. Moral Rights

104. The monist theory does not support categorization of rights to other ends than pedagogical. Thus, it might be better to mention the rights at issue as '*mainly* moral rights'.

Until the entry into force of the 1992 Law, the moral rights were based on Article 28 Swiss Civil Code and Article 6*bis* of the Berne Convention. The case law before 1993 should, therefore, be read with caution since many a traditional interrogation is no longer relevant for the rights that are provided under the new Law.

A. *Right of Paternity*

105. The author enjoys the right to be recognized as the author of his work (Article 9(1)). When it is lawful to publish an extract according to Article 25(1), then the name of the author must be mentioned, if that name is also apparent on the source document (Article 25(2)).[110]

The reverse right is no longer provided under the Copyright Act: if someone passes off his work for the work of some other author, there shall be no relief under the Copyright Act. Possibly remedies shall lay either under Article 28 Swiss Civil Code or Article 3(b) UCA which prohibits giving false or misleading indications about one's own wares, products or services.

106. The right of paternity is assignable, in this writer's view. The ghostwriter who assigned his right cannot claim it back later, and the purported author who would be fool enough to claim before a court of law that he is the author of a work which he did not write in fact, could do this on the strength of his own right. Vis-à-vis third parties, the arrangement between the true author and the purported author are of no importance, according to the principle of the privity of contracts. There might be an interest of the general public not to be mistaken about the true author's identity, but the Unfair Competition Law of 1986 would be the basis for relief in this particular case.

B. *Right of Integrity*

107. The right of integrity is the author's right to decide 'whether, when and how the work can be modified' (Article 11(1)).

It is not to be assumed that this right is assigned whenever other rights are, and the conveyance of the title to the physical item embodying the work (sculpture, painting, etc.) does not imply the transfer of the right to modify it (Article 16(2) and (3)).

In this writer's view, an agreement may assign this right to another person. Under Swiss Law, the right of integrity is not inalienable within the meaning of the French law, for example.

108. Now, the legislature was prompted to prevent the possible misuse of this newly acquired right by the assignee and provided that, notwithstanding any agreement enabling the other party to modify the work, the author may still oppose a modification which is damageable to his personality (Article 11(2)).

---

110. Barrelet & Egloff, No. 12 *ad* Art. 25 Copyright Act; ATF 131 III 480, 493 ff decides that the publication of a political article in the magazine of a different party would not be contrary to the author's right of personality, a decision which may have been influenced by the circumstances of the case. ATF 136 III 225 mentions in an obiter dictum that the right of paternity should not be transferable.

109. The Swiss Federal Tribunal has shown little respect for the integrity of architectural works in a few recent decisions.[111] Cantonal courts have been more fortunate either for architectural works[112] or for other works, such as newspaper articles,[113] audio-visual works[114] or biographical exposes.[115]

The right of integrity is less absolute for functional works, such as a guidebook.[116]

C. The Right to Authorize First Publication

110. Article 9(2) of the Copyright Act grants the author the exclusive right to decide 'whether, when, how and under which name his work shall be divulged'. With the word 'divulgation', the Swiss Law describes the first publication under whichever form, for example, the public recitation, the public display or the public performance of the work.

Therefore, the concept of 'first publication' as used in Article 6 Berne Convention appears to be narrower than the notion of 'divulgation', since for a 'publication' to take place within the meaning of Article 6(1) Berne Convention, it is necessary that a sufficient number of copies of the work be made available to the public.

The right to authorize the divulgation of the work is both of an economic and a moral nature. That right is assignable.

111. Once exercised, the authorization cannot be revoked. The Swiss Law does not recognize the *droit de repentir* admitted under German law (section 42 German *Urheberrechtsgesetz*) and under French law (Article L 121-4 French Code of Intellectual Property).

That right is probably not transferred to the buyer of a work of art unless it is expressly stipulated. The point is controversial.

111. *See* ATF 117 II 466; ATF 120 II 65; Fed. Trib. *in* RSPI 1991, 388. *See also* ATF 125 III 332; Fed. Trib., SIC 2009, 345; Fed. Trib., SIC 2012, 186 (public law zoning rules and regulations have to be respected notwithstanding a possible violation of the right of integrity of the architect); ATF 142 III 387: the only test concerning the admissibility of modifications to the original building would be whether the personality of the architect is harmed by the modification made to the building, as there would be no need for balancing the interests in presence; but in our view the integrity of the work in itself should be taken into consideration. Cherpillod, Propriété intellectuelle, Basle 2021, par. 1190 *in fine* advocates a balancing of all interests. *See* generally Thies & Spauschus, *Quo Vadis Baukultur?* (Quo Vadis Art of Architecture), SIC 2007, 881 (comparing Swiss and German law). For other works on the public domain *see* M.-A.Renold, *Dégradation et restauration des oeuvres d'art exposées sur le domaine public* (Degradation and Restoration of Works of Art Exhibited in the Public Domain), SIC 2003, 204.
112. Cant. Ct St-Gallen *in* RSJ 1991, 138.
113. Appel. Ct Zurich *in* RSPIDA 1976, 242.
114. Appel. Ct Zurich *in* RSPIDA 1981, 109.
115. Just. Commission Lucerne *in* RSPI 1994, 292.
116. Just. Ct Geneva *in* SJ 1977, 433.

II. Exploitation Rights

A. *Reproduction Right*

112. The author has the exclusive right to make a copy or copies of his work, under whatever form, shape or in whatever material. Article 10(2)(a) of the Copyright Act mentions printed copies, phonograms, videograms or other recordings (such as CD or CD-ROM). Recording a musical file or a video on a format such as MP3 or iPhone is an act of copying within the meaning of the Copyright Act.[117] This view is no longer contested, especially since the revision of the Copyright Act in 2007.[118]

113. Under Swiss Law, it should be admitted that the sheer use of software in a computer constitutes 'reproducing' within the meaning of the law. Article 24a Copr. Act that has been introduced in 2019 makes an exception for transitory copies if certain conditions are met, and Article 24d makes a further exception in case of scientific research and data mining, both of which show that in themselves, those copies fall under the right of reproduction. A 'copy' must not necessarily be a permanent embodiment of the work. The access to Internet may enable one to browse through protected materials; that would constitute 'reproduction' within the meaning of the law. Of course, the reproduction right is often infringed, as obviously happens when downloading those materials, for example. The case law is to the effect that not only a reproduction *telle-quelle* but also a modified reproduction or a partial reproduction are infringing.[119] Of course, some of the characteristic features of the original work must be recognizable.[120]

114. Nevertheless, the style as such may be copied.[121] For example, certain shapes of houses, certain solutions to technical or spatial questions may be reproduced in other architectonic works. Under Swiss copyright law, 'self-plagiarism' is

117. ATF 133 II 263.
118. *See* ATF 133 III 473, 482 (browsing falls under the exclusive right of the copyright owner as a copying act) (of course the private use exemption of Art. 19 CA may apply); Appel. Ct Berne, SIC 2001, 613, 617 & Cant. Ct BS, SIC 2003, 217 (scanning is a copying act within the meaning of the Copyright Act). *See also* H. Pfortmüller, in Müller & Oertli, *Urheberrechtsgesetz* (Copyright Act), No. 5 *ad* Art. 10 Copyright Act (the use of a software in a computer is a copying act).
119. Fed. Trib., SIC 2005, 562 (copying of the music of a movie on cassette is of course copying within the meaning of the Copyright Act). For sampling the test of 'being recognizable' may not be appropriate; *see* D. Haux, in SIC 2021, 583.
120. Sup. Ct Zurich, SIC 2001, 504 (in the case of copying a baby chair, the original model must be recognizable in order for the court to find infringement – it was admitted there); Sup. Ct Luzern, SIC 1998, 567 (protection of a digital watch); Sup. Ct Zurich, SIC 2011, 230 (unlawful copying of 5.2% of software); Sup. Ct Zurich, SIC 2013, 697 (finding a violation of copyright in a software where approx. 50% of the lines of the programme have been found to be identical). But *see* Civ. Ct Zurich, RSPI 1996, 443 (finding no reproduction in recoding a video from the US NTSC standard to the European PAL standard, because no new copy would be generated).
121. ATF 125 III 328.

not prohibited. Yet, if a contract gives a first Publisher the exclusive right of reproduction, the author who self-plagiarizes may be committing a breach of this contract. Further, if for a second publication under a different contract, the author has guaranteed that her work is original and has never been published before, there might be a breach of that second contract. However, it will be difficult to substantiate a claim for damages. Finally, outside the realm of copyright, there may be academic or professional sanctions against some scholar who would attempt to inflate his resume through repeating articles with much cut and paste.

It is important to mention that the reproduction right may be infringed if the basic structure, the table of contents or the system of a book are copied, even if there is extensive rewriting taking place.[122]

B. *Performing Right*

115. According to Article 10(2)(c) of the Copyright Act, the author enjoys the exclusive right to recite, perform or play the work. This right also covers the simultaneous performance in a location other than the original one, for example, through video.

A performance is any and all fugitive materialization of the work.[123] It is to be distinguished from the right of diffusion through broadcasting and cable, that is addressed by a different provision (Article 10(2)(d)).

116. In the practice of Swiss collecting right societies, the performing right is always exercised by the authors themselves, to whom the societies refer all applications for authorizing the performance.

Since 2007, Article 10, paragraph 2(c) also grants the author the exclusive right of 'making available' the copyrighted work. The Swiss legislature loosely followed the wording of Article 8 WIPO Copyright Treaty of 1996, without narrowing the scope of 'making available' by the addition of the word 'publicly' [available] as in the original WIPO text. Swiss case law is now exploring whether uploading and downloading works from the Internet in a file-sharing environment falls under such right of 'making available'.[124] In our view, it is certain that no simultaneous availability is necessary for the making available by third parties to be contrary to the

122. *See* ATF 88 IV 123.

123. Sup. Ct Schaffhausen, SIC 2004, 308; Sup. Ct Thurgau, SIC 1999, 404. According to ATF 145 III 72, the access provider to Internet is not liable for infringement by the end users. See J. Francey, Commentaire, SIC 2019, 686.

124. *See*, e.g., Cant. Ct Graubünden, SIC 2008, 205 (holding that hash links in peer-to-peer systems necessarily violate the copyrights, and do not fall under the exemption of private use to the extent that uploading is simultaneous with downloading). The revision of the Copyright Act in 2019 did not change the system of the law: private use, including streaming, remains admissible. This solution is valid even if the source of the streaming is illegal. The Copyright Act may be applicable to infringement of the copyright in an action filed by the copyright owner in Switzerland, even if the actions or omissions take place abroad, as long as they generate infringement in our country. Uploading as in P2P is not admissible. As a matter of fact simultaneous down- and uploading seems less current than a decade ago. *See* further below n. 126 and above text at para. 10.

copyright. An on-demand availability is sufficient. Articles 13a and 35a of the revised Copr. Act now clearly give a right of remuneration to authors and performers for Videos on Demand.

C. Adaptation Right

117. The right to adapt the work is an exclusive right of the author. The adaptation may be a sheer modification of the original work so as to better suit its purpose, or it can be a new, derivatively acquired work. In both cases, the authorization of the first author is needed, and in the second case only, the latter author will enjoy a copyright of his own.

D. Translation Right

118. The right to translate the work is an exclusive right of the author. Article 3(2) of the Copyright Act mentions as the first example of *derivative work* the translation of a work.

Of course, for copyright law to apply, the material which is translated has to be protected; this is not necessarily the case with commercial letters, or of the appendix to a contract, or a commonplace interview. For want of individuality, these texts might not be copyrightable. Then, their translation does not need the authorization of the author.

119. The translation may be a derivative *work* to the extent that it is an individual creation. If a text which is individual in its original version is devoid of any individuality in the translation because the translator missed transposing the characteristic formulation of the original author's thoughts, then the use of the translation still needs the authorization of the original author, even if no copyright action may be introduced by the translator or his publishers against third parties.

Under the 1992 Law as before, a conveyance of copyright does not extend to the right of translation unless the agreement expressly provides for transferring that right. Actually, most forms used by the Swiss publishers of library and scientific works include a specific covenant to that effect.

A translator who is an employee of a publishing company and translates a book outside the scope of his employment and during his free time is deemed to be an independent author. As it is usual that translators be paid, the publishing company must remunerate the translator, albeit at a rate less than it would to an author, if the remuneration is by means of royalties. Further, the degree of difficulty needed for the task may play a role in determining the royalty rate. For instance, payment may increase for translating texts, including the names of given public persons who are known in French-speaking countries, but less so in German-speaking countries, so that the translator has to find other names as examples of the ideas conveyed in the French text.[125]

E. Other Rights

1. Distribution Right

120. Under Article 10(2)(b), the author enjoys a right of distribution. He may authorize or prohibit any act of marketing for the copies of his work. It bears either on the sale of a copy, or on the lending thereof (before a first sale has exhausted the copyright), or on any other method to put the copies in circulation, for example, through Internet. Swiss law does not distinguish here between a distribution act against consideration and a distribution act free of charge.

2. Broadcasting

121. Under Article 10(2)(d), broadcasting the work is subject to the approval of the author. Under 'broadcasting', the law deals with any and all direct transmission by technical means such as radio diffusion, television or direct cable diffusion – which means cable diffusion by the broadcasting organization itself. This probably does not encompass Internet distribution, although the point is disputed.

122. Recording a broadcast is not allowed without the approval of the author. Swiss law does no longer know of the distinction between ephemeral recording (accepted as of right if national legislatures chose so under the Brussels text of the Berne Convention) and permanent recording, except for the new provision of Article 24b Copr. Act introduced in 2007; this provision grants to collecting right societies the exclusive privilege to collect dues for non-theatrical music deriving from the making of copies of phonograms or videograms available on the market with a view to broadcast them. (There are some controversies surrounding the notion of 'non-theatrical music' for the music embedded in movies). Switzerland, of course, follows the continental tradition according to which the broadcasts, the TV programmes as such do not work unless there is some individuality in a given programme.[126]

---

125. *See* Just. Ct Geneva *in* RSPIDA 1980, 87.
126. ATF 107 II 82; ATF 119 II 51. According to ATF 136 III 232, the law of the uploading State is determinative in order to find whether satellite broadcasts may be interrupted by advertisements, in spite of the clear text of Art. 110 para. 1 of the Act of Private International Law of 18 Dec. 1987 (SR 291). See generally L. Schüpbach, Das Schutzlandprinzip im Urheberkollisionsrecht, PhD Thesis, Basle 2018. According to Fed. Trib., SIC 2011, 305, the downloading made in Switzerland from an illegal site is a criminal offence in itself, and the accomplice may be prosecuted in Switzerland too. If the download is made from a legal source it is authorized by Art. 19 (3*bis*) CA. However, according to Fed. Trib. SIC 2011, 170 as understood in Trib. Sup. Berne, SIC 2011, 658, the activities of a private company spying on the Internet to find the IP address of possible infringers

3. Retransmission Right

123. Article 10(2)(e) provides for a specific right to authorize the retransmission of broadcasted works. The Federal Tribunal paved the way for the right of retransmission in two groundbreaking decisions in 1981.[127]

Therefore, while the retransmission right is firmly mandated by Article 10(2)(e), Article 22 of the 1992 Copyright Act contains two limitations and a precision:

(1) The *precision* is to the effect that the exclusive right entirely prevails for the retransmission of television programmes on subscription (Pay TV) or of television programmes that Swiss viewers are not able to watch on their screen. These programmes are not accessible, and their transmission within Switzerland is akin to first broadcasting rather than retransmission. There is some controversy about the test of inaccessibility: should it be inaccessible to all installations of even the most sophisticated collective retransmission network, as the intent of the legislature may have dictated,[128] or is it accessible to the normal disk antennas of the public, as this was the intent of the Third-Expert Committee?
(2) The first limitation is not a compulsory licence, but a compulsory recourse to a *collecting right society* in order to enforce the retransmission right. Although the 1989 Bill foresaw the compulsory licence system in that case, Parliament

are unlawful as contrary to the Swiss Data Protection Act (now Federal Act of 23 Sep. 2020, effective probably on 1 Sep. 2023; FF 2020 7397); thus the IP address and names of the infringer cannot be filed in the criminal proceedings. In theory the filing of a criminal action could allow to get the IP address of a serious infringer. Some foreign copyright holders were unhappy with that decision. Ten years ago there appears to have been attempts by a private company to do self-justice against possible infringers on the Internet, with cookies being put to block downloading of movies, in total illegality. The revised Copyright Act provides for a legal way to get the address of the internet infringers with a view to request the intervention of a criminal court ordering to the internet access provider to identify the user of a given IP address; *see* Art. 77*i* Copr. Act (2019) and above text at para. 10.

127. ATF 107 II 82; ATF 107 II 57. For *streaming* and *webcasting*, *see* Art. 13a (3) and 35a(3) Copr. Act; Under Art. 16a Film Ordinance of 3 Jul. 2002 as revised on 25 Nov. 2015 (RS 443.11), streaming platforms must file with the Swiss Office of Communications listings of streamed Swiss movies (or coproductions with Swiss producers) over 60 minutes with detailed information about copyright owners. A so-called Netflix law, i.e., a revised version of the Law on Cinema of 14 Dec. 2001 (RS 443.1) adopted by the Parliament with the aim of having a minimum content of Swiss movies (4%) and European movies (30%) had been waiting for the approval by the people after a successful referendum; this approval was expressed in the votation of 15 May 2022; *See* also Fed. Trib. SIC 2013, 144; Fed. Trib. in JdT 2006 I 326; Fed. Arb. Comm., SIC 2005, 641. *See also* Fed. Trib. 6B_584/2011 (Canal – I)(there is no violation of the retransmission right when a software and hardware system allows to avoid restrictions put on a decoder for viewing Pay TV, Art. 150*bis* criminal Code is not infringed either) (available at www.bger.ch).

128. *See* Barrelet & Egloff, No. 11 *ad* Art. 22 Copyright Act; Wittweiler, *Zu den Schrankenbestimmungen im neuen Urheberrechtsgesetz* (Limiting Provisions in the New Copyright Act) 588 (AJP, 1993). For the use of music in other broadcast, see Fed. Trib., SIC 2020, 554 (Tarif A Radio/Swissperform IV) (the remuneration covers use without time limitation). In any case, the impossibility to receive the broadcast exists inasmuch as the broadcast is encrypted. ATF 133 III 568. *See also* Com. Ct Aargau, SIC 2008, 24; Fed. Adm. Trib., SIC 2019, 607 (tariff 3a II) (among other criteria, tariffs decided abroad may help determine the 'equitable', that is appropriate tariffs within Switzerland).

preferred to limit as narrowly as possible the encroachment upon the author's rights. Practically, there is little difference, since the collecting right societies shall grant the authorization to whichever cable organization applies, and the tariff is approved under the usual procedure so that no individual bargaining can take place.

(3) The second limitation regards the small *cable networks*. Unfortunately, the case law was rather muddled in that respect, so the legislature was at a loss when enacting this obvious exception to the right of retransmission. A collective antenna within a small apartment house should not be subject to a separate royalty since it is only a technical device to allow every inhabitant to watch television.

However, a network covering a whole development of a thousand dwellings or more should not escape the payment of an additional royalty, since it is very similar to the municipal networks that are subject to it.

124. The qualitative test evolved in case law is the crossing of public ways or public ground.[129] It is due to the fact that the Posts and Telegrams Administration had the right to authorize or prohibit the establishment of a network cable under the public streets or public places. It is not related to copyright.

A federal decision of 1993 applying the Copyright Act of 1922 held that the networks within a hotel of more than 400 rooms would not be a public network and that it would not fall under the retransmission right. That judgment was quite recently reversed, and Swiss law is now in line with the European solution.[130] The revised Copr. Act of 2019 now follows the latter federal case, which settles the issue in favour of the copyright owners and to the detriment of the hoteliers, who have to pay a due proportional to the number of rooms in their hotel. More generally, the new Article 10, paragraph 2(f) introduced in the Copyright Act of 2007 already covered that situation. This provision provides for a 'right of receiving' the broadcast, not only 'publicly' but also in any other framework that does not fall under the exception of 'private use' under Article 19 Copyright Act. For example, a so-called private club that would show soccer games on large screens would infringe on the exclusive right of the author under Article 10, paragraph 2(f) if the viewing is simultaneous with the broadcasting. If deferred, it would infringe on Article 10, paragraph 2(e). It will be noted that the exception of 'private use' does not apply to the *replay* of broadcasts. However, there are no special fees (except the flat tax *per capita*)(not based on copyright issues) when the broadcast is stored on the broadcasting system itself for a limited period of time. The Replay TV function of the cable distributors is subject to remuneration for the replay which is included in the general

129. ATF 110 II 61.

130. *See* ATF 119 II 51 (*See* a comment by A. Kerever *in* RIDA 1994, 371 et seq.) The Fed. Trib. reversed that decision, SIC 2018, 308). Interestingly, this question was one of the few remaining points of dissent between the two Chambers of Parliament in 2019. A request for a popular referendum on the revised Copyright Act has been unsuccessful as too few citizens sponsored it..

tariff GT 12; it is explained by the fact that Replay TV may be devoid of advertising. Yet the recent threefold increase of the levies to be paid in this regard might push people away from conventional TV with replay towards subscribing even more to Netflix and Disney+.

F. Remuneration Rights

125. Of course, exclusive rights are mostly invoked by the authors in order to obtain a royalty payment.

In a sense, all copyright is for remuneration, with the obvious exception of moral rights when a ghostwriter is not at work.

Nevertheless, the Swiss Copyright Law provides for a category of remuneration which is due even in the absence of an exclusive right, be it because the legislature did not grant such right, as in the public lending for consideration, or because there is an exception by law to the absolute right, as in the case of reprography,[131] or a compulsory licence scheme, as in the case of phonograms.[132]

Article 13 subjects to remuneration the public lending of copies of the copyrighted work for a fee. The question is not whether the lending service is in the position to operate with benefits as most video clubs would be, for example, but whether there is a fee which is charged to the borrower. This test was devised mainly to exonerate state and university libraries that lend books or CDs. The exact extent of the exoneration of payment for public lending was one of the issues of the Bill for revision of the Copyright Act which had been debated in Parliament in 2019, but in the end the law was not amended in this respect.

To the extent that no exclusive right is thereby granted to authors against the public lending of their work, the Swiss solution is not compatible with the European Directive 92/100 of 1992[133] and later texts.

126. The Swiss law makes an exception for software programs, for which the exclusive right is restored against any sort of public lending.

Finally, common sense exemptions of the remuneration duty have been made in favour of the owners of architectural works and of applied artworks.

131. *See* paras 133 et seq. The right to a remuneration is deemed to be a 'quasi-contractual' claim, with the time limit of five years as for debts owing periodically, and a transfer is possible as for all contractual claims (and most claims in tort too); *see* ATF 124 III 370 c. 3 b. As a consequence, once the copyright owner has transferred his claim to a third party, the same claim cannot be put forward by a collective right society; *see* F. Wigger/M. Handle, *EuGH: Keine Reprographievergütung für Verlage* (EuCJ: No Remuneration for Copying in Favour of Publishers), SIC 2016, 251, 263 n. 105. In Switzerland, however, collective right societies do directly remunerate publishing houses for their share.

132. *See* paras 136 et seq. A similar solution has been advocated for the embedding of live-streams deemed to be a rebroadcasting that should be subject to the collective exploitation of rights in favour of the broadcasting operator; *see* R.M. Hilty, O. Schmid, M. Weber, *Urheberrechtliche Beurteilung vom 'Embedding'* ('Embedding under Copyright Law'), SIC 2016, 237.

133. Council Directive 92/100/EC of 19 Nov. 1992 on rental right and lending right and on certain rights related to copyright in the field of Intellectual Property, OJ No. L 346/61.

Further exempt from the lending right are the copies of works that have been rented in order to facilitate the use of a work which has been authorized by the contract entered into with the rightful owner of the copyright. That may be the case for musical scores, for example, or for the distribution of cinematographic works.

III. Other Rights of the Author

127. The third category of rights exists under Swiss law; rights that are neither exclusive rights aiming at confronting the author's economic position nor sheer entitlement to compensation, but rather ancillary rights that complete the moral and economic privileges of the author and help him fully enjoy his main rights. These rights regulate the relationship between the author and the owner of the main or the main embodiment of his work.

A. *Right of Access*

128. According to Article 14(1) Copyright Act, the author may request from the owner of his work access to the work inasmuch as that access is indispensable to enjoy his copyright, provided that no legitimate interest of the owner prevents access to the work.

For example, if the author has to have an inventory of his complete works with photographs or measurements, he may gain access to his painting, sculpture or building.

The *proviso* about the owner's legitimate interests aims at protecting him, for example, against the invasion of his privacy, the possible divulgence of trade secrets or the publication of photographs of a portrait which he would rather keep hidden.

B. *Right of Display*

129. Article 14(2) gives the author the right to request from the owner the temporary transfer of the work for exhibiting it in Switzerland. The author may have to post a bond, or a security deposit in order to guarantee the return of the work undamaged; in case of damage, the author who has invoked that right shall compensate the owner even if no fault on his part can be established (Article 14(3)).

'Exhibition' within the meaning of the law is not a performance, such as the showing of a motion picture, but a static display, at least according to some commentators.[134] Nonetheless, if the performance of a cinematographic work in a *cinémathèque* or a movie theatre is clearly excluded from the right of the display, the showing of the same work within an exhibition might be covered by the right of the display. For example, the display of some static works by Andy Warhol may be

---

134. Barrelet & Egloff, No. 8 *ad* Art. 14 Copyright Act.

accompanied by the showing of one or several of his audio-visual works. This writer does not see why Article 14(2) should not apply in that event.

C. Protection Against Destruction

130. Under Article 15 of the Copyright Law, whenever the owner of the sole original embodiment of work must admit that the author has a legitimate interest to keep it, he must offer to the author to take it back before destroying it.

The author shall pay only the value of the material – which might be quite expensive, for example, in case of artistic jewellery. If it is not feasible to take back the embodiment of the work, for example, because it is incorporated into a building to be destroyed in such a way that mutilation of the work would ensue if it were to be separated, then the author may request a grace period for reproducing the work, at his own costs.

As regards an architectonic work's impending destruction, the author can only ask for the possibility of photographing it, and that copies of the plans be handed over to him at his own costs.

In order to determine whether there is an architectonic work or another one, the test should be that of the functionality. A building like La Géode in Paris or La Tour Armand in Versailles is not architectonic works because they pursue no useful purpose, although they do shelter rooms and space.

131. There is no *droit de suite* in Switzerland.

§7. Limitation or Exemptions to the Copyright Protection

132. Chapter 5, comprising Articles 19 through 28 of the Copyright Act, states several exemptions or restrictions to copyright protection. Some of them are only a new version of traditional exemptions or defences in copyright litigation under Swiss law. However, the first restriction to the copyright, which concerns reprography, really does not purport to limit the authors' and the publishers' rights but to ensure that their right to remuneration be actually respected.

To these limitations in Chapter 5, there should be added the parody exemption ensconced in Chapter 3, Article 11(3), which we shall start with.

I. Parody

133. Under Article 11(3) of the Copyright Act, the use of existing works in order to create a parody or a similar imitation is lawful.

The freedom to make satiric imitations is deemed to be an important part of live cultural life. Satiric or burlesque works may imply some criticism of the underlying values on which the original work rested. Further, this criticism is protected by the constitutional freedom of speech. As such, the parody may, of course, be considered as a derivative work. To the extent that the original work is recognizable, and it is always the case in good parody, there should be an approval of the author of the original work. As that approval is unlikely for obvious reasons, the law has to provide in general terms an exemption concerning parody.

The parodic effect assumes that the public knows about the works or at least the style of the original author. Swiss law extends the defence of parody to the parody of any and all *existing* works, and not only to published works, as does the French law (Article L. 122-5 Chapter 4 French Code of Intellectual Property), for example.

There are three characteristic features in a parody, which have to be present so as to admit the parody defence in a given case:

(1) The parody aims at *ridiculing* the original work. Of course, there may be a commercial intent as well as a satiric one since no publishing will take place without the hope to derive some financial profits from the parody. If the intent is not to ridicule but rather to ride on the same wave – for example, of nostalgia – as the original work, then the defence cannot be successfully raised.
(2) The economic intention behind the parody is not to take the place of the original work on the market. There should be no substitution effect between the original and the parodic works since they do respond to different purchasing, listening, viewing, etc., motivations. In other words, the economic damage to the original author should be so small, if any, that the rule *de minimis* would apply. If the parody is really critical, there may be a change of taste among the former admirers of the original work, but that is the desired effect of allowing criticism.
(3) The parody shall be *creative*. There must be a transposition of meaning, an inversion of values, innuendos or burlesque effects. Therefore, the original work is seldom, if ever, entirely taken over in a true parody. The new features of the derivative work shall be compared to the original characteristics of the parodied work, and the parody defence will be accepted when the newer work is really original. Most *memes* should qualify for the parody exemption under Swiss law. Non-fungible token (NFT) are usually not a parody. Also, if some excepts of a text, song or other work are just taken away from the reproduction, the remaining part cannot be characterized as a parody (*see* W. Egloff in SIC 2021, 639).

II. Reprography

134. Before the enactment of the 1992 Copyright Act, the Federal Tribunal did not allow for the defence of private use to undermine the right of the author or of the publisher to prohibit the mechanical reproduction of his work, but in very narrow limits. Indeed, all reprography was illegal as soon as it aimed at avoiding commercial costs or generating income.[135]

135. *See* ATF 108 II 475. *See* now for the spirit of the compulsory payment scheme ATF 133 III 263 (MP3) and 473 (electronic press review); ATF 125 III 141 (copy within a company: legal but subject to remuneration); ATF 128 IV 201 (definition of a *narrow circle* of friends and relatives). There is no private use when for profit reproduction takes place, Fed. Trib. SIC 2018, 308 c. 5.3.2. The

There was, however, a rather wide gap between the rule of law and actual practice in the field of photography and cassette taping.

Thus, the legislature was intent on legalizing reprography but ensuring that authors and publishers would receive an appropriate remuneration.

135. The intermingling of the concept of private use with the duty to pay royalties for reprography has given rise to a rather complex set of provisions in Articles 19 and 20 of the Copyright Act. The following structuring may help explain the text of the law.

There are three rules on the admissibility of the mechanical reproduction of a protected work:

(1) Article 19(1)(a) allows for copying or other forms of private use within a narrow circle of relatives or friends (and not the friends' friends). This use is basically royalty-free, with the exception of a copyright levy on blank tapes and CD-ROMs.

(2) Article 19(3) and (4) prohibits the mechanical reproduction of various works and software. It is unlawful to copy works of fine arts, musical scores and the recording of the performance of a protected work, outside of the narrow circle of relatives and friends. Further, it is unlawful to copy the totality or the essential part of a work, copies of which are available on the market. However, there is no private copying at all allowed for software (save one copy as a safeguard). The revision of the Copyright Act of 2007 provides in an important Article 19 paragraph 3*bis* that no remuneration will be owed and that no action may be taken to prohibit the making of private copies of downloads from sources that have been put legally on the Net.

(3) Article 20 gives the legal basis for remuneration in all cases where there is a possibility of mechanical reproduction.

Under the tariff on reprography, there is a one-third rebate for educational institutions. Universities, for example, have to pay a small annual amount for each student's right to make photocopies. Tapes are charged with a levy pro rata *tempore*, varying for audio, CD-ROM and videotapes.

There is a levy on apparatuses such as MP3 players, smartphones and other material support of the copying, reproduction and storage of mainly copyrighted works,[136] but not on personal computers and notebooks. The collecting right societies have the exclusive competence to collect and distribute the royalties for reprography.

debtor of reprography royalties has to cooperate with the collecting right societies; otherwise he will have to pay more as a penalty. Comm. Ct ZH, SIC 2016, 457; that practice is criticized by A. Schnewly, *Praxis der kollektiven Verwertung nach GT 8 VII und 9 VII auf den Prüfstand* (Revisiting the Practice of Collecting Rights under Tariffs GT 8 VII and 9 VII), SIC 2017, 599. A frequent criticism against the collecting right societies are the very high costs their management entails, including high remuneration of their officers. See a cost analysis of 2015 by J. Fark, B. Meyer, D. Zöbeli, cited by C. Semmelmann, SIC 2019, at 679 fn 40.

136. ATF 133 II 263 (Tariff 4d of Collecting Right Societies – so-called iPod tariff – is applicable).

136. Among the legal exemptions to Chapter 5, the decompilation exemption has been already expounded in connection with the regime of software,[137] and the status of cable diffusion as regulated under Article 22 is described earlier.[138] The other defences are more traditional.

III. Compulsory Licences for Phonograms

137. The only compulsory licence of the Swiss Copyright Act concerns musical works, with or without text, which may be had on the market with the approval of the author: any phonogram producer having an establishment in Switzerland or established in a country granting the reciprocity to Switzerland may ask for a licence from the author (Article 23).

The performer is not subject to that compulsory licence,[139] which loses most of its use. It is recalled that the compulsory licence schema was introduced in the US and other countries for piano rolls. It seems nowadays somewhat obsolete, especially in a small country where the only hope for independent producers to survive is to market some original recordings.

138. Besides, some technical defects would be burdensome if applying the legal provision on compulsory licensing:

- There is no delay requested before the granting of a compulsory licence. In theory, the Swiss market could be immediately lost to the licensee.
- Furthermore, there is no security bond to be posted for the payment of the royalties.

IV. Archival Copies

139. In order to preserve a work, it is lawful to make a copy thereof, which copy shall be deposited in archives to which the public has no access (Article 24 (1) Copr. Act); this provision has been enlarged in the revisions of 2007 and 2019 to make clear that Fine Arts and other non-profit museums, libraries, teaching institutions and public archives may make a copy in order to preserve the completeness of their collections even when they are accessible to the public, whenever their activities are not entertained for profits.

A safeguard copy can be made for software.[140] No contract can prohibit that. Under Article 22*b* Copr. Act on orphan works, the making of a copy or copies may give rise to a compensation to be payable to a collecting right society. Under Article 43*a* Copr. Act, in the event that a large number of published works or performing rights are at stake, the collecting right societies may collect remunerations even for

137. *See* paras 34–39.
138. *See* paras 122 et seq.
139. Barrelet & Egloff, No. 5 *ad* Art. 23 Copyright Act.
140. *See* para. 138.

authors who are not among their members or registered beneficiaries. All works in public libraries, archives and conservation institutions are deemed to have been published. Under Article 24*e* Copr. Act 'short excerpts' of a work can be published in inventories of public libraries etc., with a view to letting know about their collections, provided that this excerpt does not impinge on the normal commercial use of the work.

V. Right of Quotation

140. Under Article 25, a quotation may be lawfully made if it serves as a comment, a reference or a demonstration and inasmuch as the aim of the quotation justifies its extent. The quotation is possible only in literary or scientific works, as well as in newspaper articles, but not in plastic works such as a sculpture or a painting. Sound sampling is prohibited to the extent the melodies are recognizable. Cinematographic works can be quoted for comment, demonstration or reference purposes.

The sheer taking over of a whole paragraph without indication of a discussion, criticism or comment is not lawful.[141] In the same manner, a 'thumbnail' is not a citation within the meaning of that exception to the rights of the copyright owner.

The right of quotation cannot be raised as a defence for the copyright of unpublished works.

VI. Catalogues of Museums, Exhibitions and Auctions

141. The catalogues may themselves be a work which is protected by copyright. The question at this juncture is, however, to which extent they can reproduce the paintings, sculptures and other works of art without infringing on the copyright of the authors of the various works shown in the catalogue.

The Swiss legislature followed the German solution: the public museums, as well as the galleries for their temporary exhibitions and the auction houses, may publish a catalogue without the approval of the author. The museums do not have to own the works of art on display.[142] However, this exemption does not apply to postcards, posters, T-shirts and other products of merchandising, nor does it apply to copies of catalogues printed after the exhibition is over. It does apply to catalogues made available on CD-ROM. In practice, some ill-advised museums pay royalties for the catalogues while some other museums do not because of the correct interpretation of the law which is recalled here at the beginning of this paragraph.

VII. Panorama

142. The right to publish postcards and other views of city places and urban landscapes, although they may encompass the occasional sculpture or fresco which

141. ATF 133 III 480, 489.
142. ATF 127 III 26.

adorn them, is well established in the German tradition of copyright. Under Article 27 Swiss Copyright Act, it is therefore lawful to 'copy' in two dimensions the copyrighted works that are located on public ground or ground accessible to the public – such as the patio of a museum if it is open to everyone at any time.

On the contrary, models or mock-ups of these works cannot be reproduced in three dimensions.

VIII. News Reports

143. The copyrighted works that are visible or heard during events on which the media report may be recorded, reproduced, shown, broadcasted or retransmitted in any way.

Press reviews may quote from published articles or television or radio reports. The source and the author must be mentioned, as is the case for all quotations.[143]

§8. Duration of Protection

I. General Rule

144. The protection starts with the creation of the work (Article 29(1)). No achievement, no fixation requirement is set by the Copyright Act, which protects drafts as well as final versions (Article 2(4)).

The protection stops seventy years after the author's death. These years are counted from 31 December of the year of the author's death.

145. The works that fell into the public domain before entry into force of the Copyright Act on 1 July 1993 are no longer protected.[144]

II. Special Rules

146. Software programs are protected for fifty years *post mortem auctoris* (Article 29(2)(a) Copyright Act).

147. The protection for an anonymous work or a pseudonymous work whose author remains unknown, stops seventy years after the first publication. If that work has been published as a serial story, the delay starts from the last publication.

148. The protection for collective works lasts fifty years (for computer programs) or seventy years from the death of the last co-author, unless the respective contribution of each of the authors can be separated, in which case each contribution will enjoy its own status.

143. *See* paras 104 and 139.
144. ATF 124 III 266; Appel. Ct Ticino, SIC 2004, 20.

149. For motion pictures and other audio-visual works, the only date taken into consideration is the death of the art director. For photographs devoid of originality, the protection is fifty years from their creation. Should a photograph be deemed to be original, the protection follows the general rule.

150. If the author disappears but his death is not certain, or if the author does not reveal his identity in case of an anonymous or a pseudonymous work, the protection will stop when there is reason to believe that the author is deceased more than seventy years ago (or fifty years ago for computer programs).

III. Moral Right

151. The *droit moral* enjoys the same duration as economic rights. It is not perpetual as under French law. If heirs can show that their own right of personality is harmed by a violation of the moral right occurring later than seventy years after the death of the author, the heirs have their own claim in redress and remedy based on Articles 27 and 28 Civil Code.

§9. Neighbouring Rights

I. The Swiss Copyright Law and International Conventions

A. National Copyright Law

152. The third part of the Copyright Act, Articles 33 through 39, is dedicated to neighbouring rights.

As usual, the neighbouring rights are those of the performer (Article 33), the phonogram producer (Article 36) and the broadcasting organization (Article 37). Slightly more original is the extension of the neighbouring right to the videogram producers (Article 36), as well as the right of remuneration for On-Demand video performances (Article 35*a* Copr. Act). Although it was proposed in the 1986 Draft, there is no neighbouring right for the organizers of theatrical plays. In the twentieth century, the Swiss legislature never envisaged a neighbouring right for printers or publishers. Under the 2017 Bill for revision of the Copyright Act, a new neighbouring right for press publishers might have been introduced, but it was finally rejected. As a *quid pro quo,* press photographs and other nonindividual photographs are now protected under a new special regime (Article 2 (3*bis*) Copr. Act).

B. International Conventions

153. Switzerland acceded to the Rome Convention of 1961 for the protection of performers, producers of phonograms and broadcasting organizations,[145] to the Brussels Convention of 1974 relating to the distribution of programme-carrying signals transmitted by satellite,[146] and to the Geneva Phonogram Convention of 1971.[147] Switzerland also ratified the TRIPS Agreement, Article 14 of which gives minimal protection to neighbouring rights, as well as the WIPO Performances and Phonograms Treaty (WPPT) of 1996; the 2007 revision of the Copyright Act brought Swiss legislation in line with our international obligations. The effective date of the revised Act was 1 July 2008. There is still a requirement of reciprocity for foreign nationals, as is allowed by Article 16 paragraph 1(a)(iii) and (iv) of the Rome Convention. Further, upon adoption of the revised Copyright Act of 2019 Switzerland ratified the Marrakesh and Beijing Treaties, with effective date 11 May 2020; (under Article 81 Copr. Act Articles 13a and 35a do not apply to contracts with authors and performers that have been concluded before the entry into force of the revised Copyright Act on 1 April 2020). A reservation to the Beijing Treaty corresponds to the requirement of reciprocity towards foreign nationals or entities under Article 35 Copr. Act.

II. Rights of Performers

A. Performer

154. The rights of the *performer* are afforded to the 'physical person who performs a work or shares in the performance on an artistic level'. In other words, both the interpreter and the performer (for example, within an orchestra) are protected. It is no longer necessary to enquire whether the performance is creative, as it should be for it to be a *creation* protected as such by Articles 2 et seq. of the Copyright Act. In this regard, Swiss commentary has long been reluctant towards neighbouring rights to the extent that they protect run-of-the-mill performances devoid of creativity. (The same reluctance would affect the status of databases or publishers' rights nowadays. Some would like to protect them under Unfair Competition Law, if at all). Only the 2007 revision introduced the right of paternity for performers (Article 33*a* Copyright Act).

155. Nevertheless, the distinction between a 'performer' and an author is still difficult. For example, the director of a theatrical performance might be deemed to be a performer or a co-author, depending on which level of creativity he works. Similarly, wherever there is no previous work to perform, there can be no performer's rights for the director or the actor, for example, in many *Son et Lumière*, circus

145. RS 0.231.171.
146. RS 0.231.173.
147. RS 0.231.172.

representation, etc. DJ's will often be deemed to be authors and performers, or otherwise only performers.[148] Then, the extent of their legal protection shall turn on the creative aspect of the director's activities.

156. However, the sheer technical activities are not protected by the performer's rights. For example, the technicians who mix the sounds or direct the lights will not be protected as performers.

B. Rights on Collective Performance

157. The nebulous rules on collective authorship have not been taken up for the performance by more than one performer, a frequent occurrence.

158. Article 34(1) of the Copyright Act assuredly states that if several persons performed work, the right of protection belongs to them jointly and severally. Nevertheless, Article 34(2) determines who is to give his consent in the event that the performance is made by an orchestra or a choir: the soloists, the conductor, the director and a representative of the group of performers; if no one has been appointed as representative, the consent of the group leader shall suffice. According to Article 34(3), if the group leader is not known, the organizer of the performance or of the show, the phonogram producer or the broadcasting organization can protect the interests of the group as *negotiorum gestor*. That last competence is broader than the system established under Article 34(2), which addresses the authorization to *use* the performance, whereas Article 34(3) addresses all possible acts in relation to the performance. Therefore, the organizer, the phonogram producer and the broadcasting organization have more powers than the co-performer who is not a group leader, the soloist, the conductor or the director.

159. The idea was to facilitate the various methods of using the collective performance notwithstanding any – not so seldom – uncertainty about the person who is entitled to grant authorization and the possible application of legal rules on the agency (Articles 32 et seq. CO).

C. Primary Use

160. Performers enjoy economic rights similar to those of the authors. They have under Article 33(2) the exclusive rights to all *primary* uses of their performance: any diffusion, any cable diffusion, any recording and manufacturing of phonograms or videograms, any marketing of those, any reception of the diffusion.

---

148. *See* Trib. Cant. Neuchâtel, SIC 2013, 93 (DJ is both an author and a performer, so that both types of royalties are due); *see* further, in general, A. Steiner, *Urberrechtliche Schutzfähigkeit der Zirkus und Varietékunst* (Copyright Protection for Circus and Music Hall), thesis (Basle, 1998).

161. The determination of these rights is exhaustive; in other words, until 2007, the performers had no moral rights on the basis of the Copyright Act: no right of paternity, no right against modification of their performance. Article 33*a* Copr. Act now endows them with the moral right of paternity. Further, they do have, like every person, the rights which are derived from Article 28/281 of the Swiss Civil Code if their personal interests are put into jeopardy by alterations.

D. *Secondary Use*

162. According to Article 12 of the Rome Convention and Article 35 of the Swiss Copyright Act, the performers have a right of remuneration for the secondary use of their performance; that is, the use of phonograms or videograms for diffusion, retransmission, public reception or 'performance' (e.g., the musical part of a ballet).

163. The right against secondary use can be exercised only if that use is made through a record which is available on the market. If the record is not lawfully on the market, the protection against its use is based on Article 33(2)(d) Copr. Act – a right of distribution which does not exist under the Rome Convention but has been provided for by the Swiss legislature with a broader spectrum since it protects performers as well as phonogram producers.

E. *Collecting Rights Societies*

164. The rights of performers inhere even in those performances of works that are in the public domain.

165. These rights are compulsorily exercised by a collecting right society. In Switzerland, the Society *Swiss perform* represents all natural persons and legal entities entitled to neighbouring rights.[149]

III. Rights of Phonogram Producers

166. Switzerland granted phonogram producers both an exclusive right of reproduction and an exclusive right of distribution (Article 36 Copr. Act). There is for

149. *See* D. Aschmann, *Fünf Jahre Verwertung von Leistungsschutzrechten in der Schweiz* (Five Years of Collecting Rights for Neighbouring Rights), SIC 1999, 364 et seq. Note as concerns the rights of Phonograms Producers the requirement of reciprocity under Art. 35 (4) Corp. Act: the decision by Fed. Adm. Trib. on the Tariff A radio (Swissperform), SIC 2017, 538, states that the owner of the rights to a recording that has been first published abroad in a State Member to the WPPT will be entitled to remuneration in Switzerland unless the foreign State has made a reservation to Art. 15 WPPT which would exclude rights in favour of Swiss right owners.

secondary use a right of remuneration, to the extent that performers and phonogram producers share in the royalties deriving from secondary use of the phonograms (Article 35(2)).

167. No formality is requested for the protection of phonogram and videogram producers.

168. The protection is granted even if the phonogram or videogram does not record a 'work' within the meaning of the Copyright Act. The sounds of whales, or the murmur of the sea can be recorded and published as a phonogram and shall enjoy the protection of Article 36 Copr. Act.

169. The *sampling* is prohibited under Swiss law, as it is technically a reproduction of the recording, to the extent the original recording is recognizable to the average listener. Swiss law does not know of any quantitative criterion in this regard. Just recreating a certain sound is acceptable in this writer's view.

170. The use of a phonogram to prepare the soundtrack of a movie would require the authorization of the phonogram producer as well.

171. Finally, indirect piracy, that is, not the bootlegging of a live performance but the recording of a broadcasted phonogram or videogram, is also prohibited under Swiss law.

IV. Rights of Broadcasting Organizations

172. Article 37 of the Copyright Act gives the broadcasting organizations four exclusive rights:

(1) the right to retransmit their broadcasts;
(2) the right to let people see or hear their broadcasts;
(3) the right to record their broadcasts on phonograms or videograms and to copy such recordings;
(4) the right to distribute in any way copies of the broadcasts.

173. The rights so conferred are broader than those of the Rome Convention, since cable diffusion and retransmission are expressly mentioned by the Swiss Copyright Law. Further, the broadcasting organizations share also royalties stemming from the levy on video cassettes.

174. A broadcasting organization enjoys those rights as soon as it qualifies as such under Article 37.

The broadcasts must aim at the public. Technical broadcasting services inside a corporation, police, etc., are not 'public' in that sense.

175. A cable organization is not a broadcasting organization to the extent that it simultaneously transmits signals and programmes broadcast by other organizations.

Now even a minimal expense in view of establishing autonomous programming shall put the organization in the category of broadcasting organizations.[150]

Foreign broadcasting organizations having part of Switzerland within their range are protected.

It is not necessary for the broadcast to contain a protected work in order to be protected. Article 37 does not extend protection to the interview, the sports event, etc.

§10. Infringement and Remedies

I. Administrative Authorities

176. The customs authorities have the right spontaneously to intervene in case of importing or exporting wares and goods whose distribution in Switzerland would contravene copyright or neighbouring rights (Article 75).

The copyright owner may request the customs to stop the said wares and goods (Article 76 Copyright Act). The customs will retain the goods for two periods of ten days at most, so as to enable the injured party to apply for interim measures.

II. Courts of Law

A. *Civil Actions*

177. The Copyright Act enumerates four actions:

(1) action to state and declare the respective rights of the parties (Article 61);
(2) action to prevent harm and wrongful acts (Article 62(1)(a));
(3) action to cease and desist (Article 62(1)(b));
(4) action to get information about the source of the infringing goods and wares (Article 62(1)(c)).

The Copyright Act refers to the Code of Obligations for the actions to compensate losses:

- action for damages (Article 41 Code of Obligations);
- action for compensation of moral damages (Article 49 Code of Obligations);
- accounting of defendant's profits (Article 423 Code of Obligations or possibly Article 62 ss Code of Obligations on unjust enrichment).

150. *See* Mosimann, *Die verwandten Schutzrechte* (The Neighbouring Rights) *in* SIWR II/1, 393.

178. An order to seize and destroy infringing goods may be issued if those wares are in possession of the defendant. No definitive seizure can be ordered at third parties' premises but interim measures to that effect are not to be ruled out. Practical applications of this procedure are rather seldom, but this writer knows of cases in which pirate videos and CD-ROM' Masters were seized and destroyed.

Further, the machinery and production facilities exclusively dedicated to forgery and counterfeiting could be seized and destroyed or closed. Of course, buildings infringing the copyright of an architect cannot be seized nor destroyed; the plans and measurements could be.

179. The conditions for each of those actions vary. Generally speaking, the defendant's fault must be proved to the court in order for the defendant to have to pay monetary damages. Accounting for profits does not necessitate the showing of such fault, but of course, expert testimony shall be brought as evidence of the amount of net profits due to the infringement. As this and other detailed evidence in these financial matters are difficult to show, the courts are often content with an award of royalties at a usual rate.[151]

180. In case a collecting right society files a suit against an unauthorized performance of another infringement, the tariffs usually increase the amount of royalties up to double of what is due when authorization is requested beforehand.[152]

It is a frequent occurrence that the court uses its power to adjudicate *ex aequo et bono* the claims for monetary damages.[153]

151. *See* ATF 25 II 533; ATF 37 II 486. One of the highest settlements ever (in a case of CD-piracy) reached the amount of approximately USD 1 million (1999). More recently, in the case of the Federal Railway Watch unlawfully copied by Google, the settlement is rumoured to have been 20 mio. CHF (2013). *See* generally Y. Benhamou, *Dommages–Intérêts suite à la violation de droits de propriété intellectuelle (méthode des redevances)* (Compensation for Infringement of Intellectual Property Rights/royalties method) 362 (Zurich, 2012). According to App. Ct BS, SIC 2016, 594, when an author puts his photo on Wikicommons he cannot claim as damages for loss profits the amount of royalties that he would have been able to claim from an infringer in the event that the photo had been protectable. *See* also Fed. Trib. SIC 2020, 353: applying both Art. 423 CO and 62 (2) CO in the event that the infringement of copyright is concomitant to a criminal offense towards a third party; only the profit of the respondent equivalent to a loss by the copyright owner can be claimed by him, not the profit corresponding to the loss of the other party. Where the basis of accounting for profits is to be found in the protection of personality under Art. 27 ff. CC the respondent, e.g., a publishing company, has to give full details about his profits and expenses.

152. *See* Cant. Ct Graubünden *in* RSPI 1989, 74; Fed. Trib. *in* SIC 1998, 33. However, such double royalties are not due where there is neither tariff nor contractual provision allowing for it. Stricter limits as to the fiction of approval of the estimates established by the collecting right society have been decided of late by the Fed. Trib., SIC 2021, 543: the collecting right society must prove that the respondent filed inexact or incomplete information as to his use of the protected musical works in order for the court to uphold the fiction that he approved the reckoning up by the collecting right society.

153. *See* ATF 60 II 62. According to Fed. Trib., SIC 2008, 430, the venue for actions concerning remuneration for lawful use (for authors as well as for performers probably) is not identical to the venue for action in damages for torts (Art. 25 of the Federal Law on Venues of 24 Mar. 2000 [SR 272]).

181. If the defendants acted together in the infringement, they will be jointly and severally liable for the payment of compensation.

For example, where a travel agency and an advertising agency infringed on the copyrights of Otl Aicher for the pictograms of Olympic sports, they were found jointly and severally responsible.[154]

182. As to the judgments on 'moral damages' to compensate for an infringement of the author's' moral rights, the awards are not very high, ranging from CHF 300[155] to CHF 10,000.[156] Where the infringement is minimal, the court may even reject all claims for moral damages, as was the case when a newspaper omitted to cite the source of the first publication of an article that was reprinted in conformity with the 1922 Law.[157]

B. Criminal Actions

183. Under Articles 67–73 of the Copyright Act, stronger protection has been introduced by the legislature.

Only intentional acts of infringement are punishable. Defined as infringing acts are all the acts contrary to the rights mentioned from Article 9(2) through 11 of the Copyright Act, as well as the measures aiming at circumventing the technical protection of copyrights.[158] These criminal offences are 'felonies' with the exception of the omittal of the indication of source, which is a mere 'misdemeanour'. There are different sanctions attached to these categorizations: imprisonment up to one year for a misdemeanour or a fine. If the infringing acts are so frequent and deliberate as to appear as a professional practice, the fine may be higher, the imprisonment might be up to five years, with also a fine, and the prosecuting authority necessitates no complaint by an injured party in order for the case to be put to trial.

184. There is an interesting misdemeanour: the unauthorized activity of collecting right society, which needs a complaint by the Federal Institute of Intellectual Property, in order for it to be prosecuted.

---

154. Appel. Ct Aarau *in* RSPI 1988, 128. For the case of a general partnership (*société simple*), there is joint and several liability for the royalties due to collecting right societies; Sup. Ct ZH SIC 2017, 133.
155. Appel. Ct Zurich *in* RSJ 1944, 344 (violation of the right to integrity). A case of libel is known to this writer, in which the court allowed over 100,000 Swiss francs of compensation, part of which amount was indemnity for lost business.
156. ATF 84 II 570 (violation of the right of paternity). A moral entity may be entitled to claim compensation for *tort moral. See,* e.g., ATF 138 III 337 c. 6.1; Fed. Trib. case 5A_100/2015, c. 2; Com. Ct. Saint Gallen, SIC 2019, 39 at 33 c. 10.
157. Fed. Trib. *in* RSPI 1989, 68.
158. Art. 69*a* Copr. Act as introduced on 5 Oct. 2007, effective date 1 Jul. 2008. For 'cardsharing' (circumventing dues for Pay TV) *see* ATF 139 IV 1 (Art. 150*bis* Penal Code only applicable). *See* paras 101 et seq.

§11. Overlapping and Relation to Other Intellectual Property Laws

185. Reference can be made to the Law on Designs of 2001,[159] as well as to the Act against Unfair Competition of 1986. On the one hand, the Law on Designs is not exclusive to the Copyright Act for creations of applied arts, that may enjoy copyright protection if the Copyright Act's prerequisites are met. On the other hand, the Law on Copyright does not exclude the application of the Act against Unfair Competition if the latter's prerequisites are met. Nonetheless, the application of the Unfair Competition rules cannot remove from the public domain something that has been put to it under the principles of the Copyright Act. This is sometimes termed as the 'subsidiarity principle', which is a misleading terminology; all laws are equal. However, as a matter of practical methodology, courts and counsel first start examining the facts of a case under the more specific Act, such as the Copyright Act or the Law on Design, then come over to discuss those facts under the Act against Unfair Competition.

159. *See* paras 547 et seq. It should be noted that the Act Against Unfair Competition of 19 Dec. 1986 as revised (SR 241) is not subsidiary to any special intellectual property legislation, as has been stated in ATF 135 III 446, c. 4 not reported in the Official Reporter but cited by the Fed. Trib. in SIC 2018, 162 at 164.

Chapter 2. Patents

§1. Sources of Legislation

I. Legislation and Treaties

186. The Patent Act was adopted on 25 June 1954, and entered into force on 1 January 1956.[160] The ordinance regulates mainly the procedure for registration, and the examination that the Intellectual Property Institute is allowed to do.[161] The Patent Act was amended most notably on 17 December 1976, 16 December 1994, 3 February 1995, 9 October 1998, 24 March 2000, 5 October 2001, 19 December 2003, 17 June 2005, 16 December 2005, 4 October 2007, 19 December 2008, 21 June 2013 and 18 March 2016 (the last version entered into force on 1 January 2019). Presently, the Swiss Government is preparing an important revision of the Patent Act with a view to introduce a full examination of the Swiss applications and protect utility models (*see* FF 2020, 8275 ff). However, after that, interested parties were consulted, the government appeared to abandon the idea of introducing utility models and it now wishes to institute instead two categories of patents for inventions, one with and the other without substantive examination. Parliament debates are expected for 2023 at the earliest. The Patent Ordinance of 19 October 1977 has been amended approximately twenty times in thirty years. On 1 March 2010, the Federal Law of 20 March 2009 on the Federal Patent court (RS 173.41) entered into force. This court adjudicates all matters of validity and nullity of patents, for any and all litigation arising in Switzerland, with an appeal to the Federal Tribunal. It is an exclusive jurisdiction as it concerns the validity and infringement of a patent for invention and the actions for compulsory licensing, as well as the interim measures and exequatur pertaining to such litigation. The Federal Patent court enjoys a non-exclusive jurisdiction to adjudicate other civil disputes that are related to patents, especially litigation regarding the ownership of a patent or its assignment. In this second category of cases, the Cantonal courts are concurrently competent. If a Cantonal court must rely on a decision concerning the validity of a patent or its infringement, it will stay its proceedings until the parties have introduced action before the Federal Patent court. English may be used with the agreement of the Patent court and the parties, although the decisions and judgments are in one of the four official languages. Cases that were pending before Cantonal courts on 1 March 2010 have been transferred to the Federal court whenever the main instructions hearings had not yet taken place. Its business started on 1 January 2012. In practice, many litigations are brought before institutional or ad hoc arbitral tribunals. In Switzerland, arbitral awards on the validity of a patent may be recorded on the Patent Register. Arbitration clauses are very frequent in the assignment and licensing agreements.

Switzerland is a party to the Paris Convention for the Protection of Industrial Property of 20 March 1883, as revised in Stockholm on 14 July 1967;[162] to the

160. RS 232.14.
161. RS 232.141. For the jurisdiction of the Federal Patent Tribunal *see* Fed. Trib. SIC 2018, 162; ATF 139 III 110.
162. RS 0.232.04.

Patent Cooperation Treaty (PCT) of 19 June 1970, as amended on 28 September 1979,[163] including Chapter 2 since 1995; and to the Convention on European Patents of 5 October 1973 in the modified version of 29 November 2000, applied in Switzerland since 13 December 2007.[164] Switzerland is also party to the WIPO Patent Treaty of 1 June 2000, applicable since 2007. Under Article 16, Patent Act Swiss nationals may invoke the Paris Convention whenever its provisions are more favourable than the Swiss law. Foreign nationals have the same right by virtue of the character self-executing of the Paris Convention.

II. Historical Background

187. The Patent system was not agreeable to the Swiss Parliament in the nineteenth century. Be it that the first Patent Act of 25 April 1799 had been enacted at a time when France was occupying Switzerland – and that Act was abrogated in 1802 when the French left; be it that many economists were doubtful then as to the true benefits of the patent system, the first draft Federal Patent Act of 1849 was curtly rejected. As the people had to vote in 1882 on the constitutional provision that would enable the Central State to provide for patent protection, most citizens and two-thirds of the cantons were opposed to it. But five years later, they accepted a restricted version of protection for models and designs, 'as well as those inventions that can be shown in a model and are of industrial application'.[165] Therefore, the first law on patents was adopted on 29 June 1888. There was no protection for process, which prompted Germany and its chemical industry to exert pressure on Switzerland at the turn of the century. Hence, the people adopted a broader constitutional provision in 1905, and a new Patent Act was adopted on 21 June 1907. The present Patent Act dates back to 24 June 1954. The people have rejected on 7 June 1998 a constitutional provision aiming at prohibiting the grant of patents for genetic inventions.

§2. Patentable Subject Matter

188. 'Patents for inventions shall be granted for new inventions applicable in industry (…).'[166]

163. RS 0.232.141.1.
164. RS 0.232.142.2.
165. *See* A. Troller, 40, 43, 47. The lack of a substantial patent protection does not appear to have impeded the industrialization of Switzerland. *See* E. Schiff, *Industrialization Without National Patents* 102 et seq. (Princeton U. Press, 1971).
166. Article 1(1) Patent Act.

I. Invention as a Rule

189. Every invention is a *rule*; that is, an indication to the human mind calling attention to a given causality.[167] As such, it must be apt to be repeated a number of times with the same result.[168] In no case is the invention a machine or a process, but the idea of some machine or process may be patentable.

190. The invention is not a *discovery*, but it is an addition to the world. To recognize a law of nature is not to invent. Switzerland does not know of 'scientific property' and did not adhere to the now defunct Geneva Convention of 1978 on the Protection of Scientific Property. Nonetheless, under the general provision of the Swiss Civil Code on the safeguard of personal interests (Article 28), there may be some protection against the misappropriation of a discovery.[169] The distinction between invention and discovery is an acute problem for genetic technology:[170] recombination of already existing genetic material can, however, be envisioned as an invention of combination, a category that was already well-known before;[171] in the combination invention, each individual element must not necessarily be novel and inventive. It is enough that the end result be inventive.[172] Further, many genetic inventions do not recombine genes that are in nature, but materials that are produced in laboratories.[173] Finally, the revision of the Patent Act in 2007 acknowledges the patentability of the genetic discovery itself, when it is technically presented and accompanied by the claim of a useful effect and the description of a definite function (Article 1*a* paragraph 2 and 1*b* paragraph 2 Patent Act). The new Article 8*a* paragraph 2 admits the patentability of new biological products and the patent, when issued, will cover also products deriving from the multiplication of the patented material that evince the same characteristics. Since the protection is now broader, Articles 9 and 40 provide for new exceptions to the rights of the patentee, especially for the use of genetic material (and other inventions) in research and development.

167. *See* A. Troller, 1152. *See* for other definitions W. Kuster, *Zur Frage Definition des Erfindungsbegriffes* (On the Definition of the Invention's Notion), RSJ 1975, 69 et seq.
168. *See* ATF 120 II 312; ATF 95 I 579 and two decisions of the Chamber of Appeal of the Office of Intellectual Property in PMM Bl 1981 I 71; *in* ATF 79 I 77 a process to obtain roses has been deemed unpatentable because it was not certain that the same result could be obtained after each working of the invention. For the protection of plant varieties nowadays, *see* hereinafter paras 597 et seq.
169. ATF 113 II 306, esp. 311–312.
170. Compare F. Perret, *Introduction*, in *Biotechnology and Patent Law*, CEDIDAC No. 31, at 19–20 (F. Dessemontet ed., Lausanne, 1996).
171. A. Troller, 186–189 with cit.
172. ATF 69 II 421, esp. 422–423.
173. F. Perret, *supra*, 20.

II. Invention as a Technical Rule

191. It is almost unanimously accepted that the invention shall pertain to the field of technology in its largest meaning.[174] What is meant by technology is the use of nature laws and resources towards a practical end. This excludes the protection of methods; for example, an accounting method,[175] the rule of a game, a system of public lottery, a shorthand method, tables of logarithms, a business method, etc.[176]

192. The most obvious victim of this notion of invention as belonging to technology is computer software, that is not patentable under Swiss Law.[177] The protection of copyright and that of the Act against Unfair Competition are available to the makers of the software.[178]

193. However, it is not deemed contrary to that notion of the invention that the product or the process applies to the human body, for example, in the case of drugs or cosmetics.[179] Further, Article 2 paragraph 2(b) Patent Act protects microbiological processes and products so obtained, if they are not limited to one animal species or plant variety. Article 2 embodies a long list of exceptions of 'public order' (*ordre public*), most of which embody the exceptions embedded in the Federal Law on the Research of Embryonic Cells of 19 December 2003 (SR 810.31). The new Act still prohibits the patenting of methods of diagnosis or curative methods applicable to men or animals, and the patenting of an animal species and essentially biological processes to obtain plants or animals. It should be noted that the exception of public order, as mentioned in Article 2 of the Patent Act, is actually larger than what its text could lead to believe, since the court applying it is not limited to the specific statutory cases mentioned in the Patent Act, but may base its judgment on the contrariety to *public order* and *good mores*.

III. Industrial Application

194. Article 1 Patent Act requires the invention to be capable of industrial application. That application must be possible through the means that are described in

174. One of the very few dissenting voices is that of F. Perret, *La protection des prestations en droit privé suisse* (The Protection of Investments in Labour under Swiss Private Law), RDS 1977, 262–263.
175. ATF 72 I 368 (giving that example).
176. ATF 95 II 579 (examples given by the Court). However, the Fed. Trib. allows for the patentability of the graphical representation of information, e.g., the variation of the size of the lungs of a patient in a mechanical ventilation device; SIC 2021, 30.
177. ATF 98 Ib 396.
178. *See* paras 34 et seq.
179. ATF 72 I 368. On a different point, concerning the ambit of protection, the Fed. Pat. Trib. recently adjudicated that there is no restriction to the legal exclusivity conferred by the patent or the additional certificate of protection when the authorization to use the medication has been granted for two different applications where the pharmacological action is identical; SIC 2018, 415.

the patent application, and those means must be related to 'industry' – which covers not only the manufacturing of goods but also the mining and agricultural activities.[180]

Under this heading, the cases usually reject the patentability of inventions that are of doubtful seriousness, such as a device to protect the bearer of cosmic radiations,[181] a machine to compute biorhythm,[182] a *perpetuum mobile*,[183] an impossible way to improve the productivity of a hydroelectric power plant.[184]

195. However, no possibility of mass production or working of the process is required,[185] and the profitability of working the invention is, of course, even less relevant.[186] Hence, an invention is capable of industrial application even if the State would not allow marketing of the invention, for example, due to provisions on public health or State monopolies. Nonetheless, if working on the invention or marketing the invented product should be deemed to run contrary to *bonos mores*, no patent shall be issued as is stated in Article 2(a) Patent Act.

§3. Conditions of Patentability: Novelty and Non-obviousness

I. Novelty

A. Legal Definition

196. Article 1 Patent Act requires the invention to be *novel*. This could have different meanings, but it is provided in Article 7 that 'novel' means 'not included in the state of the art', the state of the art being made of *all which has been made accessible to the public before the date of the application or a prior date, through a written or verbal description, use or any other means.*

Article 7(a) Patent Act was abrogated in 2007. It is included in the *state of the art* the invention which is the subject matter of a patent issued for Switzerland by reason of a prior application or of an application having a priority status. This point is now mentioned in Article 7, paragraph 3 Patent Act, which also includes in the state of the art the contents of a prior patent application and of a patent application which

180. *See* Art. 57 European Patent Cooperation, which is not contradicted by a provision of Swiss Law, and therefore has been deemed to be relevant under Swiss law as well by K. Troller, 78. *See* for the prevalence of the European Convention's notion of patentability over the Swiss notion Fed. Trib. *in* RSPI 1992, 95 et seq., esp. 98–99.
181. ATF 91 I 152 (patentability rejected).
182. ATF 96 I 401 (patentability admitted).
183. ATF 72 I 368 (example cited).
184. Appeal Committee for Intellectual Property, *in* RSPI 1996, 139. Same jurisdiction, SIC 2004, 791 (rejecting the patenting of a vaguely described invention consisting of a steam engine without rejection of CO_2). *See* Fed. Trib., SIC 2018, 651, for the requirement of a complete description of the technical rule.
185. ATF 63 II 277 (Rolex Oyster watches).
186. K. Troller, 79.

is based on a foreign or international prior application then extended to Switzerland, to the extent that the necessary fees have been paid and certain requirements of form have been met.

Article 7(b) Patent Act gives a grace period of six months in case the disclosure of the invention is due to an evident misuse committed against the applicant or his predecessor in title, or if the disclosure has taken place at an official international exhibition.

Article 7(c) Patent Act allows for the patentability of a new application in the field of medical treatment of a known substance or compound, when the use of the substance or compound is new and protection is claimed only for the purpose of that application. If, later on, a new application is discovered, then it can be patented as a dependent invention (Article 36 Patent Act).[187]

Article 7(d) was introduced in 2005 precisely in order to allow for the patenting of a second application; for example, a medicine useful for *preventing* heart attacks through the lowering of the blood pressure may later be found to have *curative* effects for patients having already suffered a heart attack. It has been an important debate whether the patentability of the second application would not increase the costs of social insurance schemes but the Swiss Parliament voted in 2005 to overrule these objections and favour research and development in the area of second applications as well. With a view to reach this piece of legislation favourable to the pharmaceutical industry, it was necessary to redefine the invention not only as a rule on a compound or substance but also as a rule on the *use* thereof.

197. All these statutory definitions circumscribe a *formal* requirement of novelty:[188]

- the novelty depends on the state of the art. The state of the art includes everything which is understandable for the man skilled in the art in Switzerland. All publications and disclosures to the public are included, even if that disclosure has fallen into oblivion;[189]
- the determining date for taking into account the state of the art is the date of the national patent application or the foreign patent application enjoying priority in Switzerland;[190]
- novelty is destroyed through publication only if the publication discloses all particular elements of the invention as claimed;[191]

187. *See* paras 298–302. For a case of new procedure to administer a patented drug, see ATF 137 III 170. The patent will be dependent on the prior patent on the substance. The procedure must itself be novel and non-obvious.

188. *See* ATF 133 III 229, 233 (novelty of a manufacturing process); Appel. Ct Ticino *in* RSPI 1989, 99–100.

189. *See* Fed. Trib. *in* RSPI 1993, 97, esp. 144; same court again in SIC 2019, 97 for a document over 100 years old. However, see below fn. 198.

190. ATF 95 II 363. The grace period of Art. 7(b) starts from the filing of the European Patent Application: ATF 117 II 480.

191. ATF 133 III 229, 232; Fed. Trib. *in* RSPIDA 1971, 124; Swiss Institute for Intellectual Property *in* RSPIDA 1977, 4. In practice, however, old publications are sometimes disregarded; ATF 94 II 319; ATF 95 II 363. In order to know whether the anteriority destroys the novelty of the patent application, it may be necessary to interpret the anterior publication; then, it will be construed according

– novelty may be due to a novel effect of a known process;[192]
– even if a publication is due to the inventor, it shall destroy the novelty.[193]

B. *Disclosure Through Patents*

198. The first and foremost source of publication to be opposed against the novelty of an application or a patent is the whole body of patents and patent applications that have been published in the world.[194] It shall be noted that the whole invention, that is, the technical rule protection of which is claimed, has to be found in one publication; it is not allowed to have a piecemeal approach in finding one element destructive of novelty in one document, the following one in a second document, etc.[195]

C. *Other Disclosure*

199. The disclosure otherwise than through publication is defined under Article 7(2) Patent Act as the event giving a sufficient possibility that men skilled in the art be aware of the invention in such a manner that they can work it.[196] An act of use, such as the sale of a product embodying the invention to a customer, is sufficient, even if only a limited number of specialists have access to it, provided, however, that they are not under a contractual obligation of confidentiality.[197] A line of cases[198] holds that no evidence is necessary to show that someone actually took notice of the disclosure and knew of the invention.

200. It is obvious that the opinion of the inventor on the novelty of his or her invention is irrelevant, but it should be remembered that, when dealing with a

to the so-called objective or normative interpretation, such as is applicable for legislation and the statutes and by-laws of a public company, e.g., and not according to the usual interpretation method for contracts that is based on the common will and intent of the parties, or their hypothetical intent otherwise; *see* ATF 132 III 83, 87.

192. ATF 93 II 504.
193. Cant. Ct Schwytz *in* RSPIDA 1977, 8.
194. *See* ATF 94 II 319 (French, US, Belgium and English patents cited against the novelty of a pocket watch).
195. *See*, however, Com. Ct Zurich *in* RSPI 1996, 105, esp. 112–113 (leaving undecided the question whether two documents can be read together if the second one refers to the first one).
196. ATF 117 II 480.
197. ATF 117 II 480. *See* Fed. Trib. case 4A_427/2016 (to be consulted at www.bger.ch) judging that the inclusion of a document disclosing the invention in a bid for contract sent without any confidentiality agreement destroys novelty.
198. From ATF 68 II 396 through ATF 117 II 480. Against the notion of a sheer possibility to know as sufficient to destroy the novelty, *see* ATF 58 II 286; ATF 60 II 472.

motion for provisional relief *pendente lite*, the owner of a patent enjoys a presumption that his or her patent is valid; the defendant arguing that it is not novel has to show evidence that excludes the novelty 'with some certainty'.[199]

II. Non-obviousness

A. *Terminology*

201. The Patent Act of 1954 did not explicitly require non-obviousness; the cases and commentary spoke of 'inventive level', as a condition implied by the use of the word 'invention' in Article 1 of the 1954 Act.[200] Following the European Patent Convention, Article 1(2) of the 1976 Act states that:

> *Anything that manifestly follows from the state of the art (Article 7) shall not be patentable as an invention.*[201]

202. Behind this, somewhat awkward formulation is the idea that Swiss law should be construed in line with the Munich Convention. Although various commentators had voiced the opinion that the standard of non-obviousness would be lower than the former rule of 'inventive level', case law is now to the effect that both standards are identical.[202]

B. *Non-obviousness as Creativeness*

203. According to one of the latest cases of the Federal Tribunal, non-obviousness would not simply mean that the invention is not 'obvious'; that is, 'readily at the disposal of the man skilled in the art' (as suggested by the English 'obvious' and the French 'évident'). Rather, the German notion of 'difficult to find' (*nicht naheliegend*) would better embody the true intent of the legislature.[203] The

199. For this burden of proof, *see* ATF 133 III 229, 233. Com. Ct Zurich *in* RSPIDA 1984, 47; same court *in* RSPIDA 1984, 53, with cit. (a short expert report may be adduced to the evidence in summary proceedings). According to ATF 132 III 83, a private expert report would not be sufficient to obtain interim relief. However, in order to admit the invalidity of a patent, a foreign judgment or expert report may suffice (Fed. Trib., SIC 2008, 367–368). A foreign decree on interim measures could even be adduced as evidence, according to Cant. Ct BL, SIC 2008, 368–369.

200. *See*, e.g., ATF 102 II 292.

201. Art. 1(2) Patent Act.

202. *See* ATF 123 III 485; ATF 121 III 125, esp. 137; Fed. Trib. *in* SIC 1998, 203 with cit. of commentary at 204. *Contra*: ATF 108 II 325 citing preparatory materials to the effect that a lowering of the standard was envisioned by the legislature (*see* FF 1976 II 66).

203. ATF 123 III 490. It is to be recalled that under Swiss law, all three versions of any Federal Law in German, French and Italian are of identical value. *See* F. Dessemontet, *Le droit des langues en Suisse* (The Law of Languages in Switzerland) 88–91 (Québec, 1984).

invention could be worthy of a patent if the inventive activity 'went out the ordinary way of the permanent innovation' and 'had taken new ways that derive from a creative effort'.[204]

204. All this is based on the assumption that patents for inventions are not to reward the craftsmanship or specialized competence of one who is skilled in the art, but true originality departing from the usual practice. There should be an inventive step ahead rather than incremental innovation.[205] In some cases, the test of the 'enrichment' of the technology is applied.[206] The reward theory is not the only theory that may justify this severe standard; the need to leave a field open to everyday innovation is a social necessity, especially in a country such as Switzerland where a large number of small and medium-scale enterprises thrive in the field of mechanics, watch making and electronics, while a few large companies lead chemical and pharmaceutical research worldwide – and for those, when making so-called analogical inventions in the field of chemistry and drugs, the standard of inventiveness is lower.[207]

205. Nonetheless, the inventive step is not a judgment to be passed upon the effort or merits of the invention itself, or on the method following which the invention was made.[208]

206. On the contrary, the inventive step is to be considered in an objective manner. The question is: could the ordinary person skilled in the art make that invention taking into account the state of the art as defined for the purpose of evaluating the novelty of the invention?

The key to this reasoning is properly to define the 'person skilled in the art'.

C. The Person Skilled in the Art

207. The person skilled in the art is not a real human being, but a standard against which to compare the inventiveness of the invention.

208. Although some cases define the person skilled in the art only with the terms 'having an ordinary training',[209] the Federal Tribunal now specifies that the person skilled in the art is supposed to be a 'specialist' of that particular technology.[210]

---

204. *See* Fed. Trib. *in* SIC 1998, 205. *See also* ATF 138 III 111 (while mere additions to the stock of technical knowledge are obvious, the combination of known characteristic may be conducive of a non-obvious invention).
205. *See* ATF 122 III 279; Fed. Trib. *in* RSPIDA 1973, 122; Fed. Trib. *in* RSPIDA 1974, 73 with cit.; Fed. Trib. *in* RSPI 1993, 144; Fed. Trib. *in* SIC 1998, 203, esp. 205.
206. *See* Cant. Ct Ticino *in* RSPI 1989, 97.
207. *See* ATF 93 II 504.
208. *See* Fed. Trib. *in* RSPIDA 1973, 118; Fed. Trib. *in* RSPIDA 1976, 171.
209. *See*, e.g., ATF 102 II 370.
210. ATF 114 II 85.

209. The 'person skilled in the art' is indeed supposed to have had a different background and a more or less advanced training depending on which particular field of technology the invention pertains to. For example, in chemistry, the man skilled in the art shall be deemed to have an academic degree and to have experience of some years in the laboratory of a private company or at the university.[211] However, for an invention in the textile industry, the person skilled in the art shall be an engineer of textile machines.[212] For an invention on a parking system, a mechanic having finished his apprenticeship or his technical high school and enjoying an experience of a few years would be the man skilled in the art.[213]

210. In the case of an invention combining technology in two areas, such as the technology of glue and the technology of synthetic fabrics for a self-sticking diaper, the person skilled in the art is supposed to be able to resort to a team of specialists in both areas.[214]

D. The Methodology of the Person Skilled in the Art

211. The person skilled in the art would have applied the usual methods to undertake research and development in the field of the invention. If this would not have led to the innovation at stake, then it is a patentable invention. However, the case law is rather restrictive as it concerns the idea of combining two different bodies of technical knowledge. For example, it has been decided that an engineer active in the building of textile machines would certainly apply aerodynamics to improve a given piece of machinery.[215] If an invention bears on a given way to apply lake to pieces of furniture, it would be normal for the man skilled in the art to resort to a solution for applying paint, which is already known for the painting of earthenwares, tiles and tin boxes.[216]

The sheer fact that a process which is well-known may lead to a substantial progress may be evidence of an inventive step.[217] The same might be said of a new crystalline form given to a known chemical substance.[218]

211. Fed. Trib. *in* RSPIDA 1976, 171.
212. Fed. Trib. *in* RSPIDA 1974, 73.
213. Com. Ct Zurich *in* RSPIDA 1977, 14.
214. Fed. Adm. Trib., SIC 2017, 415 at 418: for a given anticancer medication an oncologist and a chemist may have to combine their knowledge, so that they are the 'man skilled in the art'. *See also* ATF 120 II 71; *see* already, for a painting pistol with an electrical engine, ATF 89 II 108.
215. Fed. Trib. *in* RSPIDA 1974, 73.
216. ATF 92 II 49. *See* Com. Ct Zurich *in* RSPIDA 1977, 18.
217. ATF 93 II 504, esp. 514 (systematic R&D efforts for the synthesis of chloramphenicol out of the reach of the 'man skilled in the art'); Fed. Pat. Trib., SIC 2018, 85: if a man skilled in the art would have only a chance of 50% to reach the invention on the basis of the prior art, that invention is not obvious.
218. ATF 97 I 423.

E. The State of the Art

212. The person skilled in the art does not necessarily have at his or her disposal the entire state of the art as defined under Article 7 Patent Act for the purpose of novelty, but he should possess enough ability and knowledge to be able to find information in the relevant area.[219]

213. In this regard, the expert witness and the court are authorized to use a *mosaic*, piecemeal approach, taking one element of the invention in one publication and another one in another publication – except if that publication has fallen into oblivion.[220]

F. Ancillary Criteria

214. All the aforementioned observations show that some uncertainty shall result from the stringent requirements of patentability as laid down in the cases.

Therefore, various tests have been proposed as ancillary criteria to reduce the uncertainty surrounding the main test of the non-obviousness.

There are some ancillary tests that have been developed by the commentary and have no absolute value under Swiss law, for the time being.[221]

In practice, these are facts which should not be relied upon in favour of the patentability of an invention. Nevertheless, parties often refer to them in order to have the court deduce from established facts a judgment favourable to the patentability.

1. Overwhelming Technical Prejudices Against the Feasibility

215. In the world of technology, people can entertain prejudices about the feasibility or the inconvenience of a given process or product. For example, physicians objected for decades to administering amino acids to human beings in order to lower blood pressure because they considered that the needed quantities would have toxic

219. ATF 123 III 485; ATF 120 II 71. See also Fed. Trib. SIC 2020, 643 (*Pemetex III*): it is not necessarily acceptable to combine the different chapters of a treatise written by different authors with a view to prove the obviousness of the invention; ATF 95 II 363 is superseded; this case assumed that the man skilled in the art would know all the state of the art within the meaning of Art. 7 Patent Act, an obvious impossibility for anyone in particular.

220. ATF 94 II 319 (The doctrine of the mosaic does not compel to take into account a publication that fell into oblivion). For the doctrine of the mosaic, *see also* ATF 133 II 229, 233 (extent and consequences of the presumption that a patent that has been granted is valid unless it is proven to be invalid); ATF 120 II 312, 318; Fed. Trib., SIC 2003, 603, 604; Fed. Trib. SIC 2001, 749, 752–753 (the interpretation of the claims of the prior patents may be indispensable in order to decide whether the new invention is patentable).

221. *See* Fed. Trib. *in* RSPI 1994, 328.

side effects. If an inventor is able to reduce the needed quantities through the separation of more active elements and he applies the result to the human body successfully, his invention goes against the general opinion and that is inventive enough. The Federal Tribunal already accepted such reasoning.[222]

216. In most cases, however, the courts are reluctant to link any merit to the overwhelming of technical prejudice. They consider at times that the conservatism of the industry or other factors sufficiently explains that no one thought of or used the invention before the inventor, so that non-use is no indication of inventiveness.[223] Several cases reject the patentability of new developments, although it had been argued that prejudices prevented competitors from applying the novel ideas.[224] For the same reasons, the 'surprising simplicity' of an invention is no sign of its patentability.[225]

2. Uncovered Need

217. When the research for an invention has been going on for a long time, or even when the need for it was felt without any development covering it, it should be deemed proof enough that the 'men skilled in the art' could not reach the invention by themselves. Being out of their search, the invention is not obvious. With one exception,[226] the Federal Tribunal precedents reject, however, the notion that unsuccessful trials and parallel R&D efforts tend to prove the non-obviousness.[227]

The judges are reluctant to accept that test probably because they feel that they would otherwise be deprived of their authority to declare a patent null and void for lack of non-obviousness.

As it has been shown in the literature,[228] an uncovered need either shows that the interested industry sought the solution without finding it for a long time – then the invention is not obvious; or shows that the industry did not even understand the problem, then did not search in the area in which the invention was finally made; then the invention should be patentable. Thus, the judiciary might harbour some reluctance to being held hostage in such circular reasoning. Further, one might add another objection against that ancillary test: the Federal Tribunal does not accept

222. *See* Fed. Trib. *in* RSPIDA 1976, 171.
223. ATF 92 II 49.
224. For example, ATF 102 II 370 (new construction of skis); Com. Ct St-Gallen, *in* RSPIDA 1976, 162 (automatic control of fuel level in a tank). Fed. Pat. Trib., SIC 2013, 237 s. 4.6.
225. ATF 114 II 82; *contra*: ATF 69 II 188; *see also* Fed. Trib. *in* RSPI 1990, 126 (accepting *in abstracto* the overwhelming of prejudices as a sign of patentability); Fed. Trib. *in* RSPI 1993, 144; Fed. Trib. *in* RSPI 1995, 358; Fed. Trib. *in* RSPI 1996, 128.
226. ATF 69 II 188.
227. *See*, e.g., Fed. Trib. *in* RSPIDA 1963, 41, esp. 44.
228. *See* A. Scheuchzer, *Nouveauté et activité inventive en droit européen des brevets* (Innovation and Inventive Operation in European Patent Law), thesis, 410 (Lausanne, 1981).

that simply putting the right question is an inventive step, on the (in this writer's view, fallacious) premise that the invention as defined in the Patent Act is a solution rather than a problem.[229]

3. Prior Patents

218. Prior patents that have been issued to other inventors may reflect the need that was felt to achieve a workable solution for a given problem. The Swiss courts may at times see it as evidence that the invention at stake constitutes a technical progress.[230] As such, they would recognize the patentability.[231] Otherwise, it is not a certain sign of non-obviousness, since the very existence of so many prior patents shows that some of them must not have been inventive enough. Then why not say the same of the patent at stake?

4. Foreign Patents

219. It is, of course, very frequently the case that one or several foreign patents have been issued to the applicant on the same invention abroad. As it only fits a small, isolated country proud of its independence, the Swiss courts deem that fact to be irrelevant; most cases reject the argument that patentability may be best judged by foreign patent offices.[232] Some old decisions hold to the contrary.[233] Of course, it should depend on the field of technology and on the foreign Patent Office: a prior decision by a foreign court could be taken into consideration if the file would be adduced as evidence in the Swiss proceedings.

229. ATF 114 II 82; *see* ATF 81 II 292.

230. *See* Fed. Trib. *in* RSPIDA 1993, 144 (fifteen patents were cited as prior art). More restrictive: Fed. Trib. *in* RSPIDA 1963, 41, esp. 45.

231. *See* paras 220-221.

232. *See* ATF 114 II 82; Com. Ct Zurich, *in* RSJ 1955, 361; Com. Ct St-Gallen *in* RSPIDA 1976, 162. *See also* Fed. Pat. Trib., SIC 2012, 649 (an expert opinion filed with a foreign court is simply an allegation by the party filing it with the Swiss Patent Tribunal). Recently, it has been correctly admitted by the Fed. Pat. Trib. that where the Claimant bases its action only on its Swiss patent and the Respondent argues that this patent is invalid, the Court should not apply the case law of the European Chambers of Appeal; *see* P. Felhbaum, La jurisprudence du Tribunal fédéral des brevets (*The Case Law of the Federal Patent Tribunal)*, SIC 2014, 313, at 327 fn 137.

233. ATF 58 II 57, esp. 78; ATF 58 II 266, esp. 272; ATF 67 II 57; Examination's Section of the Federal Intellectual Property Office *in* RSPIDA 1963, 46. A more recent case gives weight to the foreign decision on a foreign patent application in the context of judging the *novelty* of the invention; Fed. Trib. SIC 2008, 327. Another one considers the consequence of a Düsseldorf decision on the rejected request for *ad lite* restraining orders; Fed. Pat. Trib. 2019, 169.

5. Technical Progress

220. Under the Acts of 1907 and 1954, technical progress was a requisite of the patentable invention.[234] It is no longer considered as such under the revised Act of 1976, but it is taken as a sign of inventiveness.[235] It is, of course, left to the appreciation of the court whether the technical progress sufficiently evidences the non-obviousness.[236] In fact, the bigger the technical progress, the less important it seems to be the question of non-obviousness.[237]

221. The commercial success of the invention, and the fact that customers and competitors alike adopted it is not seen as a sign of non-obviousness. The Swiss courts seem to consider that a good advertising campaign can sell any product, so that there is no causality at all between the commercial success and the merits of the invention.[238] Recent authors[239] point out that such a view is even contrary to the Patent Act itself, as shown by Article 36 Patent Act which sets out as a test to compel the patentee to give a licence for the working of a depending invention on the 'technical progress', then directs the judge to look at the 'economic need' to which the inventions correspond in order to decide if the first patentee may receive a compulsory licence on the second invention.[240]

§4. Formalities

I. Procedure for Granting of a Patent

222. The Swiss law applies to a dwindling number of patent applications. In 2021, 1,555 Swiss patent applications were filed with the Swiss Institute for Intellectual Property (in comparison with 3,720 patent applications in 1995). But only 724 national patents were granted.[241] By way of comparison, the European Patent Office (EPO) received 8,112 Swiss applications in 2020. Part of the problem lies with the absence of a procedure for substantive examination within the Swiss Institute. The European examination procedure is deemed to be very timeconsuming and expensive by the small and medium enterprises. Furthermore, those enterprises deplore the relative uncertainty surrounding the validity of present Swiss patents as

234. ATF 102 II 370; Fed. Trib. *in* RSPIDA 1974, 73.
235. Fed. Trib. *in* RSPI 1991, 198; Fed. Trib. *in* RSPI 1993, 144; Fed. Trib. *in* RSPI 1996, 128. *See also* ATF 123 III 485 (mentioning that the '*leap forward*' test has not been rebuked as it seemed in ATF 108 II 325 (cons. 1b published only in JdT 1983 I 355, 356), but the issue would have been left undecided). *See* Com. Ct Zurich, SIC 2007, 208.
236. Fed. Trib. *in* RSPI 1991, 198.
237. *See* A. Scheuchzer, *supra*, 418–419; Pedrazzini, von Büren & Marbach, para. 60 *in fine*.
238. *See*, e.g., Com. Ct St-Gallen *in* RSPIDA 1976, 162.
239. Pedrazzini, von Büren & Marbach, *supra*, para. 60.
240. *See* F. Dessemontet, *La notion d'invention dépendante en droit suisse* (The Notion of Dependent Invention under Swiss Law), in *Mélanges Paul Piotet* 240 (Lausanne, 1990).
241. *See* Swiss Federal Institute of Intellectual Property, *Jahresbericht* (Annual Report) (1996/97), 14–15; the latest figures are taken from www.lawcareerstart.ch, visited on 13 Feb. 2022.

they are not examined for novelty and non-obviousness. Hence, the Swiss Government is preparing a revision of the Patent Act, with will also entail some upholstering of the resources of the Federal Patent Tribunal.

To sum up, ten times more European patents are now granted to Switzerland than Swiss patents, and the proportion is growing. Therefore, in a publication such as this one which aims at an international readership, and at a time when new rules might come quickly into effect, it seems to be appropriate to delineate the Swiss procedure for granting patents only in a most general manner.

A. Patent Applications

223. According to Article 49 Patent Act, the patent application shall consist of the application proper requesting the grant of a patent, as well as of a description of the invention, one or more claims, technical drawings and an abstract.

224. The abstract is needed to help with research. It does not have any legal import. The technical drawings illustrate the invention and may have the same relevance as the description for construing the claims and enabling the man skilled in the art to work the patent.[242] The patent application contains the usual data about the date of the filing, the priority date if any,[243] the owner, the inventor, the patent attorney; it is necessary to appoint a patent attorney only if the applicant is not domiciled within Switzerland.

225. The core of the application is the claim or claims. The claim consists of a definition which determines the type of invention and the general features of the invention, and a specific listing of the ways and means to reach the technical result that is envisioned by the inventor. The claim sets out the area which shall be covered by the exclusive rights of the patent holder.

Swiss law admits the theory of equivalents as is known, for example, in the US.[244]

Article 58*a* Patent Act that was introduced in the 2007 revision provides for the publication of the patent application immediately after the expiry of the time limit of eighteen months since the filing of the application or the date of international priority, whichever is earlier. The applicant may request an earlier publication. The publication will take place through electronic means only. As soon as the patent application is published, the file is no longer confidential. The inventor will have to be mentioned in the publication of the patent application. Finally, there may be no

242. On the import of the description, *see* Com. Ct Zurich *in* SIC 1997, 208. The question is acute wherever the court eventually decides to narrow the claims, redefining the invention on the basis of the description. *See*, e.g., ATF 95 II 364, ATF 120 II 71; ATF 121 III 279. *See* ATF 138 III 76 (the detailed description of the invention for which a patent has been applied may be the subject matter of a 'discovery' procedure). In SIC 2017, 477 (*Nespresso VI*) the Fed. Trib. declined to extend the ambit of the protection of a patent claim on the basis of technical drawings.

243. The indication of the date cannot prejudice the rights of third parties; ATF 94 I 182.

244. *See* Pedrazzini, von Büren & Marbach, No. 120. On the importance of the claim to define the extent of the protection, *see* ATF 125 III 29.

postponing of the issuance of the patent on the grounds of public interest. Even the Swiss Confederation no longer enjoys the right to keep strategic inventions secret without limit of time as was formerly the case.

B. Examination by the Institute of Intellectual Property

226. Switzerland follows the system of a formal, immediate examination. From 1959 through 1995, there used to be a substantive examination concerning the novelty and non-obviousness of patent applications in the field of time-measuring and improvement of textile fibres. Under Article 87(2) Patent Act that entered into force on 1 September 1995, patent applications filed from 1 October 1995 do not undergo substantive examination. A full substantive examination may be reintroduced with the next revision of the Patent Act which is scheduled to be debated by Parliament in 2023.

227. Formal examination bears on the completeness of the application. Further, it addresses the issues of industrial applicability, lawfulness and *bonos mores*. If the invention is contrary to *bonos mores*, for example, because it might be deceptive for the consumers, the Institute shall reject the application. Such could have been the fate of an invention aiming at protecting the human body against the supposedly noxious effects of electromagnetic radiations.[245] The Institute could also reject an application where neither the claim nor the description gives sufficient indications as to the working of the invention.[246] If the invention cannot be worked on the basis of the application or, later, of the patent, this is a ground for invalidity.[247] Nonetheless, it is not required that the applicant would have understood the full meaning of his invention, nor would he have explained the detailed causality of the events leading to the results.[248] Claims and descriptions are to be construed in an objective manner conforming to the overriding principle of good faith.

228. As there is presently no substantive examination, there is only a limited opposition procedure against Swiss patents, in contrast with the European patents that are subject to the opposition after the grant.[249] The industry requests that no opposition procedure at all be foreseen under the revised Patent Act to be carried on starting in 2023.

245. Fed. Trib. *in* RSPIDA 1977, 3 (patent application rejected for lack of industrial application).
246. ATF 97 I 423.
247. Art. 26 (1)(3) Patent Act.
248. *See* ATF 92 II 280. *See* further ATF 132 III 83, 87; ATF 122 III 81, 83–84 (in general, the views of the applicant on the interpretation of his claims are not binding on the courts. Only the meaning that the man skilled in the art would give to the claims is determinative).
249. *See* below para. 234. Formerly, under Art. 101 Patent Act, opposition was possible after the substantive examination by the Institute in the two areas where such examination was provided, upon publication of the application, before the grant.

229. If the application is found defective, the Institute allows for the applicant to improve it, for example, by drawing up a new claim.[250]

II. Grant of the Patent

230. Once the prerequisites of the grant have been met, the Swiss Institute writes to the applicant that the examination procedure is completed and sets a deadline to pay the patent fee. When the fee is paid, the patent is issued. There is an intricate case law on the point of the time of the payment, especially for annuities.[251] Further, the possibility of withdrawal of the application is open; such a withdrawal might be invalidated under the doctrine of error (Article 24 Code of Obligations), but the mistake cannot consist in a wrong appraisal of the economic return on the working of the invention due to changing market conditions.[252]

231. The patent is registered in the Register of Patents with all usual indications. The patent will last twenty years from the filing of the application, and certificates of extension may be requested for pharmaceutical inventions; the proper construction of the original patent claims will determine if the subsequent product is covered by the certificate of extension. Transfer of the patent to a new owner shall be mentioned in the Register. That requirement is not a condition precedent to the validity of the transfer. However, if a transfer has not been mentioned, the suits against the patent owner under the Patent Act may be brought against the person who is registered rather than against the transferee.

232. Further, the *bona fide* third parties who rely on the Register in the event of a further transfer or licensing agreement shall be protected (Article 33(3) and (4) and Article 34(3) Patent Act).

233. Moreover, the Register records all modifications in the claims due to a narrowing of their wording, for example, due to a litigation, or a partial withdrawal, or a judgment or an arbitral award invalidating a claim.

250. *See* Fed. Trib. *in* RSPIDA 1977, 37 et seq.
251. *See*, e.g., Fed. Trib. *in* RSPIDA 1969, 52; Fed. Trib. *in* RSPI 1996, 361. Article 12 Ordinance has been changed in 1995 in the hope of allowing for a better understanding of the grounds leading to non-payment. See now Fed. Adm. Trib., SIC 2022, 120 ('Patent Registration cancellation II').
252. Fed. Trib. *in* RSPIDA 1975, 297 (petro-chemical industry). The applicant will have two months to supply a possibly missing translation of the European patent into one of the Swiss national languages, which time limit runs from the time the applicant becomes aware that no translation has been supplied (Fed. Trib., SIC 2008, 817). For a possible subsequent modification of the patent claims see ATF 146 III 177 (*Apple*). The public shall not be surprised by an extension of the patent monopoly through reference to the technical information which is contained in drawings and description; the courts will apply the *gold standard* of the understanding by a man skilled in the art concerning what he would understand as covered by the claims; Fed. Trib., SIC 2021, 616. A partial relinquishment of some patent claims is possible in a litigation for infringement only until the last exchange of memorials; Fed. Trib., SIC 2021, 85. It will be noted that a partial relinquishment of a patent claim or a narrower ambit thereof can also be filed with the Swiss Institute for Intellectual Property.

234. The grant of the patent, together with its text, is published as a separate document and the grant is recorded in the electronic Official Bulletin of the Swiss Institute of Intellectual Property (swiss.reg.ch).

Article 59c of the Patent Act provides since 2007 a limited *opposition procedure*. Only Articles 1*a*, 1*b* and 2 Patent Act may be invoked against the granting of a patent; this entails that only inventions concerning parts of the human body and genetic sequences are at stake, or inventions the working of which might harm human dignity such as a more ferocious torture device for countries that do not outlaw torture or accept it in practice, or the integrity of living organisms, or would be otherwise contrary to public order.

The opposition must be filed within nine months of the publication of the grant of the patent. Any person may file an opposition, but it must be in writing. The Federal Institute for Intellectual Property will examine the opposition and find on it, and an appeal to the Federal Patent court is possible.

§5. Ownership and Transfer

I. Title to the Patent

235. The title to the patent belongs to the inventor, to his successor in title, or to a third party to whom the invention belongs by reason of another regulation or contractual provision (Article 3 Patent Act).

A. *Before the Patent Application*

236. Before the patent application is filed, the inventor enjoys the protection of trade secrets under Articles 162 and 273 Penal Code, as well as under the Act against Unfair Competition of 19 December 1986, Articles 4(c) and 6 which protect against the misappropriation of trade secrets and the corruption of the inventor's employee to obtain the disclosure of trade secrets. Possibly, Article 28 Swiss Civil Code on the protection of personal interests, notably privacy, may offer some protection.

237. The protection mostly rests on secrecy. For secrecy to be protected, however, the invention must not be generally accessible to the competitors, and the inventor must show that he intended to keep the invention secret.[253] For the time being, there is no explicit requirement of *value* as set out in Article 39 TRIPS, but Swiss law must be construed to conform with this requirement;[254] as cases already

253. ATF 103 IV 283; Fed. Trib. *in* RSPIDA 1984, 281. *See* further hereinafter para. 676.

254. *See* F. Dessemontet, *Protection of Undisclosed Information*, in *Intellectual Property and International Trade: The TRIPS Agreement*, 339–358 (C. Correa & A. Yussuf eds., 3d ed., 2016). According to the Federal Tribunal, some provisions at least of TRIPS would not be self-executing; SIC 2010, 86 (copyright case involving Art. 41 TRIPS which is far more general than Art. 39). *See* generally Ch. 9 hereinafter.

request that the owners of trade secrets have a legitimate interest to maintain them under the cloak of secrecy, it should not be difficult to equate 'economic value' under the TRIPS and 'legitimate interest' under Swiss law.

B. During the Procedure

238. Besides the protection of secrecy, the Patent Act itself gives to the inventor or his successor in title or some entitled third party a right as against the state. If someone files an application with the Swiss Institute of Intellectual Property, he or she is deemed to be entitled to obtain a patent, all legal conditions being otherwise met (Article 4 Patent Act). This is a presumption that cannot be rebutted in the administrative procedure. However, the third party who argues that he is the person who is actually entitled to obtain the patent can go to a court of law and petition the court for a judgment stating that he is the true inventor and not the person who is mentioned on the patent application (Article 5(3) Patent Act). The patent might even be invalidated if the original applicant had no title to the patent (Article 26(1)(6) Patent Act), or it might be transferred to the true owner (Article 29(1) Patent Act).[255]

239. In another aspect, there are no *interference* proceedings for granting the patent in Switzerland, which follows the system of the 'first-to-file' and not of the 'first-to-invent' – as was previously known in the US.

C. Notion of Inventors and Co-inventors

240. The person who is the inventor is the person who has 'made' the invention, as this word is used in Article 3(2) Patent Act. Actually, it is a cognitive process which allows the inventor to recognize the main features of the invention and their relevance for the technical result to be reached hereby. The sheer fact of having given a good piece of advice is not enough to be considered as the 'inventor'.[256]

241. However, the Patent Act acknowledges that several persons, a team of researchers, for example, or even two teams having united their efforts as is often the case in R&D joint ventures, may have concurred to finding the invention (Article 3(2) Patent Act).

While the law speaks of a right 'jointly held' by the co-inventors, there is no indication as to the specific legal nature of that community.[257]

---

255. ATF 127 III 461, 467–469 (by application of the law of Liechtenstein).
256. *See* Just. Ct Geneva in RSPI 1992, 102; Fed. Adm. Trib., SIC 2017, 421.
257. *See* generally E. Ramoni-Fitting, *L'invention commune* (The Joint Invention), thesis (Lausanne, 1974).

The general opinion is that it is a 'co-property' under Articles 646 et seq. Civil Code, unless there is a partnership (Articles 530 et seq. Code of Obligations) implying the joint and several properties of Articles 652 et seq. Civil Code.[258]

242. In many academic research facilities, there is no real partnership between the various collaborators of the institute, whereas a partnership may be convened between an academic institution and a private company[259] or between two companies.

Within a private company, the labour law shall regulate the entitlement to the patent (Article 332 Code of Obligations).

D. Employees' Inventions

243. The inventor is always named in the patent application. It seems that no application ever named the 'company' as inventor.[260] There is a strong interest of the physical inventors to be mentioned as it improves their reputation and may help them to find a new job.[261] Within the public sector and academic research activities especially, it has even been suggested that professors and other researchers indicate which patent they obtained in the publication of their academic reports,[262] and of late, this suggestion has been followed in some Swiss Universities, in Lausanne most notably.

244. The status of employees' inventions under Article 332 Code of Obligations is the following:

(1) Inventions are deemed to 'belong' to the employer whenever they have been made by an employee who was hired to invent in the course of performing his contractual duties (Article 332(1) Code of Obligations). No specific remuneration is due to the employee (which is a solution going back to 1911 and is absolutely outmoded). In 2006, Parliament rejected an amendment to this rule. However, in case of litigation abroad, foreign courts may find this regulation repugnant to their public order, since almost all European legislations provide for the adequate and equitable remuneration of dependent inventors.
(2) If an invention is 'reduced to practice' after the end of the employment, it is no service invention,[263] unless the employee would be found guilty of some misuse of his right to terminate the contract (Article 2 Civil Code repressing any 'misuse of right').

---

258. *See* Pedrazzini, von Büren & Marbach, para. 85.
259. *See* generally F. Dessemontet, *Inventions in Swiss Universities,* 338 et seq. (Indus. Prop. 1982).
260. M. Rehbinder, *Berner Kommentar* (Berne Commentary), 1992, No. 4 *ad* Art. 332 Code of Obligations.
261. A. Troller, 68.
262. *See* F. Dessemontet, *Inventions in Swiss Universities* 385 (Indus. Prop. 1982).
263. *See* M. Rehbinder, *supra*, No. 7 *ad* Art. 332 Code of Obligations.

(3) However, the place and the time where and when the invention was made is of no relevance to define a service invention.[264] The decisive point is whether the hiring was made with the understanding that inventions or innovations could be expected from the employee.[265]

(4) By the way, as the status of employee's inventions is regulated within the title on labour relations of the Code of Obligations, the fact that the invention is patentable or not is irrelevant. The same rules apply to all technological inventions.[266] In this writer's view, however, the same should not be said for *commercial* know-how and trade secrets, as the legal basis for their protection is different[267] and the interests to be balanced against each other are not necessarily the same as in the realm of technology.[268] The conveyance of the title to the patent is automatic for service inventions, there being no need for a deed to be executed.

(5) The inventions that fall outside the scope of the service inventions but are related to the performance of his or her duties by the inventor basically belong to the employee, who was not hired to make them but somehow did invent (so-called 'occasional inventions').

(6) Nevertheless, if the employer beforehand provided through a specific provision executed in a written deed that he might claim the invention for his own, then the employee is under a duty to announce the invention by a letter or another written notice served upon the employer; the employer enjoys hereafter a delay of six months' time to claim the invention for his own, through a written notice served upon the employee. In that case, a specific remuneration is due to the employee. As always, Swiss commentary is impressed by the thoroughness of German law, the Guidelines that are valid in Germany.[269] These Guidelines are in fact based on a sound methodology to appraise the value of the invention, allocate it between the merits of the inventor and the support of the employer's organization, and make an analogy with a license, but are of course not binding on a Swiss court of law.

(7) The inventions that fall outside the scope of the service inventions and the occasional inventions are generally called the 'free inventions', which is somewhat misleading in two respects:

---

264. *See* Fed. Trib. *in* RSPIDA 1984, 259, esp. 262–263 (under Art. 343 Code of Obligations, the former provision applicable until 1971).
265. ATF 100 IV 167 (under Art. 343 Code of Obligations). The employment contract must not explicitly impose an inventive activity to the employee; it is enough if this is implied in fact under the circumstances. *See also* Fed. Trib., SIC 2013, 240, summary in F. Dessemontet & R. Dessemontet, La propriété intellectuelle en 2012, JdT 2013 II 123 No. 15 (no compensation due under present law when the inventor has been hired to invent); *see also* Fed. Trib. 4A_691/2012 (unreported, available at www.bger.ch); Fed. Pat. Trib., SIC 2019, 266 (likelihood of the existence of a service invention by reason of the function of the respondents, one being 'R & D Manager', the other one 'Engineer in electronics').
266. Cant. Ct St-Gallen, *Jahrbuch des schweizerischen Arbeitsrecht* 193 (Y.B. Swiss Lab. L. 1989).
267. *See* Art. 321a (4) Code of Obligations, Art. 162 Penal Code, Art. 4(c) and Art. 6 UCA.
268. *Contra*: M. Rehbinder, *supra*, No. 1 *ad* Art. 332 Code of Obligations, wishing to apply Art. 332 Code of Obligations *per analogiam* to non-technical know-how.
269. *See* M. Rehbinder, *supra*, No. 12 *ad* Art. 332 Code of Obligations with cit.

(a) the 'occasional inventions' that were not claimed by the employers are also entirely 'free', that is, at the full disposal of the employee;
(b) the 'free inventions', even if not related to the performance of his duties by the inventor, are nonetheless susceptible to further competition in the field in which the employer is active. Therefore, in exceptional circumstances, the general duty of faithfulness resting with all employees towards their employer under Article 321 Code of Obligations may lead a judge to consider that the inventor might have a duty to concede a non-exclusive licence to his employer so as not to impede the development of his employer's business, of course against market-priced royalties.[270]

E. Inventions in the Public Sector

245. The Swiss Confederation and some large cantons had enacted rules that either referred to the above-mentioned legislative solutions for the private industry or improved upon them. Such improvements were provided, for instance, for the service inventions that are of economic or military importance (Article 16(2) of the Federal Status of the Public Servants of 30 June 1927[271]),[272] but the new Act on the Personnel of the Swiss Confederation of 24 March 2000 (SR 172.220.1) abrogated them, and the usual rules of the Code of Obligations now apply to public servants (Article 6 of this Act).

246. In this author's view, the title to the patent may be expropriated under Article 32 Patent Act which expressly provides only for the expropriation of the patent itself whenever the public interest requests it, against due indemnification.[273] The 'public interest' is to be understood here in the narrowest meaning of the words as the military interest of the Confederation, the interest to maintain law, order and public health. Neither fiscal consideration nor a policy to lower the costs of medical help could suffice in that respect. According to the commentators,[274] no patent expropriation has ever taken place in Switzerland.

Finally, the noteworthy Article 49*a* Patent Act makes it compulsory for the applicant to mention which are the sources of traditional knowledge and genetic resources that have been tapped to invent the subject matter of the application. If he ignores it, he will have to certify in writing that he does not know of such a source and that the inventor ignores it too.

270. M. Rehbinder, *supra*, No. 14 *ad* Art. 332 Code of Obligations; *contra* Ch. Englert, *L'invention faite par l'employé dans l'entreprise privée* (The Invention Made by an Employee in a Private Company), thesis (Basle, 1960), 158; Blum & Pedrazzini, vol. I, 298–299, No. 14 *ad* Art. 3 Patent Act.

271. Formerly RS 172.221.10.
272. For cases *see* ATF 76 I 380; ATF 22, 630.
273. Blum & Pedrazzini, vol. II 269, do not consider that Art. 32 Patent Act allows for expropriation of the patent application or the title to patent.
274. Blum & Pedrazzini, vol. II 267.

II. Assignment

A. Personal Interests

247. For most Swiss authors, the right to be named as the inventor is a personal interest akin to the *droit moral* of the author; therefore, it would not be conveyed to another person.[275] Some of them accept the transfer *mortis causa* to the heirs of the inventor;[276] however, the practice is opposed to the notion of an inventor's heirs validly giving up the right of the deceased inventor to be named,[277] so that it is not possible to accept the idea that the right as such has been transferred to the heirs, since they cannot exercise it. In any event, the more modern commentary on copyright leans towards the transferability of the right to be named as the author of a work, in order not to leave defenceless the works that have been authored by ghostwriters.[278] Until that view has become prevalent, however, the practical approach is to regulate the issue in a deed; lacking such an express provision, the right to be named shall be considered as belonging to the inventor and to him only. Of course, the right to be named includes the right to give up the designation as the inventor. Such waiver cannot be made 'in advance';[279] that is, before the invention is reduced to practice. A provision contrary to the law in an employment agreement shall not be valid. The waiver is to be made in writing, with specific mention of the title of the invention, the number of the application, if known, and the date.[280] If the inventor is not named, nor his or her renouncement filed with the Institute, the application shall be rejected.[281] If a wrong inventor is named, the patent should not be held invalid, but can be corrected through a court judgment (and not through an administrative procedure before the Institute).[282] It is even possible to obtain a criminal condemnation for falsification of an instrument (a felony under Article 251 Penal Code).[283] The patent could be transferred by a court judgment to the person truly entitled to the patent as the case may be (Article 29(1) Patent Act).

B. Assignment Through Contract

248. The *transfer* of the patent, as well as the transfer of the entitlement to the patent, is possible under Article 33 Patent Act.

275. *See* R. von Büren, *Der Übergang von Immaterialgüterrecht* (Transfer of Intellectual Property Right), in *SIWR I/1*, at 254 (2d ed.).
276. R. von Büren, *Der Übergang von Immaterialgüterrecht* (Transfer of Intellectual Property Right), in *SIWR I/1*, 254 & 257 (for authors of copyrighted works); A. Troller, 771–772.
277. *See* PMM Bl 1966 I 6.
278. *See* F. Dessemontet, *Le droit d'auteur* (Copyright Law), CEDIDAC No. 39 (Lausanne, 1999), 985. *See* hereabove para. 105.
279. *See* Art. 6(2) Patent Act.
280. Art. 38 Patent Ordinance.
281. Art. 35(3) Patent Ordinance.
282. Art. 5(2) Patent Act.
283. Blum & Pedrazzini, vol. I, 323.

249. This transfer can consist of a *partial assignment*, as provided for in Article 33(1) *in fine* Patent Act; nevertheless, the commentary cautions that the patent can hardly be divided into segments that would be separately assigned. For example, the various claims of a patent cannot be assigned separately.[284] However, the various rights flowing from the patent (i.e., the right to manufacture and the right to sell or to lease) are unpractical to assign separately. What the legislature envisioned must have been the assignment of shares of ownership (i.e., the inventor assigning 50% to A, 25% to B and keeping 25% for himself).[285]

250. The transfer shall be made *in writing* (Article 33(2*bis*) Patent Act, entered into force on 1 January 1978) as is also required for the transfer of a trademark. The assignment of all other intellectual property rights is not subject to any form of requirement.

251. The rules applicable to the assignment are that of the *sale*. Therefore, the provision of the Code of Obligations (Articles 192 et seq.) regarding a warranty against the better rights of third parties may be applied if the patent is assigned by A but belongs in fact to B. *Per analogiam*, the same rules shall apply if the patent is invalid, unless of course the assignment has been made with a specific disclaimer of the assignor as to the validity of the patent.[286]

The main import of that rule is that the third party asserting his rights to the patent, or, if applied *per analogiam*, the patent being invalidated more than one year after its assignment, the assignee can *still enjoy* the protection of the law under Article 192 Code of Obligations as long as the statute of limitations does not preclude it (generally ten years from the execution of the assignment contract); whereas, if the rules on warranties and guarantees on physical deficiencies under Articles 197 et seq. Code of Obligations were to apply, the time limit of two years starting from the sale (Article 210 (1) Code of Obligations as revised in 2012) would apply, which would be most unfortunate for the assignee.[287]

252. The *recording* of the assignment in the Register of Patents is possible, but not compulsory.[288] Of course, the advantage of registering the assignee as a new

---

284. Blum & Pedrazzini, vol. II, 290–291; R. von Büren, *Der Übergang von Immaterialgüterrecht* (The Transfer of Intellectual Property Rights) *in* SIWR I/1, 258 n. 47 (seems to admit a partial transfer but does not mention the splitting of claims, which seems to this writer unacceptable in view of the nature of the patent, that is construed taking into account all claims in order to better understand one claim if there is a litigation as to its exact meaning and scope); K. Troller, 773.

285. Blum & Pedrazzini, vol. II, 299 *in fine*.

286. ATF 111 II 455 (invalidity for lack of industrial application); ATF 110 II 241 (invalid patent); ATF 57 II 403 (invalid patent).

287. *See* ATF 57 II 403, esp. 406–407.

288. *See* R. von Büren, *Der Übergang von Immaterialgüterrecht* (The Transfer of Intellectual Property Rights), *in* SIWR I/1, 263. According to ATF 135 III 656, the consent of the grantor of a licensee to the registration must be shown in writing, and the original written contract of license does not suffice. Lacking an express authorization to register the license, the Registrar must give to the licensor a time limit to accept or to reject the registration. The same common sense rule should apply to assignments.

holder is that third parties shall thereby be put on notice of the transfer. If not registered, the assignment cannot be opposed to a third party who relied in good faith on the Register to buy the patent through a second assignment by the registered owner (Article 33(4) Patent Act).

253. The *Law on sales of goods* shall apply as well for an unpatented invention[289] or technological know-how,[290] although there can probably be only a guarantee given for technical deficiencies under Articles 197 et seq. Code of Obligations, rather than a guarantee against the better rights of third parties under Articles 192 et seq. Code of Obligations.

254. When the invention is not yet reduced to practice or even not made at all, there can be a contract providing for *the future assignment* of the invention that will derive from the R&D operations.

255. There are no specific rules establishing which party is to enjoy the right to apply for a patent. Each agreement should be examined to determine what the parties really wanted at the time. Nonetheless, several commentators consider that the future invention shall belong to the company which commissioned the R&D operations.[291] A more subtle approach should be to see if the aim of the contract is to procure the benefit of a patent, or only a licence under a patent; if a licence is proper, should it be an exclusive, a sole or a non-exclusive licence?[292]

III. Licensing Agreements

A. *Definition*

256. Under Swiss law, the licensing agreement is the contract by which the licensor authorizes the licensee to work the invention (or to use another intellectual property), usually against the payment of royalties.[293]

289. A. Troller, 774.
290. *See* H. Giger, *Berner Kommentar* (Berne Commentary), vol. VI, No. 23 & 27 *ad* Art. 187 Code of Obligations (Berne, 1979).
291. *See* von Büren, *Der Übergang von Immaterialgüterrecht* (The Transfer of Intellectual Property Rights), *in* SIWR I/1, 195 with cit.
292. *See* E. Nebel, *Les contrats de recherche scientifique et technique* (Scientifical and Technical Research's Agreements), thesis, esp. 104–105 (Geneva, 1973).
293. *See* Pedrazzini, No. 14.6.2.2; U. Zenhäusern, *Der internationale Lizenzvertrag* (The International License Agreement), thesis, 3 (Fribourg, 1991). According to a recent decision by the Fed. Trib., the assignment of the title to a patent is governed by the law of the assignor, except under exceptional circumstances that must be admitted with the greatest restraint; the same solution prevails for the more usual license agreement; *see* ATF 140 III 473. For the FRAND ('Fair, Reasonable and Non-Discriminatory') licenses, Fl. Brunner, 'FRAND', SIC 2019, 1 at 6, notes that the choice of law implies that the declaring party intends to be contractually bound. See for authors of different countries on the applicable law, J. de Werra, Les licences FRAND, SIC 2019, 77 at 79 fn 11.

B. Economical Importance

257. Switzerland is one of the few countries that, most of the time, enjoys a positive balance of royalties: It is receiving more royalties from abroad than it pays abroad. This is no doubt due in part to a favourable tax climate, inciting foreign entities to open subsidiaries in Switzerland to which many royalties shall eventually flow. It also reflects the comparative strength of Swiss companies in some areas such as food, textile, tooling equipment, watchmaking and chemical as well as pharmaceutical industries.

C. Legal Basis

258. Article 34 Patent Act is the only provision bearing on the technological licensing agreement, besides Tax Law and conventions against double taxation. According to that provision, the licensing agreement is also an *authorization given to a third party to work on the invention.* It is possible to conclude from that provision that the licensing agreement gives rise to a 'relative' right, that is, a right having no effect towards third parties.[294] Therefore, even if there is an exclusivity granted to the licensee, no 'absolute' privilege will be enjoyed by the licensee[295] (in the meaning of the licensee having some rights against third parties and the automatic possibility of suing them for infringement or counterfeiting).

259. Further, the commentary is to the effect that the licensing agreement may be regulated by the courts *per analogiam* with the contracts that are most akin to the licensing agreement which is at issue in a given litigation. Sometimes, there can be an analogy to the leasing of productive assets, sometimes to the partnership.[296] In any event, the characteristic elements of a licensing agreement are not regulated by written law. Therefore, the reasoning *per analogiam* with any other definite contract is not binding upon the courts, and they will not follow such reasoning whenever the recourse to the General Part of the Code of Obligations and the reasonable interpretation of the parties' intentions suffice to reach a solution.[297]

---

294. M.M. Pedrazzini, No. 14.6.2.1; ATF 115 II 255 (the fact that Art. 34 Patent Act mentions the licensing agreement does not mean that the agreement would have a status defined by written law; it is up to the courts and commentary to define that status).
295. *See* R. von Büren, *Der Lizenzvertrag* (The License Agreement), *in* SIWR I/1,302; ATF 113 II 190. On 8 Jun. 2007, the Patent Act was amended, *inter alia,* in order to allow the exclusive licensee to file infringement actions if the licensing agreement does not expressly preclude it (Art. 71 para. 1 Patent Act). Non-exclusive licensees can be joined to the cause, all claims in damages being consolidated in one litigation.
296. Pedrazzini, No. 14.6.2.2. *See also* G. Modiano, *Le contrat de licence* (The License Agreement), thesis, 47 et seq. (Geneva, 1979).
297. *See* ATF 92 II 299; *see also* Just. Ct Geneva *in* SJ 1970, 616; ATF 42 II 10; Fed. Trib. *in* ZR 1908, 213; Fed. Trib. *in* RSPIDA 1973, 132; Fed. Trib. *in* RSPIDA 1979, 69. For the new requirement of granting licenses in a 'fair, reasonable and non-discriminatory' manner for standard-setting technologies, *see* Fl. Brunner, FRAND, SIC 2019, 1.

D. General Characteristics of the Licensing Agreement

260. In most cases, the licensing agreement provides for royalties to be paid, so that it is not an agreement free of charge.

However, there is no requirement under Swiss law that a contractual obligation be undertaken for consideration. Besides, even if no royalties are to be paid, other duties may befall the licensee; for example, to keep the licensed techniques under the cloak of secrecy, or to refrain from given acts (especially if the free licence is granted through a settlement agreement or when the cross-licenses are granted to each party by each party). Therefore, the licensing agreement is generally a bilateral contract.[298]

261. The licensing agreement is, as a rule, a contract under which given performances of each party are due at the same time. For example, where confidential technology is disclosed to the licensee, the latter has to maintain secrecy from the onset; where royalties are to be paid according to the production figures of the licensee, those figures have to be reckoned from the very first day of the agreement entering into force, etc. Therefore, the licensing agreement could be deemed to be a synallagmatic agreement under Articles 107 et seq. Code of Obligations (setting a precise procedure for one party to depart from the contract when the other party defaults on his obligations).[299] The point is also relevant to decide if Article 82 Code of Obligations is to apply (a defence that the other party did not perform his obligations), and for Article 119 Code of Obligations regarding the absolute impossibility to perform.[300]

262. There is unanimous consent on the fact that the licensing agreement is a contract usually having a long duration.[301] Too little attention has been brought to the fact that, as such, the usually compulsory procedure to terminate the contract in case of default (discharge by breach) under Article 107 Code of Obligations should not necessarily be followed when a licensing agreement has already been performed for some time and then some difficulty arises in the performance. According to one opinion, which is shared by several commentators, the termination of the contract would then be possible simply by following *per analogiam* the procedure

298. G. Modiano, *supra*, 45.
299. *See* G. Modiano, *supra*, 45–46.
300. R. von Büren, *Der Lizenzvertrag* (The License Agreement), *in* SIWR I/1, 306. It is important to note that under Swiss law, when a notice for termination has not been validly given, the contract continues and parties are requested to perform their contractual duties. Damages may come above and over that duty to discharge in fact, or instead of such a duty ('discharge by breach', a notion unknown to our Code of Obligations, but often applied in arbitral awards). *See* Fed. Trib., SIC 2012, 632 s. 10 (a trademark delimitation agreement case).
301. Pedrazzini, No. 14.6.2.2; R. von Büren, *Der Lizenzvertrag* (The License Agreement), in *SIWR I/1*, at 302 (2d ed.).

under Article 337 Code of Obligations, bearing on the termination of the employment agreement.[302] According to cases, the question is not entirely settled, however.[303] In an interesting arbitration sentence, it has been held that the licensor should always serve upon the licensee a notice setting out the grounds for deeming the performance of the contract by the licensee to be poor and inadequate, and giving him a period of time in which to improve his production; only at the expiry of that period could the licensor unilaterally terminate the agreement.[304]

Nonetheless, even if this procedure more or less conforms to the provisions of Article 107 Code of Obligations, it must not follow it in all details. For example, whereas Article 107 Code of Obligations requests an *immediate* termination or other choice by the creditor at the end of the grace period, the licensor may omit to impart immediately a second notice terminating the agreement.

263. In this writer's view, however, the termination could still be valid even if the aggrieved party writes later on, to the extent that it is not Article 107 Code of Obligations which is binding here, because the licensing agreement is a contract lasting a long time, whereas Article 107 Code of Obligations was foreseen mainly for short-term sales and similar agreements.[305] All this shows that no dogmatic conclusions should be drawn from the classification of licensing agreements as 'synallagmatic contracts'.

E. Obligations of the Licensor

1. Duty to Refrain from Filing an Action for Infringement

264. The main duty of the licensor in all licensing agreements bearing on a patented invention is to abstain from filing an action for infringement against the licensee or authorized sub-licensees.

This obligation is important because any work of the invention by the licensee that falls outside the scope of the licensing agreement can be the proper subject matter of an infringement action. In other words, for any act of working exceeding the

302. Gauch & Schluep, *Schweizerisches Obligationenrecht, allgemeiner Teil* vol. II, No. 3090, 193 (6th ed., Swiss Law of Contracts, General Part); Urs Zenhäusern, *supra*, 36; I. Cherpillod, *La fin des contrats de durée* (The End of Long Term Contracts), CEDIDAC No. 10, at 83 et seq. (Lausanne, 1988).

303. ATF 97 II 58, esp. 65–66. An interesting unpublished recent decision accepts the application of para. 314 BGB (a German provision dating of the *Bürgerliches Gesetzbuch* revision of 2002) as German law had been declared to be applicable to that licensing agreement; the result was in that case identical as the solution which would prevail under Art. 337 CO (Fed. Trib. 4A_367/2008 of 14 Nov. 2008). That approach has been reached as well by the Fed. Trib. in the case of a trademark delimitation agreement; SIC 2012, 632 c. 7.

304. ICC Award in the Case No. 4496, LES Nouvelles 1988, XXIII/I, 23 (a trademark case). That viewpoint is rejected by Fed. Trib., SIC 2012, 632 c. 7 (for a trademark delimitation licence). *See* generally for the arbitrability of issues 'arising before termination of the licensing agreement' ATF 140 III 134.

305. *See* ATF 92 II 299. In the same sense *see* now Fed. Trib., SIC 2012, 632, c. 7.

authorization as given by the licensor, there is not only one action deriving from the law of contracts but also one action deriving from the Patent Act.[306] This is a unique feature of licensing agreements.

2. Duty to Disclose Technological Information

265. Although some patents are explicit enough to be worked as the description of the invention stands, most licensing agreements provide for some disclosure of additional know-how to work the invention. This know-how may or may not be protected by the law of trade secrets, but it is usually a technical knowledge for which the licensee has bargained with great interest. The correct and candid disclosure of such know-how should not be deemed to be an ancillary obligation of the licensor opening only the general remedy of damages (under Articles 97 et seq. Code of Obligations). Rather, it is, in most cases, one of the main obligations of the licensor,[307] and failure to discharge at the outset of the contract shall open the specific remedies of withdrawal from the contract for non-performance by the other party (Articles 107 et seq. Code of Obligations, as contrasted with the case where there has been a performance of the contract during quite some time).

3. Duty to Obtain or to Maintain Patent Rights

266. Where the licensing agreement has been entered into in consideration of the exclusive rights that belong to the licensor or for which the licensor already applied or promised to apply, there is certainly a duty to take the necessary steps in the procedure, either to apply or to resist opposition by a third party. Of course, annuities to uphold the rights shall be paid.[308] No renouncement of the patent claims should be decided without consultation with the licensee, as a total or partial renouncement may give rise to the termination for cause by the licensee. However, in case the patent is declared invalid by a court of law, the licensing agreement is deemed to serve as a sufficient basis for the payment of royalties up to the time when the licensee had 'serious doubts' about the validity of the patent.[309] Therefore, as the aforementioned consultations may well raise 'serious doubts' about the validity of the patent, and thus authorize the licensee to stop paying royalties, a separate agreement should be sought with the licensee to take the changing situation into account.

306. For trademark licensing, *see* the same solution as embedded in Art. 8(2) of the EC Directive No. 89/104 on Trademarks of 1988; *see* further below para. 413. For infringement suits *see* paras 322 et seq.

307. *See* Tercier & Favre, *Les contrats spéciaux* (Contracts) No. 7981 at 1202 (4th ed., Zurich, 2008).

308. R. von Büren, *Der Lizenzvertrag* (The License Agreement), *in* SIWR I/1, 341. As a rule the debtor having pledged a right has to maintain it through registration and annuities if needed; the creditor can do it *in lieu of* the defaulting debtor. *See* Report of the Swiss Group of the AIPPI, Security Interests over Intellectual Property, SIC 2016, 547, 550.

309. ATF 85 II 38. *See also* para. 279 hereinafter.

4. Warranties and Guarantees

267. At the time of entering into the licensing agreement, the licensor has to give precise information on the performance of the technology. The legal effect of those detailed warranties is to bind him. No specific provision of the licensing agreement is necessary to this end.[310] Such an implicit guarantee covers only the technology as described during the negotiations and most often corresponds to the parameters that are set out in an appendix to the contract. For example, the patented equipment for filtration of a broth in a pharmaceutical plant is said to allow x m^3/hour of broth to be filtered. Such technical warranty is part of the contract. Besides, if the disclosure of the information would have been misleading, annulment of the contract for misrepresentation could be considered at the request of the licensee.

268. Generally speaking, the licensor guarantees the working of the technology in the environment in which the technology has been developed and has been used up to the conclusion of the contract. In other words, the warranties and guarantees do not bear on the working of the technology in the plant and workshops of the licensee, possibly under a different climate, with other raw materials or a differently educated labour force. The licensor may undertake to show how the technology should then apply, but this is clearly another agreement for technical assistance.

269. Further, the warranties and guarantees do not usually cover the marketing and financial return of the exploitation of the invention. In the absence of specific provisions in that regard, there is no 'economic guarantee' in the sheer licensing agreement.[311] However, it happens that the licensing contract may be only part of a broader transaction, such as a joint venture, a turn-key sale of a factory, a management contract and/or some other scheme. Then, the economic outcome of the cooperation between parties may be the proper topic for express or even implied warranties and guarantees.[312]

270. Further, the necessity for patented inventions to market them under a trademark may result in the licensor and the licensee having to collaborate both for maintaining the quality of the wares and, possibly, a certain level of pricing for the targeted consumers. The same aim could also lead to obligations of supplying the licensee with given raw materials or semi-manufactured components. Competition law is applicable.

310. *See* R. von Büren, *Der Lizenzvertrag* (The License Agreement), *in* SIWR I/1, 368–370.
311. Blum & Pedrazzini, vol. II, No. 87 *ad* Art. 34 Patent Act; U. Zenhäusern, *supra*, 39.
312. *See* UNIDO, *Warranties and Guarantees Provisions in Transfer-of-Technology Transactions* (Vienna, 1989).

5. Exchange of Information, Licensing of Improvements

271. It is quite common for the licensor to undertake to maintain a steady flow of information towards the licensee. That obligation of updating the technological data is not to be seen as ancillary to all patent licences.

First, some patent licences do not imply such a continuing inflow of information.

Second, the obligation, if existing and not complied with, could lead to a termination of the agreement for cause because non-compliance is an event that undermines the legitimate expectations of the licensee and his trust in good faith of the licensor.

272. By the way, the licensing agreement can provide for the licensee to disclose all relevant information that has been gained in the working of the invention to the patent owner. There are no restrictions for grant-back provisions under present Swiss law. However, absent specific provisions to that effect in the licensing agreement, the licensing of improvements by the licensor is not an obligation, nor are grant-back licences to be given by the licensee to the licensor for the improvements.

6. Exclusivity, Sole Licence, Non-exclusive Licence

273. Regarding the exploitation of the invention, the licensing agreement can provide two further obligations for the licensor:

(1) under an *exclusive licence*, the licensor undertakes not to work the patented invention in the area and for the products that are licensed to the licensee, nor to grant further licences;
(2) under a *sole licence*, the licensor undertakes only not to grant any further licence to a third party for the products and for the geographic area that is mentioned in the licensing agreement.

According to the better view,[313] there is no presumption in favour of the first obligation here above when the contract is ambiguous in this regard. Licensing agreements have to be construed with due respect for the objectives of the rules on competition. This is not to say that in one particular case, a licensing agreement which is not entitled 'exclusive license' nor contains the word 'exclusive' could not be construed as assuming exclusivity; on the contrary, its general set-up, the circumstances surrounding negotiation and execution, the subsequent practice of both parties can help interpret the true intent of the parties and point towards an exclusive licence.

313. Blum & Pedrazzini, vol. II N. 39 *ad* Art. 34 Patent Act; *see contra*: R. von Büren, *Der Lizenzvertrag* (The License Agreement), in *SIWR I/1*, at 314 (2d ed.,) and cit. at n. 110. For the duty of the exclusive licensor to stand by the exclusive licensee in case of infringement by a third party *see* Fed. Pat. Trib., SIC 2017, 745.

274. If no exclusivity nor sole licensee position was intended, the licensee can later be in the situation of competing with third parties having received a licence from the patent owner at a lower rate. In order to prevent the ensuing distortion of the competitive background between the first licensee and the following licensees, the Swiss practice tolerates the 'most-favoured licensee' provisions that are common under US law. This means that, if licensee A has to pay royalties, for example, at the rate of 2% and licensee B, later on, gets a licence for 1.5%, licensee A may request from the licensor the readjustment of his contractual obligations, lowering the royalty rate at 1.5%, provided however that the contract embodies a most-favoured licensee clause.

7. Other Restrictions of Competition

275. Under Swiss law, the licensing agreement can validly contain other restrictions barring the licensor from using the technology under licence, but they have to respect the limitations that are set out in the Communication of the Swiss Competition Commission of 28 June 2010.[314] Of course, when the licensing agreement is otherwise subject to the European law of competition or to the American Antitrust Guidelines, to subject it to Swiss law in case of dispute shall not allow the Swiss court (or arbitration tribunal)[315] to disregard the European or American rules.

F. Obligations of the Licensee

1. Royalties

276. Under private law, there is no maximum royalty rate, and the arrangements widely vary from one industrial sector to the next one, depending on the technology at stake, the process or the product concerned, the level of exclusivity, the duration of the project and various other parameters. Variable royalties are not uncommon.

277. It is worthwhile mentioning a thorough study on Remuneration in Technology Transfer which was based on a large practical experience acquired in the heavy chemical industry.[316] The general concept is that of *profit-sharing*, which allows for the determination of running royalties taking into account the assessment of the

314. Feuille fédérale 2010, 4625. *See* generally P.-A. Killias, *L'application de la législation cartellaire au droit des marques* (The Application of Trust Law to Trademark Act), thesis, 291–303 (Fribourg, 1996). The most important case is now Fed. Trib. SIC 2017, 484 (Gaba): A licensing agreement is characterized as a distribution agreement for purpose of applying the Swiss antitrust legislation; exceptions allowing restrictions by reason of technology transfer under EU law are not applicable to an agreement submitted to Swiss law. *See* generally R.M Hilty & A. Früh, *Lizenzkartellrecht* (Antitrust and Licensing), (Berne 2017).

315. *See* for Art. 85 Treaty of Rome ATF 118 II 193; for Art. 86, an award in the case ICC No. 7181 *in* ICC Bull. 1996, 99.

316. H.A. Janiszewski & M. Besso, *Remuneration in Technology Transfer*, in *1982 Licensing Law Handbook,* 3–118, (New York, 1982).

respective shares of the licensor and of the licensee in the gross profits or the net profits on sales accruing from the given project for which the licence is required. Of course, in practice licensing agreements tend to transfer the risk of unprofitability to the licensee, with fixed lump sum payments, down payments as a prerequisite of entry into force of the agreement, minimum annual royalties, disclosure fees, option fees, service and technical fees, engineering and consulting fees; all of these are basically authorized under Swiss law, and there should be no substantive control by the court or the arbitral tribunal once the parties have validly agreed upon the remuneration.

278. Under international taxation law, however, no royalty arrangement could result in a misuse of the network of bilateral treaties affording relief against double taxation.[317] Further, a national authority may adhere to given guidelines in order to accept royalties as deductible costs. For example, an exclusive licence in the food industry may have running rates of 4%, whereas a non-exclusive licence may have an acceptable rate of 2% only. Of course, the true intent of the parties concerning the exclusivity of the licence will take precedence over any misunderstandable wording, if the proof of such an intent can be adduced to the tax authorities.

279. It is no peculiarity of Swiss law that royalties are due and can be kept when already paid even if the patent underlying the licensing agreement has been declared invalid.[318] According to one precedent,[319] the duty to pay the running royalties ceases with the first serious doubts about the validity of the patent. As to lump sum payments, etc., there appears to be no general statement in that regard in the case law. According to this writer, the accounts corresponding to a down payment (so-called front-end payment), or to the grant of an option right, or to the disclosure of know-how, or a share of R&D costs should not be returned. On the contrary, the lump sum, when having been regarded by the parties as the capitalized value of running royalties should not remain undivided in the hands of the licensor, but an apportionment on time basis should be undertaken.

317. *See* Th. Steinmann, *Les transferts de technologie et de marques en droit fiscal international* (Technology and Trademark Transfer in International Tax Law), thesis (Lausanne, 1991). The new international endeavour to tax multinational companies to a minimum rate of 15% starting 2023 might have some consequences for the licensing contracts that are used to transfer profits from one jurisdiction to another one.

318. *See* ATF 75 II 166; ATF 85 II 38; ATF 116 II 191. For the same solution in France *see*, e.g., Cour appel Lyon (2 Jan. 1989, Dalloz 1990 S.C. 152).

319. ATF 85 II 38, cited with approval by R. von Büren, *Der Lizenzvertrag* (The License Agreement), *in* SIWR I/1, 398.

2. Obligation to Work the Invention

280. According to most authors, it would be compulsory for the licensee to work on the invention whenever the licence is exclusive.[320] The general notion is that the licensor is no longer in a position to put his invention to use, be it by working it himself or through other licensees.

281. Of course, this argumentation does not convince whenever there are minimum running royalties or down payments in lieu of minimum royalties. Further, it does not seem appropriate to set up general rules in an area which is only subject to the common intent of the parties; their intent may vary from case to case. The licensee may, for example, wish to receive an exclusive licence in order to prevent third parties from working on the invention. As Swiss law does not have a general provision on patent misuse as, say, section 271(d) US Patent Act (35 U.S. Code § 271), there seems to be no reason not to enforce such an agreement.

G. *Common or Reciprocal Obligations*

282. Both parties may further undertake obligations such as:

- furthering the development of the market, for example, through advertising campaigns;
- obtaining the administrative authorizations that are possibly compulsory to work the technology, to assure the respect of the environmental regulations, and to put the product on the market;
- clearing administrative export-import regulations (requesting the licences for export or import) and receiving the certificates of origin, etc.;
- abiding by an arbitration clause, or a choice of venue, undertaking to pay penalties if convened upon and admissible under the law applicable to the contract;
- within the limits of applicable competition law, an exchange of information and licences on improvements can be provided in the original licensing agreement.

320. B. Stocker, *Benützungsrecht und Benützungspflicht des Lizenznehmers bei technischen Lizenzverträgen* (Rights and Duty of Use of The Licensee in Technical License Agreement), thesis, 190 et seq. with cit. (Zurich, 1971).

§6. Scope of Exclusive Rights

I. Interim Protection

A. *Before the Application*

283. Before a patent application has been filed, there is no protection under the Patent Act. There might be protection as dictated by the trade secret law,[321] or contractual duties of someone who is entrusted with the preparation of a prototype, series O, OEM manufacturing or further R&D studies.[322]

B. *Upon the Application*

284. Upon the filing of his or her application, the inventor or his or her successor in the title does not yet enjoy the exclusive rights of the patentee. Nevertheless, Article 73(3) Patent Act enables the patentee, once the patent has been issued, to claim damages also for the period of time that the defendant had knowledge of the patent application. Actual knowledge of the patent application is required, unless there has been publication of the application, which then puts the competitors on notice. For a long time, that latter case did no longer happen for Swiss applications[323] but for European patent applications; Articles 73(3) and 111(2) Patent Act provide, therefore, that damages may be obtained from the time of actual knowledge by the infringing party, but at the latest from the publication of the application by the EPO. This is the minimal protection that has to be afforded under Article 64 Munich Convention, rather than the full-fledged protection, including the right to an injunction against further use of the technology covered by the patent application.

II. Definitive Rights

A. *Exclusive Right to Use the Patented Invention*

285. Under Article 8 Patent Act, the patent gives the grantee the right professionally to use the invention. 'Professionally' (*gewerblich*) means within the practice of an activity which either aims at yielding profits or benefits third parties.[324]

321. *See* paras 670 et seq.
322. *See*, e.g., ATF 77 II 263; F. Dessemontet, *Les accords de confidentialité* (Confidentiality Agreements), in Mélanges P. Engel esp. 28–32 (Lausanne, 1989).
323. Examination procedures with third party opposition were abolished as of 1 Sep. 1995 and the opposition procedure had remained unknown from then until 1 Jul. 2008. The starting revision of the Patent Act may lead to a different situation.
324. For example, an apparatus to play an organ or ringing bells benefits a religious community. *See* A. Troller, 627. On a different point, note that Swiss case law accepts a theory of equivalence to define the scope of the protection which is granted by the patent; Fed. Trib., SIC 2017, 71; *see also* Fed. Adm. Trib. SIC 2017, 415 at 419. Fed. Trib. SIC 2020, 562: in order to properly construe the main

Under Article 8*a* Patent Act, the patent on a manufacturing process affords an exclusive right onto the product directly made by the process (*see,* e.g., Fed. Trib., 4A_160/2013, www.bger.ch).

Experiments in educational institutions are not 'professional', but experiments in the laboratories or workshops of commercial companies or institutes working in cooperation with private companies are.[325] Unlike French law, for example, Swiss law did not know until 2008 a defence based on scientific and technological research, in this writer's view at least.[326] Article 9 Patent Act, as revised in 2007, now provides for this defence. It is no prerequisite to the success of a suit for infringement that the defendant be a competitor of the patentee. Thus, we do not believe that under the former law, the industrial research would have been to be outside the scope of the patentee's exclusive rights when there is no relationship of competition between the patentee and the research laboratory or facilities.

286. Under *use*, the legislature understood working of the invention itself or use of a product which is the result of working the invention. Of course, once the product has been lawfully put onto the market, the first-sale doctrine applies. Reversing a Zurich Commercial Court decision,[327] the Federal Tribunal has confirmed the national exhaustion of rights for the patents.[328] There are no rules addressing the activities or inactivities of *patent trolls*.

---

patent claims, the dependent claims can be taken into account. On yet another point: under Art. 9*g* Pat. Act as introduced in 2016, with effective date 1 Jan. 2019, medical doctors and pharmacists have received the right to prescribe the use of a patented medicine for a second medical use, which may be seen as an exception to the rights of the patent owner; *see* Ch. Willi, Sturm im Wasserglas, SIC 2019, 405. This freedom to prescribe has been granted in exchange for the introduction of the pediatric protection certificate and the longer duration of the certificate of extension for pediatry (*see* Art. 140 n and 140t Pat. Act). For defining the ambit of the protection granted by the certificate of extension, the Fed. Pat. Trib. requests that the original patent claims contain the mention of the active substances of the product or that the claims necessarily cover those substances (summary in SIC 2019, at 227).

325. A. Troller, 627.

326. *See*, however, A. Troller, 627–628 fn. 71; Blum & Pedrazzini, vol. 1, 393–394. These authors maintain that the inventions can be worked by someone who endeavours to find a 'dependent' invention; under Art. 36 Patent Law, if he finds such an invention, he will be entitled to a compulsory license. Thus, so the argument goes, he should be free to work the patented invention beforehand. Of course, the argument can be reversed: as long as the stringent prerequisites of Art. 36 Patent Law are not met, there is no defence against a suit for infringement.

327. Com. Ct Zurich *in* ZR 1998, 289 et seq.

328. ATF 126 III 129. On 19 Dec. 2008, the legislature limited the bearing of this ruling mainly to pharmaceutical products and other patented items the price of which is regulated by the State, if any. *See* Art. 9*a* paras 4 & 5 Patent Act, in force since 1 Jul. 2009 (ROLF 2009, 2615); under Art. 9*a* Patent Act the parallel import of patented products is prohibited only if the patentee may prove that the patented part of the imported device is essential to the functioning of the item; *see* Pat. Fed. Trib. case S2016_006, SIC 2016, 678; *see* already F. Dessemontet, *L'épuisement en droit des brevets: un arrêt de principe* (Exhaustion of Rights for the Patents: A Leading Case). Bulletin du CEDIDAC No. 32 (Lausanne, December 1999). *See also* ATF 115 II 279. National exhaustion might be the rule for Chips Semi-Conductors and Plant Varieties. On the contrary, there is international exhaustion of rights for copyright (*see* para. 120 & fn 534) and for trademark (*see* para. 419 & fn 534). For the first-sale doctrine for computer software, *see* para. 36, and for semiconductors fn 789.

B. Prohibited Acts

287. Article 8(2) Patent Act details the acts that infringe upon the patentee's rights:

- use and working of the invention;
- offering for sale;
- sale;
- distribution.

288. Article 8 Patent Act allows the patentee to stop the marketing of the infringing goods at any level (importer, wholesaler, retailer).

289. The Patent Act applies only to acts taking place within the Swiss territory. A customs-free zone may be Swiss for that purpose,[329] but not if it is located outside Switzerland due to the exiguity of the country.[330] Goods and wares in transit through Switzerland are not subject to the Swiss Patent Act, so that even if they change from one flight to another in a Swiss airport, no marketing will be deemed to have taken place within Switzerland.[331] However, even if only the execution of the contract (e.g., signature) takes place in Switzerland, the Swiss Patent Act applies and the sale is an infringement.[332] Of course, manufacturing in Switzerland with a view to selling abroad is an infringement as well.

§7. Limitations and Exceptions: Compulsory Licences

I. Defence of Personal Working

290. Under Article 35 Patent Act, the patent cannot be opposed to the person who, in good faith, professionally used the invention in Switzerland before the date of the patent application, or had undertaken specific preparations towards that end. Most European patent legislations provide for that defence, as they are based on the 'first-to-file' system. This defence used to be unknown from the US Patent Act before the revision of 2011, abandoning the 'first-to-invent' system. Articles 35*a*

329. ATF 92 II 293. If there are no actual sales nor offer to sell yet, but the respondent has registered an infringing medication in a Swiss register for pharmaceutical products, a temporary injunction will be issued against him as this registration will be deemed to be an 'offering for sale'; *see* Fed. Pat. Ct., SIC 2019, 617 ('*Tadafil*'). For process patents as for product patents the result of the infringement must take place within Switzerland; see ATF 129 III 588 at 591.
330. ATF 115 II 279 (the Airport of Basle-Mulhouse is not part of Swiss territory).
331. ATF 115 II 564, esp. 588–578.
332. Blum & Pedrazzini, vol. 1, 403. However, ATF 92 II 293, esp. 298 states in an obiter dictum that such will not be the case if the only contact between Switzerland and the sale is the place of execution of the agreement (presumably, such would be the case for two foreign nationals residing abroad and meeting in Switzerland to sign an agreement). It will be noted that experts view 'franking' (that is letting the infringing wares be marketed elsewhere when compensatory damages have been awarded in one court) is not supported by present Swiss law in any area of intellectual property; *see* Report of the Swiss Group of the AIPPI, SIC 2019, 648.

and 35*b* Patent Act also allow farmers to use patented seeds in order to produce further seeds. This rule originates with the Law on Protection of Plant Varieties (*see* below Chapter 7). The exemption does require the farmers to work themselves the patented seeds and the resulting new seeds can be planted only on the farmers' own farms. Otherwise, it does not follow the regime of the general defence of personal working as is described hereinbelow.

A. *Professional Use*

291. The concept is the same as under Article 8 Patent Act,[333] so that working, offering for sale, sale and marketing are included.

The defendant must be aware that he or she uses a new process or manufactures a new product.[334]

292. The precise determination of the user has already taken place before the grant of the patent is important because it is only to the same extent that the defence of personal use will apply.[335]

B. *Specific Preparations*

293. Even if no use has taken place at the filing of the application, the defendant may raise the defence that he had then already undertaken specific preparations to work on the invention. It does not mean that he had to invent himself the invention,[336] but rather that, in good faith, he was busy preparing its use. By then, the invention itself must have been fully known, so that R&D endeavours are not 'specific preparatory steps' within the meaning of Article 35 Patent Act. Such steps are rather, the tooling, the erection of production facilities, the administrative requests to put the invention onto the market, as well as hiring skilled labour.

294. There is no specific amount of expenses that would be required as evidence of those preparatory steps; of course, as the protection of the investments made in good faith before the filing of the application by the patentee is the only ground for that defence, the defendant who can prove large investments is more likely to convince the courts that he deserves to continue working the invention.

333. *See* para. 286.
334. *See* ATF 121 III 125.
335. Blum & Pedrazzini, vol. II, 553 et seq.; A. Troller, 628.
336. *See* ATF 20, 677, esp. 685.

C. *Good Faith*

295. The good faith exists whenever the defendant cannot be shown to have known of a violation of the rights of the applicant through which the invention becomes known to himself or an intermediary.

D. *Legal Nature of the Defence*

296. There is some controversy about the legal nature of the right to use the patented technology. For some authors,[337] it would be an intellectual property right, valid against all third parties. The better view is rather that it is a limitation that the legislature decided in order to circumscribe the rights of the patentee.[338] Where the business of the defendant is transferred, the vendee can continue to raise the defence, but it is a factual mastery of the technology and not a property interest that could be asserted vis-à-vis third parties. It should be noted that Article 35 Patent Act does not require that the defendant be the rightful owner of the invention; he could be, as well as the licensee, a third party. The result is that Article 35 Patent Act does not grant a further intellectual property right but only protects the investment made in good faith. Finally, the heirs of the defendant do not inherit a right to use the invention, but only the possibility to raise the same defence if they inherit the business.

II. Defence of Automobiles Temporarily in Switzerland

297. Article 35(3) Patent Act protects the owners or renters of cars that are only temporarily driven within Switzerland against suits for infringement of a patent concerning an invention which is embodied in the car. Under an old administrative guideline, 'temporarily' means six months at most.[339]

III. Dependent Inventions

298. Under Article 36 Patent Act, a compulsory licence on a patented invention may be granted by a court to the inventor of an invention that has been later granted patent protection and that is not to be worked without infringing the prior patent, provided, however, that the second patent has to fulfil an entirely different goal, or that it constitutes considerable technical progress.

299. Since the 1976 revision, there is no need to wait for a given period of time in order to obtain a licence.

---

337. Blum & Pedrazzini, vol. II, 533–534.

338. A. Troller, 631–632.

339. Zurich, *Mitteilungsblatt des Strassenverkehrsamtes* (Report of the Traffic Office) of 29 Jul. 1958, W/nb 2000, as cited by Blum & Pedrazzini, vol. II, 567.

300. Under Swiss law, the prior invention shall not necessarily be used each time that the second invention has worked. It is enough if the prior invention has sometimes worked during the use of the second invention, or only for some of the acts that are covered by the exclusive rights of the patent owner.[340]

301. It has been stated by the Federal Tribunal that the public interest would be irrelevant; only the private interests of the second patentee might justify the grant of a compulsory licence.[341] This view may not be entirely outdated, but this writer assumes that the public interest is best served when the conflicting private interests of the two inventors are reconciled. The harmonization of their interests is based on the grant of a compulsory licence, by order of the court if need be, and the payment of the royalties and further indemnities.[342] It is not mentioned that such royalties shall be 'fair and equitable', but such is certainly the meaning of that rule. Under Article 4 Civil Code, the court shall apply the rules of equity whenever the law entrusts the courts with a power of appreciation or requests them to take into account circumstances or good causes. The market price of the licence is the indicator of the royalties to be paid.[343] As a matter of fact, there is precious little case law concerning the compulsory licence, perhaps because the threat of obtaining such a licence through a court order is enough for the prior patentee to grant a voluntary licence under usual business conditions.

302. The licensee may have to grant a licence under his own patent to the prior patentee when both inventions correspond to the same economic need (Article 36(2) Patent Act). The legislature thus provides for 'reverse compulsory licensing'.

IV. Compulsory Licence for Want of Working

303. Under Article 37 Patent Act, a compulsory licence may be granted by order of the court when the patentee has not sufficiently worked the invention within Switzerland, without having good cause therefor. A period of three years since the issue of the patent, but at least four years since the application must have elapsed. 'Working' the invention is a broad concept, that covers also sufficient importation to Switzerland from abroad.

304. The licence is non-exclusive and pertains to the business, which works the invention, so that neither a separate conveyance of the rights under the licence nor the grant of a sublicence may be validly made without the simultaneous transfer of the business.

340. *See* Blum & Pedrazzini, vol. 2, 573; F. Dessemontet, *La notion d'invention dépendante en droit suisse* (The Notion of Dependent Invention under Swiss Law), in *Mélanges Piotet* 238 (1990).
341. ATF 29 II 564, esp. 588–578.
342. Art. 35 (3) Patent Law.
343. *See* ATF 52 III 30 (under Art. 22 former Patent Law of 1907, now Art. 36 Patent Law).

305. As the ordinary trial may last a long time, the court may order the interim grant of a licence, if the claimant:

- has filed an action;
- has shown the likelihood that he has an interest to work on the invention immediately rather than upon a final judgment (some five or ten years later); and
- has shown the likelihood that the legal prerequisites are met in the particular case.

In that event, the court shall request the posting of a bond by the claimant to guarantee the defendant against damages suffered by reason of the interim licence.

306. In the final judgment, the court determines the royalties, the duration and the exact scope of the licence.

307. There are almost no precedents for the application of Article 37 Patent Act. The only case that had been mentioned to this writer has been settled out of court.

V. Forfeiture of the Patent

308. Under Article 38 Patent Act, when the granting of compulsory licences does not allow for the Swiss market to be sufficiently supplied, the court may order the forfeiture of the patent if petitioned to do so by any person showing an interest thereto, but not prior to two years starting from the grant of the first compulsory licence.

309. Swiss law is therefore restrictive: in the normal case, it is not before six years from the filing of the application, or five years from the grant of the patent, whichever is longer, that an action for forfeiture of the patent may be filed. Therefore, by way of reverse reciprocity, the law provides that, when the patent owner is a national or resident of another country in which forfeiture may be requested already after three years from the grant of the patent, such a shorter delay will apply: the petitioner may then dispense with showing that compulsory licences have been granted to no avail; he must only show that the prerequisites of granting a compulsory licence are met and petition the court for an order stating that the patent is forfeited.

310. No judgment is known to this writer.

311. With countries that grant reciprocity, the Government may order that Articles 37 Patent Act on compulsory licences and 38 Patent Act on forfeiture do not apply. Such a declaration has been made towards nationals of Germany and the US.[344]

344. Treaty with Germany of 13 Apr. 1892/26 May 1902 (RS 0.232.149.281); Decision of the Federal Council of 28 Jan. 1908 on the Reciprocity with the United States of America (RS 232.149.336).

VI. Licences in the Public Interest

312. Under Article 40 Patent Act, if the patentee rejected the request for the grant of a licence, the interested person may petition the court to order such a licence to the extent that the public interest requires it. Against German and American citizens who own Swiss patents, Article 40 Patent Act gives the only remedy for the insufficient supply of the market. The public interest is narrowly understood as the public health or very pressing needs for environmental protection. No judgment granting a licence in the public interest seems to have been reported.[345]

The 2007 revision of the Patent Act provides for three new cases of compulsory licences in the public interest. The first two cases are a safeguard against the ill consequences of patents being now granted for genetic technology: the law provides for a non-exclusive licence for research using patented biotechnical material; and a non-exclusive licence for inventions relating to a product or a process applicable in the diagnosis of human ailments if competition law requires the monopoly of the patent holder to be lifted (*see* Articles 40b and 40c Patent Act).[346] The third case is a consequence of the Doha Provisions of 2001 and 2003, aiming at facilitating the sale of medicines against pandemics such as acquired immunodeficiency syndrome (AIDS) and other medicines, the acquisition of which is a priority under the public policy of less developed countries (Article 40d Patent Act). The Swiss Government has opposed the application of this regime to the vaccines and medications against COVID-19 but in Spring 2022 a compromise has been decided by WTO in favour of the pharmaceutical industries of developing countries.

Further, the new Article 40e Patent Act provides for common rules bearing on all compulsory licences.

VII. Purchase by State Compulsion

313. Under Article 32 Patent Act, the Swiss Confederation might expropriate the patent owner against due compensation, in case the public interest would require it. Weaponry and public health might justify it, but such a purchase by compulsion was never ordered, as far as could be ascertained by this writer. Switzerland does not know entirely 'secret patents'; there will always be a registration in the Register of Patents.

345. *See* ATF 42 II 269 (it was really a case of dependent inventions, to be adjudicated under Art. 36 Patent Law).

346. Two cantonal courts have given two differing answers to the question whether using a patented invention in the administrative proceedings that lead to the authorization to market a medicine is an infringement of the exclusive rights of the patent holder: positive (Com. Ct St-Gallen, SIC 2005, 31) or negative (Sup. Ct BL, SIC 1998, 78).

§8. Duration of the Protection

I. Ordinary Duration

314. Swiss patents are granted for a duration of twenty years since the application has been filed (Article 14 Patent Act). The Swiss legislation was adapted in 1976 to the Munich Convention so that the TRIPS did not entail any legislative modification in that regard.

II. Premature Termination

A. Non-payment of Annuities

315. As most patent systems in the world, Swiss law preconditions the continued duration of the patent to the timely payment of annuities, so as to favour the relinquishment of patents that serve no useful purpose. Still, there are 140,093 European patents in force on 1 January 2022, to which 6,623 Swiss patents may be added.[347]

B. Partial Relinquishment

316. A partial giving up of claims may limit the validity of a patent. It is possible only within four years from the grant of the patent unless the limitation occurs through the joinder of sub-claims to an independent claim (that will necessarily be much narrower thereafter).

317. The limitation may leave claims deserving of protection without the authorized scope of the patent under Articles 52 and 55 Patent Act on main claims and sub-claims. Therefore, one or several new patents may be granted to cover such an isolated claim, with reissue under the original date of the first patent.

318. After a litigation, a judgment may circumscribe more narrowly the justified scope of claims under the patent.

C. Annulment of Patents

319. Under Article 26 Patent Act, the invalidity *ab ovo* may be stated by a judgment – or an arbitral award[348] – upon the petition of any interested party.

347. It will be noted that an expired patent cannot be seized in bankruptcy proceedings, Fed. Pat. Trib., SIC 2016, 531.

348. *See* F. Dessemontet, *The Specificity of Intellectual Property Arbitration, in Research Handbook on Cross-Border Enforcement of Intellectual Property*, ed. by P. Torremans, 607 (London 2014); F. Dessemontet, *Arbitrage, propriété intellectuelle et droit de la concurrence* (Arbitration, Intellectual

320. The grounds of invalidity are the following:

- the subject matter is not patentable, for want of novelty or industrial application or *contra bonos mores*;
- the invention is not described in the patent so as to allow a man skilled in the art to work it;
- the claims go further than the application which gives the priority date;
- the patentee is neither the inventor nor his or her successor in title.

321. Partial invalidity may be adjudicated, bearing on some of the claims only.

§9. Infringement and Remedies

I. Infringement

322. The infringing acts are circumscribed in Article 66 Patent Act, that limitedly enumerates them. The only addition is the wrongful pretence to enjoy patent protection when such is not the case, a misdemeanour under Article 82 Patent Act.

323. There can be either counterfeiting or imitation[349] of the invention. In practice, Swiss law is not alien to the theory of functional equivalents as known in other countries. The imitation is wrongful even if the defendant is unaware of the patented invention. However, criminal redress is only possible when the defendant may be convicted of intentional imitation – or outright piracy.

324. The refusal to give information on the suppliers of infringing goods and wares is also wrongful.[350]

Property and Antitrust Law) in *Objective Arbitrability*, Swiss Arbitration Association Special Series No. 6, at 55–97. ATF 125 III 241 (Zurich, 1994): The action in nullity is an action to state the legal situation and not an action to change the legal situation. This action may also be brought before an arbitral tribunal, *see* F. Dessemontet, *L'action en constatation de droit, spécialement pour les contrats de licence* (The action for declaratory relief, especially for licensing agreements), in *Wirtschaftsrecht in Theorie und Praxis* (Business Law in Theory and Practice), *Festschrift für Roland von Büren* 253–268 (P. Kunz et al., eds., Basle, 2009); *see also* ATF 129 III 295, 299: It was then adjudicated that the action to obtain a statement whereby the claimant does not infringe on a patent is admissible; however, it should not be entertained if its purpose is only to open a new venue under the Lugano Convention on the Jurisdiction and the Enforcement of Civil and Commercial Judgments (RS 0.275.11). Recently nonetheless, the Fed. Trib. seemed to reverse that opinion and to open an avenue for a 'Swiss torpedo', stating that the interest to create a venue that is useful is a sufficient interest to open access to a Swiss court for an negatory action, i.e., an action filed with a view to obtain a judgment negating infringement; SIC 2018, 356. *See also* SIC 2019, 698. ATF 133 III 282 appears to be no longer a valid precedent.

349. *See also* 125 III 29; Fed.Trib., RSPI 1991, 198; Com. Ct Berne, SIC 1999, 657; Cant. Ct Zurich, RSPI 1991, 402.

350. *See* ATF 97 II 169. *See* now Fed. Pat. Trib., SIC 2013, 770 (admission of a plaintiff's request for information even when the adverse party has offered to give some evidence, if there is a controversy on the exact amount of profit deriving from the infringement of a patent).

325. To erase the sign of a Swiss patent and its number is a separate wrong.

326. Accomplices may be convicted even if the main wrongdoer is not (Article 66(d) Patent Act).

II. Civil Actions

327. The Patent Act offers an array of remedies:

- action for a declaratory judgment;
- action for cease-and-desist order (injunctive relief);
- action for damages and accounting for profits.[351]

III. Criminal Actions

328. Most infringing acts are felonies, punishable with imprisonment up to one year or a fine.[352] Only the wrongful pretence to a patent is a misdemeanour. If the infringement is made on a regular basis, it is a crime punishable by imprisonment of up to five years and a fine.

351. For details, *see* above paras 177 *et seq.* (also valid for Patent Law). According to ATF 132 III 83, an official expert report is always required if the validity of a patent is contested. ATF 134 III 306 states that the respondent to the action in disgorgement of profits must prove the amount of the costs that he incurred and keep the accounting documents necessary to this end. Under ATF 132 III 379, it would no longer be possible to reckon the damages on the basis of the royalty rate prevailing in the industry. For criticism, *see* F. Dessemontet, *La propriété intellectuelle et les contrats de licence* (Intellectual Property and Licensing Agreements) (Lausanne, 2011), No. 364. In Fed. Trib, SIC 2012, 52, it is reaffirmed that technical documents pertaining to the novelty of the invention or other contested issues may be taken into consideration by the court even when the protection of technical secrets makes it necessary to file them under seal so as to prohibit the other party to *see* the secret information (*see* Art. 68 Pat. Act). A claimant may proceed first with a claim towards getting information on the alleged counterfeiting, then with a claim in monetary relief; further, the first claim for information may succeed independently of the proof of the counterfeiting; Fed. Pat. Trib., SIC 2016, 68. On a different processual aspect, the Fed. Pat. Trib. adjudicated that when an action is based on different national patents claimed under the Munich Patent Treaty, the Swiss court may split up the trial if the EPO proceedings are less advanced for one patent than for other patents; SIC 2016, 530.

352. As from 1 Jul. 2008.

Chapter 3. Utility Models

329. For the time being, Switzerland does not know a registration system for utility models.[353] The Swiss Government had been preparing a new legislation in order to institute a protection of utility models for a period of ten years. It would not be available for process inventions, nor biotechnological, chemical or pharmaceutical inventions. However, due to the industry's reluctance, this endeavour has been dropped from the current revision of the Patent Act.

330. To some extent, Article 5(c) of the Act against Unfair Competition[354] already now could be invoked to protect 'small inventions' against outright piracy if the 'model' is ready to be put on the market.

353. *See* paras 555 et seq.

354. Art. 5(c) UCA: '*Exploitation of the Achievements of Others: Shall be deemed to have committed an act of unfair competition, anyone who, in particular, (c) by means of technical reproduction processes and without a corresponding effort of his own, takes the marketable results of work of another person and exploits them as such.*' Art. 5 (a) and (b) UCA edict the protection for an investment in labour when a result of that labour, for example calculations, bids, blueprints or design, has been entrusted to someone or when the defendant acquired it *mala fide*.

Chapter 4. Trademarks

§1. Sources

I. The Law

331. The Federal Law of 26 September 1890 regulated the protection of trademarks, geographic denominations and mentions of industrial awards. It was replaced by the Federal Law on Trademarks and Geographic Denominations (hereinafter 'Trademark Act') of 28 August 1992,[355] which enacted many substantial modifications, so that former case law and literature should be consulted only with utmost caution. The Annex 3 of the revised Patent Act of 22 June 2007, with effective date of 1 July 2008, introduced certain important modifications for the Trademark actions (Articles 53, 55 and 57).

II. The Ordinance

332. The Ordinance on the Protection of Trademarks of 23 December 1992[356] regulates the administrative procedure before the Federal Institute for Intellectual Property in Berne and the Swiss side of the international registration. It has been often amended until 2021.

III. The Treaties

A. *Multilateral Treaties*

333. Switzerland is a party to the Paris Convention for the Protection of Industrial Property and to the Madrid Arrangement on the International Registration of Trademarks,[357] as well as to the Madrid Protocol,[358] the Nice Agreement Concerning the International Classification of Products and Services, and the Singapore Treaty of 2006 on the Law of trademarks as well as to the Geneva Treaty on the Trademarks Law of 1994.[359] Switzerland is, of course, not a member of the EU; therefore, Regulation 40/94 of 20 December 1993 on the Community Trademark[360] does not apply in Switzerland. To a large extent, the Federal Law of 1992 embodies the same solutions as the First European Directive 89/104 of 21 December 1988 on

355. RS 232.11. An English translation is to be found in Industrial Property, November 1996.
356. RS 232.111. An English translation is to be found in Industrial Property, June 1993.
357. RS 0.232.112.2 The Stockholm Version revised in 1967 is RS 0.232.112.3.
358. RS 0.232.112.4.
359. Nice Agreement: RS 0.232.112.9, as revised in Geneva on 13 May 1977; Singapore Treaty: RS 0.232.112.11; Geneva Treaty: RS 0. 232.112.1.
360. OJ No. L 11/1 of 14 Jan. 1994.

the Harmonization of the Trademark Act.[361] Although the formulation of the Swiss provisions may differ from the European text, a euro-compatible interpretation should be possible in most cases.[362]

B. Bilateral Treaties

334. The most important bilateral treaty was the Agreement between Germany and Switzerland of 13 April 1892 as revised on 26 May 1902,[363] which provided that the use of a trademark by a national or resident of a party in his State party is assimilated to the use in the second State party to the agreement. In other words, trademark owners who benefited from that convention could use their trademark in only one country and nevertheless enjoyed protection in both. It now appears that this Treaty is no longer entirely binding for Germany as it might be contrary to the obligations of Germany regarding the other European States and their citizens under the EU Treaty (*see* below paragraph 336).

335. Switzerland is bound to several countries by bilateral treaties on the protection of investments that usually include trademarks among the protected assets.[364]

361. OJ No. L 40/1 of 11 Feb. 1989. A notable difference regards the collective trademarks that can be made out of a descriptive denomination under Swiss law.
362. *See* David, No. 9 *Einleitung* (Introduction). Mr David also notes the important difference concerning the 'certification mark' that may consist under Swiss law of a generic term.
363. RS 0.232.131.913.6.
364. *See* for the Convention between Germany and Switzerland of 1892, RS 0.232.149.136; for the Free Trade Agreement with the United Kingdom of 25 Feb. 2019 see RS 0.142.113.672; for other modern bilateral investment treaties *see* generally RS 0.975 ... and most notably Albania (RS 0.975.212.3) Art. 1; Barbados (RS 0.975.216.8) Art. 1; Bolivia (RO 1991, 1624) Art. 1; Burkina Faso (RO 1969, 1084) Art. 7; Cameroon (RO 1964, 400) Art. 7; Cabo Verde (RS 0.975.216.8) Art. 1; Central African Republic (RO 1973, 1275) Art. 6; China (RO 2014 1783) Arts 1(2)(g) and Chapter 11, for trademarks esp. Art. 11(7); Colombia (RS 0.975.226.3) Art. 1 (1) (d); Congo [formerly Zaire] (RO 1973, 983) Arts 1 and 2; Congo-Brazzaville (RO 1964, 633) Art. 7; Costa Rica (RS 0.975.228.5) Art. 6; Côte d'Ivoire (RO 1963, 53) Art. 7; Cuba (RS 0.975.229.4) Art. 1 Czech Republic and Slovak Republic (RO 1991, 2079) Arts 1 and 4; Dominican Republic (RO 2006, 3915); Ecuador (RO 1969, 1089) Arts 1 and 6; Egypt (RO 1974, 1283) Arts 1 and 3; El Salvador (RS 0.975.232.3); Gambia (RS 0.975.235.8) Art. 1; Ghana (RS 0.975.236.3) Art. 1; Guatemala (SR 0.975.237.6); Hungary (RO 1989, 1376) Arts 1 and 4; Indonesia (RS 0.975.242.7) Art. 3; Jamaica (RS 0.975.245.7) Art. 1; Jordan (RO 1977, 804) Art. 5; Laos (RS 0.975.248.1); Lettonia (RS 0.975.248.7); Lebanon (RS 0.975.248.9; Liechtenstein (RO 1923, 565) Art. 5 (enactment on his territory of the whole Intellectual Property Swiss Law); Macedonia (RS 0.975 252.0) Art. 2; Madagascar (RO 1966, 1455) Art. 7; Malaysia (RO 1978, 1183) Arts 2 and 3; Mali (RO 1979, 222 and 843) Arts 2, 3 and 5; Malta (RO 1965, 225) Art. 5; Mauritius (SR 0.975.255.4); Art. 1 (3)(d) Mexico (RS 0.975.256.3); Morocco (RO 1991, 1360) Arts 1, 3 and 4; Moldavia (RS 0.975.256.5) Art. 1; Montenegro (0.975.257.3); Mozambique (RO 1980, 1560) Art. 6; Niger (RO 1963, 46) Art. 7; Panama (RO 1985, 1376) Arts 2 and 8; Paraguay (RO 1992, 2384) Arts 1 and 4; Poland (RO 1990, 917) Arts 1 and 4; Qatar (0.975.265.6); Russian Federation (RO 1991, 2196) Arts 1 and 4; Senegal (RO 1964, 718) Art. 7; Singapore (RO 1978, 1190) Arts 2 and 8; Slovenia (RS 0.975.269.1) Art. 1; South Korea (RO 1971, 731) Arts 2 and 7; Sri Lanka (RO 1983, 772) Arts 1 and 4; Sudan (RO 1975, 97) Arts 1 and 4; Syrian Arab Republic (RO 1979, 1352) Art. 2; Tanzania (SR 0.975.273.2) Arts 1 and 4; Tchad (RO 1968, 9) Art. 8; Togo (RO 1966, 1443) Art. 7; Tunisia (RO 1964, 67) Art.

C. Predominance of International Treaties

336. Article 20 Trademark Act provides that international treaties (when appropriate for direct application) shall benefit Swiss citizens and residents as well as the foreign nationals who are their first beneficiaries. For example, the Paris Convention priority can now benefit Swiss applicants even if they file their first registration application abroad. A second example is the German–Swiss Convention of 1892: a Swiss national could claim as sufficient use the use of his Swiss trademark in Germany if he or she had registered it in both countries but did not use it in Switzerland; however, for an Union trademark, since the European Court of Justice has ruled on 12 December 2013 (case '*Baskaya/Passaia*' – SIC 2014 307) that this bilateral Convention cannot create an exception to the Community Regulation on the trademarks as regards the requirement of a 'serious use', the Swiss owner could not claim the protection of the Convention of 1892; Switzerland (i.e., a country not bound by the Regulation) may recognize the use in Germany but Germany must avoid recognizing the use of the Union trademark in Switzerland as equivalent to the use in Germany; for a German trademark that a German national or resident owns, its use in Switzerland is assimilated in Germany to use within Germany and it does not seem to be contrary to European law under the ECJ C-720-18 & 721/18 ('Ferrari/Testarossa'); in the long run the Convention of 1892 will probably be terminated. For the time being, refugees and stateless persons who habitually reside in Switzerland are assimilated to Swiss nationals in that respect.[365]

§2. Subject Matter of Protection

I. Signs Which May Serve as Trademarks

A. Principles

337. According to Article One of the Trademark Act, the trademark may be each and any sign which is apt to allow for a distinction between the products or the services of an enterprise and those of other enterprises.

According to the non-limitative listing of Article 1(2) Trademark Act, the words, the letters, the numbers, the graphic symbols, and the three-dimensional shapes by themselves or in combination with colours may be registered as trademarks.

1; Turkey (RO 1990, 551) Arts 1 and 3; Uganda (RO 1972, 2524) Arts 1 and 4; Ukrainia (RS 0.975.276.7) Art. 1; Uruguay (RO 1992, 1810) Arts 1 and 3; Uzbekistan (RS 0.975.262.1) Art. 1; Venezuela (RS 0.975.278.5) mentioning 'Intellectual property rights, technical processes, know-how and goodwill' (Art. 1(2)(d); Vietnam (RS 0.975.278.9) Art. 1; Zambia (RS 0.975.282.3) Art. 1.

365. *See* Conventions of Geneva of 28 Jul. 1951 relating to the Status of Refugees (RS 0.142.30) and the Convention of New York of 28 Sep. 1954 relating to the Status of Stateless Persons (RS 0.142.40). Concerning the future fate of the 1892 Convention the Fed. Trib. did not evoke it in decision 4A_152/2020; see SIC 2021, 295 fn 11.

Further, it is worth noting that the sound symbols, that are not mentioned in the Trademark Act, are not excluded;[366] nevertheless, under Article 10 of the Ordinance, the sound trademark must be susceptible to a graphic expression, which restricts the sort of sound that may be registered. Nonetheless, the 'Olympic Hymn' is registered as a trademark in Switzerland.[367]

The sheer colour can be registered in an exceptional case,[368] and a combination of three colours may be a valid trademark in most cases, while a two-colour combination has to be well-known to be accepted.[369]

Olfactive trademarks are probably not valid trademarks unless they can be expressed in writing. Assuredly, the chemical formula of the main compound is accessible to that sort of description, but the real scent of the trademark as diluted is not.

B. Exceptions

338. Article 2 Trademark Act gives a limited list of grounds for exclusion of the registration of a sign as a trademark:

- signs that belong to the *public domain*;
- shapes that are of the nature of the product as well as the shapes that are necessary for the functioning of the product or of the packaging;
- signs that are misleading;
- signs that are contrary to public policy, *bonos mores* or the law.

1. Public Domain

339. As a general requirement, a trademark has to be apt to allow for a distinction between the products or services of the trademark owner and those of his competitors. This distinctive flavour does not exist when a trademark consists of a sign which is in the public domain. Conversely, if a sign is in the public domain, all the

366. *See* David, No. 16 *ad* Art. 1 Trademark Act; Pedrazzini, von Büren & Marbach, No. 465.
367. Swiss Mark No. 408261 (*see* Marbach, 506). *See* a different tune consisting of seven notes protected as trademark by Fed. Trib., SIC 2009, 520 (international trademark No 858,788).
368. *See* the trademark 'Lilac' for chocolate, a trademark registered because it is well-known (in use since 1901). *See*, however, the decision of the Appeal Committee for Intellectual Property, followed by an obiter dictum *in* RSPI 1996, 315, esp. No. 6: 'The text of Art. 1(2) Trademark Act mentions colours only in combination with other signs, therefore colours alone are not valid trademarks.' However, this practice has been reversed for the 'yellow' of La Poste, accepting a single colour as trademark for certain categories of goods and services, but not for the most common retail products (same Appeal Committee, SIC 2002, 242). *See* for a new colour Swiss Mark No. 402 110 – 'Mastergray'. Finally, a combination of colours together with words that are in the public domain may constitute a valid trademark according to the Appeal Committee, SIC 2000, 297. In such a case, however, all elements of the trademark taken together may become well-known, but the verbal element which is in the public domain may not be opposed to a new filing by a third party; same Committee SIC 2004, 929 (Kraft).
369. *See* Marbach, *Markenrecht* (Trademark Act), *in* SIWR III, 52.

competitors should be able to use it in order to describe their wares or services. This holds true even for signs that once upon a time were valid trademarks, but have become descriptive of wares and goods (e.g., Frigidaire, Aspirin).[370]

There are three categories of signs belonging to the public domain.

a. The Descriptive Signs

340. The descriptive signs, so-called *generic signs*, disclose some information on the nature, the geographic origin, the quality or other characteristics of the products or services, for example:

- 'Elle' for contraceptive devices.[371]
- 'Duo' for games.[372]
- 'Grand Amour'[373] (Great Love) or 'Dominant' for wines.[374]
- 'Alta tensione' (High Tension) for knitted wears.[375]
- 'Basic' for cigarettes.[376]
- 'Sibel' for clothes.[377]

---

370. *See*, however, ATF 60 II 249 ('Bel Paese' is not a descriptive mark for a cheese). In general, see the PhD thesis by A. Schäffler, Das Freihaltebedüfnis, Berne 2020, 231 p.
371. Fed. Trib. SIC 1997, 159.
372. ATF 118 II 182–183.
373. Fed. Trib. *in* RSPI 1991, 91; with all due respect, the decision of the Supreme Court of Switzerland seems more like a practical joke.
374. ATF 96 I 248. *See* Fed. Adm. Trib., B-6430/2008 ('iPhone' is descriptive for cellphones but it has acquired a secondary meaning, so that it is registered); Fed. Trib. SIC 2010, 89 ('Magnum' is descriptive for any product that is sold in bottles); SIC 2010, 91 ('Gotthard' is a geographic denomination that must be kept free for any industry or business to use even in a distant future); SIC 2010, 97 ('Terroir' is a word connoting quality for agricultural products; therefore, it must remain free for every producer to use); Fed. Adm. Trib. B4762/2011 ('FIDUCIA' suggests 'trustworthy'; it is a generic term that cannot be registered as a trademark); Fed. Trib., case 4A_343/2012: 'Ein Stück Schweiz' ('A piece of Switzerland') is descriptive for cheese and must remain free for everyone to use as a slogan); *see* however Fed. Trib. SIC 2010, 162 ('Radio Suisse Romande' is a descriptive trademark to the extent that it incorporates a geographic denomination, but it must not be held for everyone in the public to use it, because the combination of the words 'Radio' and 'Suisse Romande' may make a valid indication of a given business entity; further, secondary meaning is a question of law that the Federal Tribunal may freely pass judgment upon, and not a question of fact); Fed. Trib. SIC 2010, 797 ('Pneus-Online' is descriptive for a business that sells tires) (*see* for the financial consequences of unfair competition through use of a confusingly similar domain name and accounting for profit Fed. Trib. SIC 2013, 360). Secondary meaning must be based on use of the trademark during ten years without interruption; it may be proven by polls, that are not absolutely required in law but tend to be very frequent in present practice. To be valid a poll should mirror the views of at least 1,000 persons, and at least 50% should connect the mark to a given company; *see* Fed. Adm. Trib. SIC 2012, 451 ('Oktoberfest') and decision Keytrader, below fn. 397. *See* further Fed. Adm. Trib. SIC 2016, 61. *See also* Fed. Trib. SIC 2017, 381 (*carnet*). Generally, note that Art. 27a LPM as introduced in 2017 by the Swissness Act amends Art. 2 lit. a LPM.
375. ATF 114 II 371.
376. Fed. Trib. *in* PMM Bl 1982 I 16.
377. Fed. Trib. *in* RSPIDA 1975, 761.

– 'Tender' for tobacco.[378]
– 'Discotable' for furniture.[379]
– 'Top set' for chocolate.[380]
– 'Enterocura' for drugs.[381]
– 'Synchrobelt' for transmissions.[382]
– 'Spandex' for fabrics.[383]

A short term for a technical standard (e.g., X.2 for modems, an International Union of Telecommunications standard) should not be a valid trademark for those products for which the standard is intended.

341. Even if the generic word is misspelt, it is not apt to be a trademark.[384] Nevertheless, it is necessary that the consumers or other interested circles (wholesale dealers, industry, etc.) immediately see the relationship between the sign and the characteristics of the product or services; if some second thoughts are involved, there is no descriptiveness of the sign, which may, therefore, be registered as a trademark.
Examples of valid trademarks are:

– 'Fioretto' for sweets.[385]
– 'OKT' for a drug.[386]
– 'Rotring' for tools.[387]
– 'Jet set' for clothes and sports articles.[388]

378. Fed. Trib. *in* PMM Bl 1974 I 65.
379. ATF 99 Ib 10.
380. ATF 97 I 81. Fed. Trib., SIC 2010, 797 ('Pneus-Online' is descriptive for a business of selling tires online and cannot be a valid trademark; however, in the particular circumstances of the case, it is an act of unfair competition for defendant to take up a quasi-identical denomination that will give rise to confusions among consumers (Arts 2 and 3 (d) UCA)).
381. ATF 96 I 755.
382. ATF 95 I 477.
383. ATF 94 II 44; for some more cases decided by the Fed. Trib. in the last years *see* SIC 2019, 684 ('revelation' for hair shampoo connotes quality, therefore is not registerable; except in borderline cases, the view of foreign courts in the same matter are irrelevant); ATF 139 III 176 = SIC 2013, 440 ('you' cannot be registered as a trademark); SIC 2003, 426 ('Masterpiece' is not registerable); SIC 2009, 275 ('adRank' not registerable for software); SIC 2005, 278 ('Firemaster' not registerable for chemical fire extinguishing compounds); SIC 2003, 32 ('Première' for a TV channel and products of the media is not registerable); SIC 2004, 500 ('BahnCard' not registerable for services relating to the railways). 'Ce'Real' is descriptive for cereals, as the combination of two words in different languages (*c'est* and *real*) is not obvious to the average consumer; Fed. Trib., SIC 2014, 24. In Switzerland the mark 'THE' registered in the US for the State of Ohio would probably not be admitted. For further examples *see* David, No. 13 and 19 *ad* Art. 2 Trademark Act. Due to its worldwide fame 'Apple' has been accepted as a trademark in all categories for which it has been filed, e.g., jewellery; ATF 145 III 178.
384. *See* David, No. 6 *in fine ad* Art. 2 Trademark Act.
385. Fed. Trib. *in* RSPI 1991, 93.
386. ATF 109 II 256.
387. ATF 106 II 245.
388. Fed. Trib. *in* PMM Bl 1977 I 54.

– 'Isola' for insulating tapes, etc.[389]
– 'Brisemarine' for cosmetics.[390]

342. Of course, descriptiveness cannot be a bar to the registration of a product altogether different, such as 'Telephone' for cigars.[391]

343. Finally, the combination of two descriptive words is sometimes registrable because of some distinctive strength derived from the combination, such as Biovital for drugs, etc.[392]

b. The Common Place Marks

344. The commonplace marks also belong to the public domain. For example, the red rectangle on Levi's West jeans is not registerable,[393] nor is a dot or a star on a shoe's sole,[394] or a title like Dr iur., MBL, etc. The present-day practice is somewhat more liberal than the older case law.[395] A combination of a verbal element and circles, etc., may be a valid mark.[396] Further, a commonplace mark may get a secondary meaning through long use and advertisements on a large scale; as such, it will be registered,[397] as might be common words and phrases, to the extent that there is no need for all the merchants and industry to use these words.[398]

---

389. ATF 97 II 153.
390. ATF 93 II 261. Fed. Trib., SIC 2004, 500 ('Discovery Travel and Adventure Channel' valid for telecom services); SIC 2008, 44 ('Zero' valid for clothes); SIC 1999, 29 ('Swissline' valid for financial and insurance services). Fed. Trib. 4A_361/2020 ('SWISS RE – WE MAKE THE WORLD MORE RESILIENT' is a valid trademark). The word Eco can be added to form a valid trademark, e.g., 'ECOSHELL (fig)'; Adm. Fed. Trib., 10 May 2021, B-103/2020.
391. ATF 23, 643. *See also* Fed. Adm. Trib., SIC 2008, 293 (the mark 'New Wave' is not descriptive for clothes, because consumers would think of a musical style and not of a certain clothes style).
392. ATF 99 II 401; *see*, however, ATF 104 Ib 138 (Sano-vital); Appel. Ct Ticino, *in* RSPI 1989, 88 (Chicco d'Oro).
393. Fed. Trib. *in* RSPIDA 1984, 120; a star can be registered (ATF 43 II 677; ATF 47 II 226; ATF 63 II 282).
394. Fed. Trib. *in* RSPIDA 1978, 46; SIC 2011, 236 (Stars for rating hotels).
395. *See* Marbach, *Markenrecht* (Trademark Act), *in* SIWR III, 52 n. 139, for example.
396. Example: International Trademark No. 489381 (TEFAL with circles).
397. ATF 134 III 314; ATF 131 III 121; ATF 129 II 514, 522; ATF 128 III 441, 443–444 (Appenzell); ATF 128 III 447, 450–451. For the conditions of the acquisition of the secondary meaning, *see*, e.g., ATF 140 III 297 ('Keytrader' is descriptive and did not acquire secondary meaning); Fed. Adm. Trib. SIC 2016, 61 ('Luxor' might allude to an Egyptian origin of the goods even for microscopes and eye surgery, but a secondary meaning may result from use during 10 years on the entire Swiss territory).
398. ATF 131 III 121 (smarties); Fed. Trib., SIC 2009, 167 (Post); *see*, however, ATF 140 III 109 (no protection for ePost Select on square yellow ground); SIC 2005, 463 ('bon la vie'); for slogans in general *see* ATF 134 III 223, 232–233; for SWISS RE-WE MAKE THE WORLD MORE RESILIENT see fn 390 above. For a weak trademark embodying the name of a famous writer *see* Cant. Ct VS, SIC 2016, 343 ('Rilke').

c. The Letters and Numbers

345. The case law was rather strict for letters and numbers. Single letters and combinations that could not be uttered as a word were not registerable, according to the Supreme Court, unless a distinctive design of the letters would make them attractive enough.[399] The present practice seems less severe, to the extent that combinations of two letters of any kind are now accepted by the Register:[400] still, in a particular case, a trademark could be challenged before a court when it consists of two numbers or two letters,[401] or a number with a letter (X.2), or a descriptive abbreviation (e.g., V8 or 4WD).

2. Tri-dimensional Technical Shapes

346. It is not possible to register as a trademark a shape which is the 'nature' of the ware (Article 2b Trademark Act). This rather obscure prohibition should entail that the shape of a product cannot be registered when the shape cannot be distinguished from the product. Such would be the case for a new variety of flowers[402] or for the layout of the cover of a book. This does not extend to the packaging of the product; for example, a bottle for detergent allowing to clean remote surfaces has been registered as a trademark,[403] as well as a box for candies.[404]

347. Further, it is not possible to register a shape which fulfils a technical purpose, such as a battery, a diskette or a bottle lid, or even a position mark.

399. *See* ATF 113 II 204 ('RFS Informatic' is not registerable). Rejecting the protection, *see* Fed. Trib. *in* RSPIDA 1975, 68.

400. *See* Swiss Mark No. 406518 ('U2' for phonograms, clothes, etc.) and further examples in Marbach *supra*, 51 n. 134. ATF 130 III 328, 331 (a mark which is potentially distinctive but is not yet distinctive at the time of the filing will not be registered).

401. ATF 48 II 296 (W); ATF 52 II 300 (As). Fed. Trib., SIC 2011, 241 (accepting the validity of a figurative G mark, but rejecting the protection in the case at bar); Fed. Trib., SIC 2011, 102 (no protection for a V mark).

402. *See* David, No. 46 *ad* Art. 2 Trademark Act. For a fantasy trademark in the shape of a cartoon see Fed. Trib. 4A_483/2019, www.bger.ch (concerning int. trademarks N° 1'111'354, 1'111'357 and 1'111'359, 'plush': protection denied for toys etc.).

403. *See* Swiss Mark, No. 404040 (Marbach, *Markenrecht* (Trademark Act), *in* SIWR III, 512). ATF 134 III 547, 555 (possible protection of a special chair 'Chaise Panton'; in the same matter *see* Fed. Adm. Trib., SIC 2011, 312); *see* however ATF 131 III 121; ATF 129 III 514; Appeal Committee, INGRES News December 2006 1 (no protection for a new Coca-Cola bottle); Fed. Adm. Trib., SIC 2008, 51 (no protection as trademark for the head of a guitar); Fed. Trib., SIC 2012, 811 ('*Lego IV*') (rejection of the technical shape filed as a trademark, even if competitors could use a different shape with a very small increase in costs). *See also* the Nespresso II decision of the Fed. Trib., SIC 2012, 627 (no protection under Arts 2 and 3 Act against Unfair Competition for a shape that is technically necessary). The same shape has been finally found not to be registerable as a trademark; Fed. Trib., SIC 2022, 24 (*Nespresso VII*). Critical comment by M. Burnier & A. Schäffler, SIC 2022, 57.

404. Swiss Mark No. 416341 (Marbach, *Markenrecht* (Trademark Act), *in* SIWR III 506). For the case of a position mark as mentioned next line in the above text, *see* Fed. Trib. SIC 2017, 408 ('*Flashlight*') and SIC 2017, 557 ('*Loubutin*').

3. Misleading and Deceptive Marks

348. The consumers and other circles should not be misled by the use of registered trademarks.[405]

The test is not whether a consumer has been misled, but whether the trademark is deceptive as seen in an abstract manner, independently of additional indications such as 'type',[406] 'substitute',[407] etc. The deceptiveness may come from an *innuendo* as to the nature of the product,[408] the business of the trademark holder,[409] or the origin of the products.[410] Even century-old historical links will not placate the courts.[411] Even usual claims as to the effect on the environment may be found as

405. If some other aspects of labelling or advertising is deceptive, other remedies may exist under the Law against Unfair Competition or the Law on Food Products, for example.
406. *See* ATF 60 II 249 (Tipo Bel Paese).
407. *See* ATF 50 II 195 (Vial–Ersatz).
408. ATF 56 I 46 ('Tragiseta' for artificial silk); Fed. Trib. *in* RSPIDA 1969, 66 ('Dorcrin' and 'Portecrin' for brushes without animal hair); ATF 98 Ib 188 ('Sheila Diffusion' is deceptive for wares without any connection with the pop-singer Sheila); ATF 101 Ib 17 ('Bioclinique' if the product is not used in hospitals); Fed. Adm. Trib. SIC 2010, 635 ('Wow', deemed to be like an ad for quality); Cant. Ct Geneva, SIC 2013, 296 ('Skin Caviar' misleading for a ware devoid of any caviar).
409. ATF 98 Ib 188 ('Sheila Diffusion' if no relationship with the pop-singer Sheila); Com. Ct Zurich and Fed. Trib. *in* RSPIDA 1984, 299 ('JPs' for clothes although the producer has no relationship with the tobacconist Imperial Group Ltd); Fed. Trib., SIC 2005, 390 (*Maggi v. Romeo Maggi*; Mr Romeo Maggi was found to be using his own name in good faith).
410. ATF 56 I 469 ('Kremlin' for non-Russian oil); ATF 76 I 168 ('Big Ben' for waterproofs that do not originate in England); ATF 79 I 253 ('Swiss Greetings' for roses from abroad); ATF 93 I 571 ('Trafalgar' for American cigarettes); ATF 97 I 79 ('Cusco' for chocolate); ATF 112 II 263 ('Alpina' for Japanese watches). One of the most bizarre cases was L.I.M.A.: this name of well-known miniature trains made in Italy could not be registered as trademark because the Supreme Court found that someone could believe that it came from Peru … Fed. Trib. *in* RSPIDA 1980, 129. Further *see* ATF 132 III 770 ('Colorado' may not be a valid trademark for products originating outside the US); Fed. Adm. Trib. SIC 2013, 47: 'Austin' is not a valid trademark since it is ambiguous (is it a name or a place of establishment?). *See*, however, ATF 128 III 454 ('Yukon' would not be descriptive for the source of the products); Fed. Trib., SIC 2009, 614 ('Calvi' not acceptable for products originating outside Corsica); ATF 117 II 327 ('Montparnasse' may be registered for products originating in France); Fed. Trib., SIC 2013, 532 (Wilson, a city of North Carolina, may be a valid trademark); Fed. Adm. Trib. SIC 2009, 530 ('Albino' not being known in Switzerland as a location, it can be a valid trademark); for 'Swiss Military' under the new Swissness regulations entered into force on 1 Jan. 2017 *see* Fed. Adm. Trib. SIC 2018, 313. A gallup may be accepted to show that the name of a location is not misleading: Fed. Adm. Trib. SIC 2013, 163 ('Savannah'). *See* recently Fed. Trib., SIC 2021, 81 ('Vals', a place of which the green stones are well-known, can be registered or used for ceramic tiles that obviously are not in stone). Compare with ATF 117 II 321('Valser').
411. ATF 95 I 473 ('Slivowitz Herzegovina' for Austrian brandy); decision of the Fed. Adm. Trib. SIC 2011, 245: 'Brora' is a little known township of Scotland that is nevertheless a Protected Geographic Denomination for whiskies, and cannot be registered as a trademark; Cant. Trib. Vaud, SIC 2008, 213 ('Torino' is not a valid trademark for chocolates originating in Switzerland); but *see* Fed. Adm. Trib. SIC 2008, 108 ('Bellagio' may be registered as trademark, because the Swiss consumers would think more of the Las Vegas Hotel than of the charming township in Italy …) ; Appeal Committee, SIC 2004, 772 ('Volterra' is a town of Tuscany but may be a valid trademark for electrical power utilities).

spurious, therefore invalidating the trademark.[412] However, the long use of the trademark may give it a secondary meaning that prevents delusion of the public.[413]

4. Signs Against Public Policy, *Bonos Mores* or the Law

a. Signs Against Public Policy

349. Here, 'public policy' is not the *Ordre public* in international matters as defined in Article 17 of the Federal Law on International Private Law of 1987. It is the *Ordre public* for internal matters as referenced in Article 19(2) Code of Obligations; that is, the entire body of imperative law.[414]

350. It is difficult to distinguish between 'public policy' and *bonos mores*.[415] The following trademarks, *inter alia*, have been found to be against public policy:

- 'Buddha', Siddharta, Jesus Christ Super Star and Mahomet.[416]
- 'Deus' for things of whatever kind.[417]
- 'Golgotha' for wine.[418]
- 'Islam' for things of whatever kind.[419]
- 'Prince of Wales' for German brandy.[420]

412. Federal Office of Intellectual Property *in* PMM Bl 1972 I 54 ('Protector' rejected for washing products).
413. *See* Art. 2(a) Trademark Act.
414. According to our definition; according to some other authors, only the core of the imperative law would be *ordre public*: Engel, *Traité du droit des obligations* (Treaty on the Law of Contracts) 113 (2d ed., Zurich, 1997). *See*, e.g., ATF 102 Ia 574. For a minority of authors, only public law (as opposed to law regulating private matters) would be *ordre public* regulations under Art. 19 Code of Obligations. *See* Gauch & Schluep, *Schweizerisches Obligationenrecht, Allgemeiner Teil* (Swiss Law of Contracts, General Part) No. 648 (6th ed., Zurich, 1995). *See*, e.g., Appeal Committee, SIC 1999, 36 ('Canal': a sign that is contrary to the Law of the Protection of Public Coats of Arms of 1931 (RS 232.21) (as revised due to the *Swissness* Bill, entered into force effective 1 Jan. 2017) would be contrary to the 'ordre public').
415. *See* hereinafter para. 351.
416. Federal Office of Intellectual Property, *in Markenartikel* (Branded Articles) 1974, 199 (Buddha); Appeal Committee SIC 2001, 31 (Siddharta) citing Mahomet and Jesus Christ Super Star as other examples.
417. Federal Office of Intellectual Property, *in* RSPIDA 1951, 157.
418. Federal Office of Intellectual Property, *in Markenartikel* (Branded Articles), 1974, 199.
419. Federal Office of Intellectual Property, *in* RSPIDA 1951, 157. *See also* Fed. Trib., SIC 1997, 493 ('Anne Frank' cannot be registered as trademark; the legal basis involved is Art. 29 CC on the protection of personality, which is strange since the bearer of this name is no longer alive, and personal interests such as the name usually enjoy a legal protection that is limited to their lifetime; it would have been better to state that a trademark 'Anne Frank' is *contra bonos mores*).
420. Federal Institute of Intellectual Property *in* RSPI 1996, 487.

b. Marks Against the Bonos Mores

351. All and any sign that may hurt the feelings of the population or part thereof, or is disrespectful of the commonwealth, or of an international or humanitarian organization will not be registered.
Examples include:

– 'Marijuana' for clothes.[421]
– 'Kidnapper' for liquors.[422]
– 'Week-end sex' for a publication.[423]
– 'S.O.S.' for watches.[424]
– 'Guermundialis' for toys.[425]
– 'Madonna' for fabrics, clothes, accessories.[426]

c. Signs that Are Illegal

352. The law, of which violation can make the trademark illegal, can be an international treaty or a federal or cantonal[427] law.

Laws concerning the commerce of gold and other precious metals,[428] or the commerce of food products may be relevant for trademarks.

II. Different Categories of Trademarks

A. Trademarks for Industry and for Commerce

353. The old Law of 1890 drew in its title a distinction between trademarks for producers and trademarks for tradesmen. Most trademarks are owned by producers, but some modern department stores and most franchise networks thrive on trademarks of their own. Under present Swiss law, the distinction is of no importance.

---

421. Fed. Trib. *in* PMM Bl 1984 I 57.
422. Federal Office of Intellectual Property, as cited *in* RSPIDA 1944, 82.
423. Fed. Trib. *in* RSPIDA 1973, 44.
424. ATF 70 I 101.
425. Federal Office of Intellectual Property, *in* RSPIDA 1944, 82.
426. ATF 136 III 474. In the case of jewellery, use of some symbols is acceptable, such as the cross, the David star, the new moon; *see* Fed. Adm. Trib. SIC 2016, 521 (also for a design; which however shall not be *contra bonos mores*). Recently, the Fed. Administrative Trib. has accepted the validity of a combined figurative and verbal mark encompassing a cross on the head of a stag; decision of 5 Feb. 2020 ('Jägermeister'), B-1440/2019.
427. *See* Message by the Federal Council, FF 1991 I 20 *contra*: David, No. 78 *ad* Art. 2 Trademark Act (cantonal law should be disregarded because the Trademark Act is federal; this opinion does not take into account that Art. 2(d) Trademark Act is referencing to laws other than the Trademark Act).
428. *See*, e.g., ATF 80 I 381 ('Goldhelm', 'Goldfront' for metal items).

B. Service Trademarks

354. The Trademark Act of 1992 now protects the trademarks owned by service companies, such as banks, publishers, telecom operators, etc. Before 1993, the protection was given to service providers only under the aegis of the Act against Unfair Competition.

C. Well-Known Trademarks and Famous Trademarks

1. Well-Known Trademarks

355. Switzerland being party to the Paris Convention for the Protection of Industrial Property, and to the TRIPS Agreement, is bound to recognize the well-known marks as mentioned in Article 6*bis* Paris Convention and in Article 16(2) TRIPS. The dominant opinion appears nowadays to be that transborder advertising in print or on TV should be sufficient to make a mark well-known in Switzerland. If a trademark is well-known, it cannot be registered by a third party in Switzerland; the well-known trademark so enjoys priority without use within Switzerland (Article 3(2)(b) Trademark Act). However, if it is not registered in Switzerland, its protection against piracy shall derive from Unfair Competition Law[429] or the rules on the protection of economic personal interests (Article 28 Civil Code), or possibly those on the protection of the name (Article 29 Civil Code). According to some authors,[430] well-known trademarks are not subject to the requirement of use within five years under Articles 11 and 12 Trademark Act, which is logical to the extent that unregistered well-known foreign marks are not positively protected under the Trademark Act, with the possible exception of the action for transfer under Article 53 Trademark Act.[431] Nevertheless, once the well-known trademark is indeed registered in Switzerland, it is subject to the requirement of use within Switzerland (or Germany if the 1892 bilateral treaty is applicable).[432]

2. Famous Trademarks

356. For one century, the protection of famous trademarks derived from the Civil Code, then from the Act Against Unfair Competition. Since the enactment of the 1992 Trademark Act, a specific provision, Article 15, protects famous

429. *See* ATF 130 III 267 on the notion of a well-known trademark ('Tripp Trapp' trademark: over 50% of the interested consumers should know the trademark in order for the court to find it well-known); *see* further Fed. Adm. Trib., B-151/2018 ('BVLGARI' has acquired secondary meaning); Fed. Trib., SIC 2001, 317 ('Central Park'); Appeal Committee, SIC 2006, 177 ('Médecins sans frontières'); SIC 1999, 651 ('Galeries Lafayette').

430. Marbach, *Markenrecht* (Trademark Act), *in* SIWR III, 175 and n. 59.

431. K. Troller, 492. *See also* I. Cherpillod, *Le droit suisse des marques* (Swiss Trademark Law) 127–129.

432. *See* para. 332 *supra*.

trademarks.[433] Article 15 Trademark Act protects them against dilution through their use by a third party for other wares and goods or services than the ones for which their owner uses them.

It is against the risk of dilution that the Law has been made, and it is not supposed to help the famous trademark owners dispense with the other requirements of the Law. For example, a trademark which is in the public domain shall not be protected in areas other than those in which it is actually used[434] by virtue of its secondary meaning. Further, the famous trademark which is used for the title of a publication shall not necessarily be valid for the merchandising of other wares if there is a priority of rights by a third party for those wares and goods.[435]

However, the former case law is no longer valid to the extent that it required the trademark to be the symbol of the producers.[436] Further, even a modification of the famous trademark would not prevent the success of an action for infringement, as long as the consumers believe that the modified trademark belongs to the owner of the original one.[437]

D. Trademarks and Trade Names

357. The protection of 'house marks' and 'trade names' varies according to the registration procedures that have been elected by the owner. If a mark has been registered as a trademark, then the Trademark Act shall apply. Under the 1992 Law, no remedy of the Trademark Act may be available without prior registration as a trademark.[438]

However, if a trade name has been registered with the Office of Commerce under Articles 944 et seq. Code of Obligations and Articles 36 et seq. Ordinance of the

---

433. ATF 124 III 277 (Nike); Fed. Trib. SIC 1999, 132 ('Nike', unabridged text of the same case); ATF 130 III 267, 278 ('Tripp Trapp'); ATF 130 III 748 (Nestlé) (at 753 this judgment mistakenly mentions an 'exception to the principle of *subsidiarity*'; it should read 'principle of *speciality*'). The speciality doctrine prevents a trademark to be protected as against a domain name referencing a webpage that does not evidence any connection with the products for which the trademark is used, as has been judged by Sup. Ct Aargau, SIC 2014, 632; that case is not in line with the URDP decisions in such matter. For a summary of the Fed. Trib. cases on famous trademarks in the last 25 years *see* B. Lüthi SIC 2018, 217–218. *Add* ATF 145 III 178 (Apple).
434. *See* Fed. Trib. *in* SIC 1997, 159 (Elle).
435. *See* Com. Ct Berne, *in* SIC 1997, 164 (Play Boy); Fed. Trib. SIC 2018, 558 (Panda): there is a confusion between Panda and Pandaki, as well as between the figurative trademarks at stake; however, the claim to prevent use 'on all goods and wares' is not admissible (decision taken on a request for interim measures). Otherwise a famous trademark may be protected even if only 25% of the consumers are making a connection between the magazine and the third party's wares and goods, according to Fed. Trib. SIC 2013, 41 (Vogue); for Vogue *see* further Sup. Ct App. AR SIC 2018, 57: Vogue will be protected only as against competitors using it for print matters. *See also* below fn 463.
436. *See* Civ. Ct Jura, *in* RSPI 1993, 113, esp. 125–126 (501).
437. Com. Ct Berne, *in* RSPIDA 1981, 67 (Coca-Line); *see* for other Coca-Cola cases ATF 112 II 73 and ATF 116 II 463.
438. Under the 1890 Trademark Act, protection was afforded to trade names as trademarks whenever they were registered with the Office of Commerce. Further, use of a trademark was determinative for the priority of rights, and not registration. For the protection of trade names generally, *see* hereinafter paras 527 et seq.

Register of the Office of Commerce[439] (as amended), then the protection shall be granted on the basis of Article 956 Code of Obligations against similar trade names, when used as trade names. Further, protection may be had under the Law of Unfair Competition and under Articles 28 and 29 Civil Code. Although there appears to be a bewildering array of legal rules outside the Trademark Act, it is still simpler and by far more certain to register a trade name as a trademark whenever possible.

E. Certification and Collective Trademarks

1. Certification Trademark

358. The certification trademark is a mark which several enterprises may use in order to indicate the quality, the geographical origin, the method of production or some other common characteristics of their products or services (Article 21(1) Trademark Act).

The central control by the trademark owner is an important feature of that system. The owner is often an association of producers (e.g., a wine growers' syndicate).

The Law provides that the owner may not use the trademark for his own products or activities, so as to avoid conflicts of interests. Further, the owner may not prohibit the use of the certification mark by any entity which complies with the ad hoc regulations.

These regulations have to be filed with the Trademark Register (Article 23 Trademark Act). If they are violated, the violation would give rise to an action for liability in tort against the violator.[440]

Examples of certification trademarks include the signs ASE (Association of Swiss Electricians), VITI (Vini Ticinesi, Tessin wines); the crossbow for Swiss-manufactured products, etc.[441]

2. Collective Trademarks

359. According to Article 22 Trademark Act, the collective trademark is the trademark which is used by a number of companies that are members of a given

439. RS 221.411, hereinafter 'ORC' (as amended from time to time, last on 17 Nov. 2021). Under Art. 177 ORC however, all simple trade names should have been stricken out of the Register of Commerce within two years from 1 Jan. 2008. For the legal protection of trade names *see*, e.g., Fed. Trib., SIC 2012, 564 (Mediconsult) (a trade name that is registered will be protected even when it consists of generic terms; the posterior trade name must contain distinctive elements).

440. *See* ATF 131 III 495 (certification marks and individual marks being contrasted): ATF 52 I 192, esp. 201 (for a certification mark in use before the Law knew of that category). Now an action lies under Art. 55(3) Trademark Act, but Art. 55(2) Trademark Act declares the provisions of the Code of Obligations to be applicable to the actions in damages, so that this precedent is still valid.

441. *See* F. Dessemontet, *Protection of Geographic Denomination under Swiss Law*, in *Protection of Geographic Denominations of Goods and Services* 97 et seq., esp. 120 (Cohen Jehoram ed., Alphen aan den Rijn, 1980).

association or group. These various members are not supposed to be a conglomerate belonging to the same shareholders, but they could be; for example, the Federation of Migros Cooperatives (active in retail sales) could try and set up a number of collective trademarks.

Since 1992, the Trademark Act does no longer know of the particular 'holding company trademark', nor of the mark for a given group of companies which was provided under Article 6*bis* of the former 1890 Trademark Act as enacted in 1939.[442] Hence, a group of producers or merchants that are a sole economic entity could now conceivably deposit a collective trademark. Nevertheless, it could render itself liable to proceedings following the request of a third party to use its trademark if they comply with the regulations, which are also required in that case. The question does not arise in practice. This writer only knows of rejections of applications for collective trademarks because the required regulations as to the manufacturing of the brand products and the use of the mark were altogether missing.

F. The Protection of Public Coats of Arms and Other Emblems

360. The Law on the Protection of Public Coats of Arms and other Emblems of 5 June 1931[443] afforded a differentiating treatment to emblems of sovereignty. It did not deal with private coats of arms, or emblems of a family or of a trade association, for example. For the public arms, it is provided in the new Law of 2013 that the Swiss and cantonal coats of arms and flags cannot be registered as a trademark, nor affixed for commercial ends on products that are put into circulation. Nonetheless, the coats of arms or flags can be put on billboards, advertisements, prospectuses or commercial papers, on delivery trucks and in any other way, provided,

442. *See* F. Dessemontet, *La marque holding et les marques de groupe* (Holding and Corporate Holding Trademark), in *Marke und Marketing* (Trademark and Marketing) 121 et seq. (Berne, 1990).

443. This law used to be referenced under RS 232.2. The bill for revising this Law was adopted by Parliament on 21 Jun. 2013; the new Law on the Protection of Coats of Arms of 21 Jun. 2013 entered into force effective 1 Jan. 2017 (*see* RS 232.21 and Ordinance of 2 Sep. 2015 on the Protection of the Coat of Arms, RS 232.211). It dissociates the protection of Swiss coats of arms (the use of which will still be reserved to the Swiss Confederation) and the use of the Swiss flag, that will (new) be admissible for all Swiss users if their products meet some detailed specifications about Swiss origins (60% of value added in Switzerland). If production of an item is mainly happening in a foreign country, it cannot keep the denomination 'Swiss made' even if it had been enjoying it for decades (e.g., chocolate 'Toblerone', starting 2022). For the uses of cantonal coats of arms and Swiss coat of arms which are still prohibited under the new law *see* SIC 2017, 696 (decision by the advertisement industry self-regulating Committee for Loyal Advertising). *See* further below para. 475. Art. 8 of the 2013 Law enumerates exceptions to the rule that only the relevant public entities may use the flags and coats of arms; among the exceptions there is the use as part of a certification trademark (Art. 8 (4)(f)). Signs other than coats of arms or flags such as the sketch of a well-known mountain, castle, or bridge can be used if this is not deceptive (Art. 11). Signs that are deemed to refer to a geographic origin of products or services follow the regime of geographic denominations under Art. 47 through 50 Trademark Act. Therefore, some signs are not registerable as marks (Art. 14). A similar protection extends to foreign coats of arms and flags. Criminal sanctions are provided in Art. 28 through 31.

however, that such use be not deceptive or misleading as to the geographic origin or the value of the products, the nationality of the business or its supposed links to the Confederation or a cantonal State.

361. Similar rules protect the coats of arms of Cantons, districts and cities.

362. Collective trademarks can embody Swiss or cantonal coats of arms. Swiss public entities can register their own coats of arms as trademarks, as can publicly owned corporations.

363. Further, official quality stamps and marks may not be affixed without authority under the relevant regulations; for example, under the Federal Law of 20 June 1933 on the control of the Trade with Precious Metals.[444]

364. Other emblems are free for use, with the exceptions of the emblems of the Red Cross, the United Nations Organization (UNO) and other intergovernmental organizations and the International Olympic Committee.[445]

365. Foreign coats of arms and hallmarks enjoy similar protection on the basis of reciprocity. Even in the absence of reciprocity, it is prohibited to use such foreign coats of arms or hallmarks, when it is an indirect indication of origin, if such use would not conform to Articles 47 et seq. Trademark Act.[446] If there is an identity or similarity between the Swiss and the foreign coats of arms, both may be used in a concurring manner when the foreign one was prior in use. In other words, the use of the Swiss regional or local arms is free within the Law, in spite of a possible confusion which could occur with a foreign coat of arms that was utilized before.

366. The Law of 1931 provided for penalties; that was, a fine of up to CHF 5,000 (double upon relapse) or imprisonment not exceeding two months. The fines and time of imprisonment have been adapted in 2013 and aligned with those provided by the other Intellectual Property Acts in the new Law of 21 June 2013.

---

444. RS 941.31.

445. *See*, e.g., ATF 135 III 648 ('UNOx': the embodiment of the letters 'UNO' in a Swiss trademark is not admissible). Switzerland signed but has not ratified the Nairobi Treaty on the Protection of the Olympic Symbol adopted on 26 Sep. 1981. However, the Olympic Emblem is protected by virtue of the Agreement between the Swiss Federal Council and the International Olympic Committee of 1 Nov. 2000 (RS 0.192.122.415.19 Art. 6). *See*, e.g., the Law concerning the Protection of the Red Cross Emblem and Name of 23 March 1954 as amended 2008 (RS 232.22), strictly applied, e.g., by Fed. Trib., ATF 140 III 251; ATF 134 III 406 (this Law does not prohibit the registration of a trademark consisting of typographic characters that are not red and form a cross).

446. *See* paras 484 et seq. For the case of the use of a coat of arms similar to the Montenegro coat of arms *see* Fed. Trib., SIC 2008, 52 (no confusion because of different colours).

§3. CONDITIONS OF PROTECTION

367. The legal protection requires compliance with given formalities[447] and for the claimant to be the original owner or assignor of the trademark.[448] The claimant shall be victorious if his exclusive rights have been infringed upon by the defendant.[449]

§4. FORMALITIES

I. Registration

A. Application

368. Since 1 April 1993, any physical person or legal entity can file an application for registration of a trademark. This is a great departure from the precedent regime, under which only producers or merchants could own a trademark.

No reciprocity is required for foreign nationals or countries that do not belong to multilateral conventions, contrary to the European solution.[450]

369. It is not necessary to show the present use of the trademark. Therefore, an application may be filed even in order to provide for leeway in the future activities of the owner, and it is difficult to exclude sheer 'defensive signs', that is, signs that protect the trademark as it is really used but that are not used themselves.[451]

370. The application is filed with the Swiss Institute of Intellectual Property in Berne, in one of the official Swiss languages[452] (Article 3 Ordinance). For priority

447. *See* paras 382 et seq.
448. *See* paras 411 et seq.
449. *See* paras 423 et seq. and paras 451 et seq.
450. *See* Message of the Federal Council, FF 1991 I 30.
451. *See* ATF 136 III 102 (invalidity of a trademark for lack of use and fraudulent filing?); of course the use of trademark without one of its important constitutive elements is not sufficient to maintain the validity of the rights of the owner; *see* Fed. Trib. SIC 2014, 81; ATF 127 III 160, 164; Fed. Trib., SIC 2008, 732 (Gmail) (defensive trademarks are null and void and a court can state it before the expiry of the grace period of five years for using the trademark); SIC 2004, 325; *see also* Fed. Adm. Trib. SIC 2016, 149 (serious use for triathlon); Sup. Ct Thurgau, SIC 2005, 194; I. Cherpillod, 'Marques défensives, de réserve et dépôts frauduleux' *(Defensive and Fraudulent Trademarks),* SIC 2000, 359; F. Dessemontet, 'Droit à la marque' *(Right to the Trademark)* in *La nouvelle Loi fédérale sur la protection des marques* (The New Federal Act on the Protection of Trademarks) 52 (Lausanne, 1994); Marbach, *Markenrecht* (Trademark Act), *in* SIWR III, 145 and fn. 62.
452. For the distinction between the four national languages and the three official languages, *see* Art. 70 Federal Constitution and (under a former text of that provision) F. Dessemontet, *Le droit des langues en Suisse* (Language's Law in Switzerland) 19 et seq. (Québec, 1984). The three official languages German, French and Italian are to be used between the Confederation and the Cantons, while Romanche is to be used by the Confederation with the people speaking Romanche; to this extent and only since 1996 Romanche is an 'official' language but of limited application, as there are approximately 35,000 people speaking Romanche as their main language as of 2021. On the level of Cantonal law in the Canton of Graubünden romanche is a full official language.

claims, documents in English are admitted. Should a document be filed in a language different from the Swiss official language a time period will be granted for supplying a translation.

371. The application consists of a form with the name of the applicant and his or her address, a listing of annexed documents and a signature, plus, if relevant, the name and address of his or her professional representative, and the claim for international priority or for priority deriving from the exhibition at a fair or exposition. The trademark shall be filed in ten copies (black and white) or five copies (for colour trademarks). The list of products or services for which protection is claimed follows the Nice Agreement.

372. Until 1 July 2011, a representative established in Switzerland had to be appointed by any applicant who has neither domicile nor seat (i.e., registered offices) within Switzerland.[453] Under Article 42 Trademark Act as amended in 2018, an address for serving notification of any procedural act must be registered within Switzerland unless direct notification is possible, for ex under the Convention N° 94 of the Council of Europe.

373. The basic registration fee is CHF 550, CHF 100 more per additional class – CHF 400 for expedited examination.

374. The application takes the date of the day it was submitted to the Institute or to a Post Office (or presumably a courier) or sent by electronic mail (under Article 7a OPM). This date shall be determinative for the national priority and for the duration of the trademarks if registered with no essential modification (Articles 10(1) and 29 Trademark Act).

375. In the not-too-distant future, the Swiss Confederation will impose the use of electronic mail for all administrative procedures and most judicial procedures, under a project which is being prepared and is currently under review by Bar Associations and other stakeholders.

B. Examination

376. The Federal Institute for Intellectual Property ascertains that no grounds for rejection of the application are present. A particular care is devoted to the list of services and products that are to benefit from the protection, and even inside a class of goods or services, some specifications can be admitted while others will not be. No

453. The new Federal Code of Civil Procedure has abrogated the obligation to appoint a representative in Switzerland for *judicial proceedings* with a party who is not domiciled in Switzerland or does not have its seat here. *See* FF 2009, 123.

specific examination addresses the intricate questions of trademarks encompassing a family name (by the opposition with the restrictive practice prevailing under the 1890 Law).[454]

II. Opposition

A. Formal Requirements

377. The opposition is open to owners of prior registered trademarks within three months from the date of publication of the registration in the Federal Official Swiss Journal of Commerce.[455] The opposition must be in writing, in two copies, with usual details as to the opponent and the trademarks that are involved, as well as a short explanation as to the ground(s) of the opposition.

378. The administrative procedure follows the general principles of administrative law; that is, it is inquisitorial rather than adversarial.[456]

379. The costs of the other party are to be borne by the losing party but in exceptional circumstances.[457]

B. Substantive Requirements

380. The prior trademark belonging to the opposing party must be in current use, or the lack of use must be justified (Article 12 Trademark Act); for example, by the illness of the owner, the expropriation of the enterprise, a war, lengthy proceedings for authorization to put pharmaceutical or chemical products onto the market, a state ban on exports, etc.

---

454. *See* for present-day practice Marbach, *Markenrecht* (Trademark Act), *in* SIWR III, 84 and n. 310; for the former restrictive practice, e.g., Fed. Trib. *in* RSPI 1988, 160 ('Mr Dupont'); for further cases, *see* Fed. Trib. *in* RSPIDA 1976, 77 ('Metz'); Fed. Trib. *in* RSPIDA 1979, 255 ('René d'Aristide'); Just. Ct Geneva *in* RSPIDA 1980, 36 (use of first name); Com. Ct Zurich *in* RSPIDA 1982, 152 (use of first name); Fed. Trib. SIC 2004, 316 ('Montessori'); Fed. Adm. Trib., B-151/2018 ('BVLGARI').
455. In case of the opposition addressing an international registration with claim for Switzerland, the three-month period starts from the first day of the month following the online official publication by WIPO (Art. 50 (1) Ordinance as amended effective date 1 Dec. 2021).
456. Marbach, *Markenrecht* (Trademark Act), *in* SIWR III, 153. A gallup poll may be adduced as evidence that a trademark is known among interested circles in Switzerland whenever secondary meaning is alleged. *See* ATF 131 III 121 ('Smarties': the poll should take place in all linguistic areas of Switzerland); ATF 128 III 441 ('Appenzeller').
457. *See* Recourse Commission of the Intellectual Property Institute *in* SIC 1998, 583. According to ATF 133 III 490 the value in litigation for a dispute on the validity of a trademark without an action in damages amounts to at least CHF 50,000 and sometimes CHF 100,000, which lower limit opens the way for an appeal to the Federal Tribunal concerning the judgments on the validity of the trademark.

381. There is a valid use even if the prior mark as used is slightly modified in comparison with its registered form; for example, through the adoption of a different type for one letter, or the renouncement to a given ancillary graphic element.[458]

382. Where there is prima facie proof for the use of the prior trademark on only a limited part of the list of wares and goods or services that were claimed, there may be a partial rejection of the opposition (for all other goods or services). The opposition procedure is an administrative one, in which the facts may be established ex officio.[459]

383. As a further requirement for the sustaining of the opposition, the newer trademark has to fall under the grounds for excluding the protection of the trademark coming second in time under Article 3 Trademark Act. This risk of confusion is also the main fact that must be established in any action for infringement of a valid trademark, even outside an opposition proceeding as we now turn to see, dealing with the protection of trademarks generally once they are validly registered.

C. Danger of Confusion

384. Article 3 Trademark Act follows the general pattern of the EU Trademark Act.

385. Article 3(a) Trademark Act excludes per se from the registration the marks that are *identical* to a prior trademark, and that are claimed for *identical* products or services.

386. Litt. b excludes the registration of trademarks that are identical to a prior trademark, and that are claimed for *similar* products or services, inasmuch as there exists a danger of confusion.[460]

387. Finally, litt. c excludes the registration of trademarks that are *similar* to a prior trademark and that are claimed for *similar* products or services, inasmuch as there is a danger of confusion.

458. Fed. Trib., SIC 2009, 763 (if the trademark consists of a simple geometrical sign that in practice is supplemented with figurative elements, the use is not sufficient for the opponent to win the contest with the new trademark). On a different point: if the former trademark has not been demonstrably used in Switzerland, or under the fictive use as admissible under the 1892 Treaty with Germany (*see* above No. 334), the owner of the more recent trademark may have preferable rights; Fed. Trib., SIC 2018, 729 (appeal against a *pendente lite* decision).

459. Sup. Ct Lucerne, SIC 2009, 351, Com. Ct Berne, SIC 2009, 717, 719–720. Finally, the Fed. Adm. Trib. changed its practice in June 2019 (case 'Gerflor', B-6675/2016) in order to allow for the objection to the opposition based on non-use of the opposing trademark to be filed even before the end of the time limit for starting use. See comments in SIC 2020, 3 et seq.

460. *See*, e.g., ATF 123 III 189 (Tattoo).

388. Prior trademarks are both the registered trademarks (or the trademarks for which a valid application for registration has already been filed at the time of the filing of the application for the newer mark) and the well-known trademarks as protected under Article 6*bis* of the Paris Convention. Famous trademarks are mainly protected under Article 15 Trademark Act, and the court rather than the Swiss Institute for Intellectual Property are called upon to enforce the rights of their owners.[461]

389. Only the owner of the prior trademark can object to the registration of the newer trademark or to its protection vis-à-vis his own mark (Article 3(3) Trademark Act). Switzerland no longer follows the system of the so-called absolute invalidity, which was imposed by our courts under the 1890 Act. According to that system, where A was the owner of a prior trademark having better rights than B on that sign, C, who was sued for infringement of B's trademark, could argue that B's trademark was absolutely null and void because of A's priority, although A was not a party to the proceedings.[462]

390. The risk of confusion is given either when the consumers take one trademark for the other one, or when there is in their mind a connotation between the two marks.[463]

391. Case law (examples):

(1) Similar Trademarks with Risk of Confusion:
   - Honneur/Bonheur.[464]
   - Valvoline/Havoline.[465]

---

461. *See* David, No. 7 *ad* Art. 3 Trademark Act; in practice, opposition procedures are known to exist for marks that are alleged to be famous.

462. For the present 'relative invalidity doctrine', *see* Appeal Committee, SIC 2004, 930; Fed. Adm. Trib., SIC 2022, 114 (The grounds for absolute nullity of the registration of a trademark can be invoked by way of administrative proceedings as well as through a civil action in the courts). *See* however a somewhat different view herebelow fn 497. For the former 'doctrine of absolute invalidity' *see* ATF 92 II 112; ATF 102 II 114. *See* A. Troller, 735 and fn. 46 for citations of commentators already opposed to the absolute invalidity.

463. *See*, e.g., Com. Ct Zurich, SIC 1999, 581 ('Rivella/Apiella'). The gallup must be put in fair terms, otherwise the inquiry may constitute an act contrary to the Law against Unfair Competition of 1986 (Art. 2, General Clause against any practice contrary to good faith in business); *see* Fed. Trib., SIC 2013, 41 ('Vogue'). The questions in the gallup should be categorized by market as defined by the similarities between the goods and wares; *see* Fed. Adm. Trib. SIC 2016, 401 ('Visudyne/Vivadine'). Only one judgment seems ever to have considered that the risk of confusion plays a role in the case of identical trademarks for identical products: Fed. Adm. Trib. SIC 2018, 313 ('Swiss Military').

464. ATF 36 II 428.

465. ATF 55 II 155; ATF 122 III 382 ('Kamillosan/Kamillan') (in general, trademarks that are used for products of daily use must be more easily distinguishable). The trademarks are either strongly distinctive, weakly distinctive or of an average distinctiveness (Fed. Trib, SIC 2008, 44). *See* also Fed. Trib. SIC 2012, 106 (A weakly distinctive trademark will enjoy less protection than an average or a strongly distinctive one, thus there is no protection of *Appenzeller v. Appenberger*). The protection of a trademark is more extensive when it enjoys strong distinctiveness. Where the common elements belong to the public domain, there is less likelihood of confusion (Fed. Adm. Trib., SIC 2008, 533 ('Webstamp'); Fed. Trib. SIC 2016, 101 ('Think' vs 'Think outdoors'). If the conflicting

– Mido/Smidor.[466]
– Scandale/Sandal.[467]
– Pollux/Colux.[468]
– Bolex/Folex.[469]

(2) No Risk of Confusion, although there is some similarity:
– Nephrisan/Neotrisan.[470]
– Xylocain/Celecain.[471]
– Sihl/Cosil[472] – Pond's/Respond.[473]
– Puschkin/Mustrin.[474]
– Lego/Logi.[475]

(3) Where only generic or descriptive elements of the marks are identical, there is no risk of confusion:
– Clix/Clip.[476]
– Sollux/Solis.[477]
– Brasilva/Brasilia.[478]
– Seccolino/Escolino.[479]
– PS Prosoft/Profisoft.[480]
– Swatch/Othmar's Watch.[481]

(3) Similar Products:
– Papers/Photo paper.[482]
– Wool/Cotton.[483]

---

trademarks give a same or very similar phonetic impression the semantic difference must be strong to differentiate them; Fed. Adm. Trib. 2016, 401 ('Visudine'). If a younger purely verbal trademark is written with different typographic shapes this plays no role in the appreciation of the risk of confusion; Com. Ct. Berne, SIC 2021, 70 at 74 ('NITRO'). Some decisions sound bizarre; for example, according to Fed. Adm. Trib. SIC 2017, 135, *Havana Club* would not be very well-known, or its notoriety would be irrelevant in the opposition proceedings; whereby that is one of the oldest and best known liquor marks and has been at the centre of a lengthy WTO Dispute Resolution Proceedings between the US and the EU in case DS 176.

466. ATF 73 II 63.
467. ATF 79 II 175.
468. ATF 91 II 15.
469. Com. Ct Zurich *in* ZR 1981, 160; *see* further (ATF 127 III 160 ('Securitas/Securicall'); Fed. Trib, SIC 2008, 44 ('Zero/Zerorh +'); Appeal Committee, SIC 2006, 412 ('Minergie/Sinnergie'); Fed. Adm. Trib. SIC 2017, 410 ('The Body Shop'); Sup. Ct ZG, SIC 2018, 558 ('Panda').
470. Com. Ct Zurich *in* ZR 1951, 121.
471. ATF 84 II 441.
472. ATF 92 II 270.
473. ATF 97 II 78.
474. Cant. Ct Freiburg *in* RSPIDA 1975, 78.
475. Fed. Trib. *in* RSPI 1985, 67. *See* further Fed. Trib., SIC 2000, 194 ('Campus/Liberty Campus').
476. ATF 80 II 171. *See*, however, *Metro v. Metropol* (confusion admitted) (Fed. Adm. Trib. SIC 2014, 365).
477. ATF 79 II 98.
478. Com. Ct Aargau *in* RSJ 1973, 25.
479. ATF 112 II 362.
480. Com. Ct Zurich and Fed. Trib. *in* ZR 1992–1993, 136.
481. Civ. Ct Basle-Countryside *in* BJM 1988, 155.
482. ATF 33 II 451.
483. ATF 38 II 705.

- Domestic detergents/Car detergents.[484]
- Sparkling/Aperitifs.[485]
- Men clothes/Raincoats.[486]
- Cognac/Pastis.[487]
- Banana/Orange.[488]

(4) Products that are not similar:
- Coffee/Cough drop.[489]
- Watches/Sewing machine.[490]
- Spirits/dietetic drinks.[491]
- Food/Books.[492]
- Domestic supply/Shaver.[493]

III. International Registration

392. Following the Madrid Arrangement, seventy-eight countries are parties to the Madrid Protocol Concerning the International Registration of Marks of 14 April 1891,[494] and Switzerland is one of them.

393. The Swiss Institute for Intellectual Property may receive an application for an international trademark registration originating in Switzerland. The Institute shall ascertain that the trademark is really registered in Switzerland by the same person and for the same products or services; further, that the applicant is established within Switzerland; further that the application forms are correctly filled with their appendixes; finally, that the fees are paid.

484. Com. Ct Zurich *in* ZR 1930, 7.
485. ATF 56 II 402.
486. Com. Ct St-Gall *in* RSJ 1958, 206.
487. Just. Ct Geneva *in* RSPIDA 1975, 80.
488. Com. Ct Berne *in* RSPIDA 1983 II 47. *See* further Appeal Committee, SIC 2006, 88 ('Corsa') (cars, motorbikes, as well as cars and tires are similar products); Appeal Committee, SIC 2006, 86 ('Proteos/Protos') (pharmaceutical products and surgical/medical instruments are similar products).
489. ATF 65 II 202.
490. Just. Ct Geneva *in* SJ 1957, 161.
491. Civ. Ct Freiburg *in* RSPIDA 1975, 78.
492. ATF 99 II 104.
493. ATF 70 II 245; *see* further Appeal Committee, SIC 2006, 35 (Banking services, and software development services are not similar to a cheese grater); Appeal Committee, SIC 2004, 863 ('Harry's Bar') (identical retail channels does not entail that the products are similar); Appeal Committee, SIC 2005, 135 (the possibility of substituting a product to another one does not entail that these products are similar).
494. As revised at Brussels on 14 Dec. 1900, at Washington on 2 Jun. 1911, at The Hague on 6 Nov. 1925, at London on 2 Jun. 1934, at Nice on 15 Jun. 1957, and at Stockholm on 14 Jul. 1967 (RS 0.232.112.3). In 2021, 109 States covering 126 countries were, like Switzerland, party to the Madrid Arrangement itself.

394. This being the case, the application is transmitted to the WIPO in Geneva, where the usual procedure follows. The international trademark may not differ from the national one; otherwise, it will be invalid.

395. For foreign trademarks that are registered with WIPO in Geneva, the opposition can be brought before the Swiss Institute for Intellectual Property within twelve months from the first day of the month following the publication of the trademark by WIPO. The Institute may also reject the protection as concerns Switzerland. In both cases, Articles 6 et seq. Paris Convention must provide a good cause for denying the protection of the international trademark in Switzerland. The rejection may be total or for a limited part of the products and services. It nullifies the protection of the trademark *ab ovo* as far as Switzerland is concerned. An appeal is open to the Federal Administrative Tribunal against the decision of the Swiss Institute for Intellectual Property and to the Federal Tribunal as a last resort.[495] The list of products and services for which protection can be claimed cannot be modified during the procedure.[496]

396. If registered, the international trademark shall be valid for twenty years in Switzerland, unless the applicant chooses to pay only the fees for ten years.[497] After five years a third party may request striking off the trademark for want of use (Article 50*a* Ordinance, effective date 1 January 2017).

397. If a country has not ratified the Madrid Protocol of 28 June 1989, the central attack against the international trademark is possible, during the five-year period of the original Madrid Arrangement.

§5. Ownership and Transfer

I. Ownership

398. The registered owner of the trademark is entitled to all rights that are defined and all remedies that are provided under the Trademark Act (Articles 13 et seq. and 52 et seq. Trademark Act). The owner can be the fiduciary holder of the rights.[498]

495. *See* Marbach, *Markenrecht* (Trademark Act), *in* SIWR III, Trademark Act, 157.
496. *See*, e.g., Ct Just. Geneva, SIC 2004, 859.
497. *See* Marbach, *Markenrecht* (Trademark Act), *in* SIWR III, 166. *See* further Fed. Trib. SIC 2008, 896 (an 'action in nullity' within the meaning of the Madrid Arrangement is only a civil action; an 'opposition' is of administrative nature, thus not a civil action. Therefore, the opposition proceeding in Germany is not a valid excuse for not working the trademark in spite of the obligation of use of Art. 12 Trademark Act).
498. *See* U. Ruede-Bugnion, *Fiduziarische Rechtsgeschäfte, die ein Markenrecht zum Gegenstand haben, nach schweizerischem Recht* (Fiduciary Legal Acts in Relation with Trademark Act under Swiss Law), thesis, Geneva esp. 162 et seq. (Berne, 1978). Further, it will be noted that the rightful owner of a trademark wrongfully filed by another person may claim a transfer of the mark to her own name (Art. 53 (1) Trademark Act), and this action is also admitted for the simple filing of an application to register; Fed. Trib. SIC 2021, 69.

399. All decided cases relating to the requirements of the former Trademark Act as to the person of the registered owner – to wit, that he be a producer, a merchant or a legal entity having a going business – are irrelevant since 1 April 1993.[499] The Swiss law now follows the French and European system, the only requirement being that the registered owner be an existing physical person or legal entity; even a public corporation organized under public law, such as a city or canton, maybe the owner of a trademark.[500] Therefore, there is no longer any uncertainty about the right of the franchisor to apply for the registration of a trademark,[501] nor for the same right of a company which is established in Switzerland for taxation purposes but does not own a factory here nor a going business.[502]

II. Transfer

400. There are two methods to transfer the use of a trademark: outright assignment and licensing of the trademark. In specific cases, parties may also enter into a 'trademark delimitation agreement', that is not a licensing agreement but a settlement out of court, according to the latest cases decided by the Federal Tribunal (ATF 138 III 304 c. 11; *see* also SIC 2021, 245); therefore it is not terminable for cause unless so provided by the parties.

A. Assignment

401. Under the new Trademark Act, the assignment is free, with no longer any requirement as to the simultaneous transfer of the industrial facilities of the assignor that worked in the area for which the trademark is used (Article 17 Trademark Act). There is no *proviso* concerning the misleading use of the trademark by the assignee. This is, in our view, a drawback of the Swiss legislation in comparison with the European law.[503] The ground for diverging from the European solution appears to have been a reluctance to open the way for control by the Institute or the Judiciary of the validity of the assignments; the decided cases were rather strict[504] and the practice of the Federal Office for Intellectual Property (as it was then called) perceived as finicky, so that the majority of the Expert Committee wanted to do away with all safeguards.[505]

499. *See*, e.g., the *Tarzan* case, Fed. Trib. *in* PMM Bl 1973 I 57 (no registration for the applicant because it did not use the trademark itself, but only through a network of independent licensees); *see also* ATF 100 II 159.

500. *See Rapport Explicatif* (Explanatory Report) for the first Draft Trademark Act, 7–8 (Berne 1988).

501. *See* Th. de Haller, *Le contrat de franchise en droit suisse* (Franchising Contract in Swiss Law), thesis, esp. 83 (Lausanne, 1978).

502. *See* Fed. Trib. *in* PMM Bl 1971 I 41.

503. Art. 17(4) of the Regulation 40/94 of 20 Dec. 1993, O.J. No. L. 11/7.

504. *See* ATF 101 II 293; ATF 105 II 49 (license cases).

505. *See* Message of the Federal Council, FF 1991 I 27.

402. The authors of the Message of the Federal Council attempted to save some safeguard under the guise of a reference to Article 20 of the Code of Obligations, stating that an assignment would be void and null were it to mislead the consumers or otherwise hurt the public interests.[506] As far as 'public interests' are envisioned, the Message cannot be followed, since the 'public interests' that may be impinged upon are not necessarily protected by way of making null and void any and all contracts contrary to the public law,[507] let alone contracts that are not clearly contrary to the law as is the case here. The only provisions that may be cited in this respect are to be found in the Federal Act against Unfair Competition, that prohibits all sorts of delusive measures and behaviour.[508] However, the commentary is to the effect that those provisions suffice to prevent any wrongful effect of the assignment,[509] so that there is no need for nullity of the assignment contract itself; as a result, no protection is afforded against a misleading assignment at the moment when the Swiss Institute for Intellectual Property registers the assignment.

403. The transfer by assignment is made in a written deed (Article 17(2) Trademark Act), although the duty to assign a given mark or a portfolio may be undertaken in any form-free contract.[510] In case of a transfer of the whole business, the assignment shall not necessarily comply with the requirement of the written deed; in other words, it may even be implied in fact, and this is the presumption which is made in the law.[511] The registration of the assignment is necessary only vis-à-vis third parties.[512] In the absence of a registration of the transfer, actions can be filed against the former owner,[513] but the claimant can already file a suit against the assignee if he so chooses.[514]

404. No legalization of the signature is necessary to require the registration of the assignment. The form is to be filed with the Swiss Institute for Intellectual Property together with the written deed embodying the assignment contract, or the auction minutes, etc.

506. Message of the Federal Council, FF 1991 I 26.
507. *See*, e.g., ATF 102 II 401, esp. 404–409 and generally F. Dessemontet, *Droit à la marque* (Right to Trademark), in *La nouvelle loi fédérale sur la protection des marques* (The New Federal Act on Trademark Protection), CEDIDAC No. 27, 59–60.
508. *See* Arts 2 and 3 (b) and (d) UCA.
509. Marbach, *Markenrecht* (Trademark Act), *in* SIWR III, 219; David, No. 8 *ad* Art. 17 Trademark Act.
510. *See* Marbach, *Markenrecht* (Trademark Act), *in* SIWR III, 220.
511. Ar. 17(4) Trademark Act.
512. Art. 17(2) second sentence Trademark Act.
513. Art. 17(3) Trademark Act; *see already* under the 1890 Trademark Act, Com. Ct Berne, *in* RSPI 1990, 90.
514. Com. Ct Berne, *in* RSPI 1990, 90.

B. Licence

405. A detailed review of the general structure of licensing agreements under Swiss law is to be found hereabove.[515] Suffice it to state here that the licence agreement is entirely free, as to the form as well as the substantive issues that the parties may regulate at their will, with due attention to the antitrust law.

406. However, if the parties wish to register the licensee, their application towards this end shall be filed together with a written declaration by the licensor confirming the grant of a licence.[516] The advantage is for the registered licensee to be able to assert his rights vis-à-vis an ulterior assignee, the latter not being in a position to present the defence that he did not know of the licence.

407. Otherwise, as there are no requirements of form, licences can be implied in fact, for example, whenever a distributor has registered the trademark belonging to the foreign producer.[517]

408. Finally, it should be mentioned that a trademark may be validly pledged[518] or brought into a partnership, or a company limited by shares,[519] but a precise valuation of a trademark as an asset of the company should be attempted; otherwise, the founders of the company, its officers, even the notary public could be held liable for the overestimate and the corresponding undercapitalization of the company.

409. In bankruptcy proceedings, the trademark may be assigned to a Swiss or to a foreign party upon auctioneering or, if the law permits, through arms-length negotiations.[520]

---

515. *See* paras 86 *et seq.* and paras 256 *et seq.*, esp. 261 and 262 for the termination for cause.
516. Art. 29(1)(a) Ordinance.
517. *See* Fed. Trib. *in* RSPIDA 1974, 118; ATF 101 II 293, esp. 299; ATF 107 II 356, esp. 361, and cit. *in* F. Dessemontet, *Remarques à propos de l'ATF du 6 octobre 1981* (Remarks about the Fed. Trib. Decision of 6 Oct. 1981), RSPIDA 1982, 134. It is not always feasible to imply a license in that case; *see* Com. Ct Zurich, *in* RSPIDA 1981, 56.
518. Pestalozzi, Gmuer & Patry, *Business Law Guide to Switzerland* 433 No. 1311 (2d ed., Bricester, 1997). *See* Report of the Swiss Group of the AIPPI, SIC 2017, 547, 550.
519. David, No. 11 *ad* Art. 17 Trademark Act.
520. *See* Arts 89 et seq., 122 et seq. of the Federal Bankruptcy Act of 11 Apr. 1889 as amended on 16 Dec. 1994 (RS 281.1). In my view, a trademark right is not subject to Art. 131 Federal Bankruptcy Act on the transfer of contractual rights, since the trademark right (as distinguished from the license for a trademark) is an absolute right of intellectual property (*quasi* in rem) and not a contractual right. *See* David, No. 4 *ad* Art. 17 Trademark Act. According to a recent case, a trademark license which is not recorded in the Register cannot be opposed to the buyer of the trademark, even in bankruptcy proceedings, as the license itself is a contract with effect only between the parties; the ignorance or knowledge of the license by the buyer is irrelevant; *see* Fed. Trib. 2017, 67.

§6. Scope of Exclusive Rights

I. General Definition

410. Under Article 13 Trademark Act, the owner of a trademark has the exclusive right to use the trademark for the registered goods and services and to assign it or otherwise to contract the trademark.

411. This positive dominion over the trademark is now deemed to be a property right.[521] On the contrary, the former Trademark Act was compatible only with the theory that the trademark was protected as part of the personal interests of the holder, and was therefore not to be assigned without the entity using it.

412. The commentary is to the effect that, as for any property right, the trademark right encompasses the right to use the trademark, and that right of use of the holder may benefit the licensee who is able to derive his priority right against a third party from the right to the holder.[522] In our view, such an opinion is no longer convincing, since the new Trademark Act does not take the *use* of the trademark as the event that gives a right to the mark; rather, it is the registration. Between a licensee and a third party, the position of the licensee is better because he is authorized to use the mark by the registered owner.

II. Particular Rights

A. *Prohibition of Use by Third Parties*

413. The trademark owner has the right to prohibit any use of his mark, or a similar one, as a trademark by another party for the same or similar goods or services. If it is not a case of an identical mark on identical goods, a risk of confusion must exist (Article 3(1)(b) and (c) Trademark Act).

414. The *use* as a trademark is the use to distinguish a product or a service when those are offered on the market. There is the use of a trademark within the meaning of Article 13(2) Trademark Act where it is affixed to products or packing, when it is used to offer products for sale or leasing or to offer services, when it is used for export[523] or import transactions, or whenever it is used in business, for example, on letterheads, bills, advertisement, etc.

---

521. In German: '*Herrschaftsrecht*'. *See* Appeal Committee, SIC 2004, 232, 234 ('Bin Ladin') (as property right the right to a trademark is protected by the constitutional right of property).

522. David, No. 5 *ad* Art. 13 Trademark Act.

523. Art. 13(2)(d) Trademark Act closes a long-lasting controversy between two separate courts of the Federal Tribunal on the use of a trademark solely for export purposes (infringing: the Penal Court, ATF 109 IV 145; ATF 110 IV 108; not infringing: the First Civil Court, ATF 101 II 293; ATF 113 II 73). For cases on the notion of infringing use of a trademark generally, *see* Appel. Ct Ticino, SIC 2008, 522; same Ct SIC 1997, 583; Appeal Committee, SIC 1999, 651; SIC 2002, 242 (La Poste)

A contrario, it is not prohibited to show the trademark in a comparative survey of goods and services as is published by a neutral consumer organization, or a newspaper, as long as it is not a piece of an advertisement. However, a catalogue by an authorized dealer may refer to the trademark of several competitors only because there is a licence by the various manufacturers or trademark holders.[524] Nonetheless, although the Trademark Act does not state it in so many words, the use of a trademark as a necessary reference, for example, to offer spare parts for the car industry,[525] does not fall under the exclusive right of the owner, as long as the sale itself is not illegal.[526] Further, reproduction of the trademark together with the product in a magazine, sports journal, book or calendar is not infringing on the rights of the trademark owner.

B. Prohibition of Use by Licensee and Authorized Dealers

415. The new Trademark Act especially provides for a rule that is common to all licences and was nowhere expressed until now: if the use of the trademark exceeds the authorization given by the licensor, this constitutes an infringement that may be enjoined under the Trademark Act.[527] Actually, this new provision (Article 13(3) Trademark Act) does explicitly aim at the authorized dealers and sales representatives who first have to ask for the approval of the foreign trademark owner in order to register in Switzerland an identical or similar trademark; it would be an infringement to register it without his agreement, as it might be an infringement later to omit to request its radiation when they are no longer authorized dealers for him.

416. As a matter of case law, the question was already settled before 1992 in favour of the foreign trademark owner,[528] and Switzerland could thus comply with Article 6*septies* of the Paris Convention.

(the use of a trademark for services subject to a State monopoly is still considered use as a trademark, and as such the trademark may acquire secondary meaning). Art. 13 (2*bis*) Trademark Act makes it now a violation of the exclusive rights of the trademark owner to import or export even for private use; that does not constitute a criminal offence as is expressly provided by Art. 65a of the same Act.

524. *See* ATF 104 II 58 (decided then under the UCA). For this ancillary use of Unfair Competition remedies in trademark cases concerning the true passing-off and the misuse of someone else's reputation, *see* now A. Alberini, *L'exploitation de la renommée de la marque d'autrui* (The Use of the Renown of Another Person's Trademark), thesis Lausanne 2015, spec. 255 et seq.

525. *See* David, No. 34 *ad* Art. 13 Trademark Act; ATF 128 III 146 ('Audi'); Fed. Trib., SIC 2000, 611 ('WIR'); ATF 104 II 56 ('Singer') (however, it is an act of unfair competition to have the public believe that the merchant using the trademark as a reference is an 'authorized dealer' of that product). For the cumulative application of Trademark Act and Unfair Competition Law, *see*, e.g., Fed. Trib. SIC 2018, 162 at 166; SIC 2014, 153; further, ATF 135 III 446 ('Maltesers').

526. *See* para. 417 for the first-sale doctrine.

527. *See* para. 264 for the patent licence.

528. *See* Fed. Trib. *in* RSPIDA 1974, 118, esp. 125–126; ATF 61 II 59; ATF 72 II 422; ATF 107 II 356. *See*, however, Com. Ct Zurich, *in* RSPIDA 1981, 56.

§7. Limitation on the Exclusive Rights

I. The First-Sale Doctrine

417. The German[529] first-sale doctrine is followed in Switzerland as elsewhere in Europe. Under the former Trademark Act, both the Federal Tribunal[530] and the cantonal courts[531] have acknowledged that once the brand products are legally put onto the market, the right of the trademark owner is no longer to be opposed to the vendee of the goods. For example, the owner of the trademark cannot impose that the trademark stays affixed to the goods, or that the products be sold only through a network of authorized dealers. Consent of the owner of the trademarks is required for the sale to be a valid first-sale under that doctrine.

II. International, European or National Exhaustion

418. During some years after entry into force of the new Trademark Act, authors and cantonal courts were divided about the question of whether the first-sale doctrine applies when a brand product is put onto the market *abroad* with the consent of the owner.[532]

419. The Federal Tribunal has now settled the question: for marks[533] as well as for copyright,[534] the international exhaustion is the rule, provided, however, for trademarks, that the consumers not be deceived over the characteristics of the products.[535]

III. Prior Use of the Trademark by Third Parties

420. Although registration is the only test to know who is entitled to the trademark, the prior use by another competitor may be a good defence if the trademark

529. *See Entscheidungen des Reichsgerichts in Zivilsachen* (Judgments of the *Reichsgericht* in Civil Law) 50, 229 et seq.; *Entscheidungen des Reichsgerichts in Zivilsachen* 51, 139 et seq.

530. ATF 86 II 270, esp. 282.

531. Appel. Ct Freiburg, *in* RSPIDA 1979, 121; Appel. Ct Solothurn, *in* RSPIDA 1981, 61.

532. *Contra*: Appel. Ct Berne *in* RSPI 1995, 133 ('Pentax'); *pro*: Com. Ct Zurich *in* RSPI 1995, 107 ('Timberland' and 'Head'); Com. Ct St-Gallen *in* RSPI 1995, 126 ('Nikon'). For the literature, *see* Marbach, *Markenrecht* (Trademark Act), *in* SIWR III, 203–204.

533. ATF 122 III 469.

534. ATF 124 III 321. For patents, the Fed. Trib. confirmed the national exhaustion of rights in ATF 126 III 129, and Parliament reversed that decision in 2008 for most products but not medical drugs, *see* para. 285. The international exhaustion also means that it is not illegal to erase the original production series numbers and replace them so as to conceal the source of the parallel-imported items; Com Ct Berne, SIC 2014, 634.

535. *See* ATF 122 III 469, 481; Com Ct Berne, SIC 2014, 634 at 637 (the exhaustion of rights does not interfere with the rights of the owner of the trademark against a counterfeiting product); *see* already ATF 105 II 49. According to our Minister of Justice, this ATF 122 III 469 case would be good law even after the enactment of the new Trademark Act. *See* Stenographic Bulletin of the Swiss Parliament, Council of States 1992, 23.

owner asserts his right against the prior user. Article 14 Trademark Act provides for that exception because some small firms in Switzerland may not file their trademark.[536]

421. As is also the case under the Patent Act, this provision does not give a right to the trademark, but only a defence against an infringement action.

Further, the defence is only valid to the extent that the use has been made at the date of this registration of the trademark. No new item can be added to the list of the wares and goods for which the trademark is used, but it is possible that obsolete products be replaced within the same category by new ones.[537]

§8. Use Requirements

I. Notion of Use

422. The notion of use varies according to the provisions in which it is found. There are at least four meanings of the word 'use':

(1) the 'use' which is necessary to maintain the exclusive rights on a trademark under Articles 11 and 12 Trademark Act;
(2) the 'use' which falls under the exclusive right of the trademark owner according to Article 13 Trademark Act; this provision gives an exemplary listing of the sorts of use that are taken into account by the court, but is in no way limitative or prevailing for the application of Article 11 Trademark Act;[538]
(3) the 'use' to which a third party is entitled under Article 14 Trademark Act because it is a use prior to the registration;
(4) the 'use' which is a prerequisite for a well-known trademark under Article 6*bis* Paris Convention and Article 3(2)(b) Trademark Act.

423. The Swiss law did not follow the European provisions that require a 'serious use'[539] in order to maintain the exclusive trademark rights.

---

536. Under the former Trademark Act, the right to the trademark was based on use rather than registration. Further, trade names or company names as registered in the Office of Commerce were protected as trademark without double registration.
537. *See* David, No. 3 *ad* Art. 14 Trademark Act.
538. For example, the informational use as defined by the Fed. Trib., SIC 2000, 611 ('WIR'), cannot help define the necessary use under Art. 11 Trademark Act. To affix a trademark on leisure dress is also a valid use under Art. 11 and 13 Trademark Act; see Com. Ct. Berne, SIC 2021, 70. *See* further A. Alberini, SIC 2022, 131 commenting Fed. Trib. 4A_95/2019 ('VW-Land Toggenburg') and other, older cases. Formerly, the courts often relied on the invoices showing that a certain number of a given product had been ordered or sold within Switzerland.
539. *See* Art. 12(1) of the First Council Directive 89/104/EC of 21 Dec. 1988 to approximate the laws of the Member States relating to Trade Marks; Art. 13 of the Council Regulation 40/94 of 20 Dec. 1993 on the Community Trade Mark. *See* Fed. Trib., SIC 2009, 36 (the registration of a company in the Register of Commerce is in itself not a sufficient use of the trademark as trademark), SIC 2009, 268 (Gallup) (the use of a trademark in the title of a publication is not a use as trademark); Fed. Adm. Trib., SIC 2008, 219; same Ct, SIC 2008, 222; Appeal Committee, SIC 2004, 868

424. The use may be made under a slightly different form (Article 11(2) Trademark Act).

425. The use can be made by a licensee or an agent, sales representative, importer, etc., as long as they act with the consent of the trademark owner (Article 11(3) Trademark Act). This conforms to the former case law, under which the agent or sales representative was supposed to use the trademark for the foreign manufacturer.[540]

II. Effects of Non-use

A. Litigation

426. In case of litigation, the trademark owner cannot successfully assert his trademark rights if he did not use his mark for *five years*, starting either from the end of the time to file an opposition against his registration or from the end of the opposition procedure (Article 12(1) Trademark Act).

427. The only exception appears to be if the non-use is due to causes outside the trademark owner's power or will, as are Acts of God, for example, destruction of a factory by a volcanic eruption (a rare event in Switzerland), a general strike (even more seldom), or a decision of the Administration,[541] banning the brand product from the market or waiting a long time to give the necessary authorization (e.g., for an agrochemical product). A partial non-use, the trademark being used for some of the claimed products or services, and not for the other ones, leads only to a partial loss of the trademark rights. Such a partial loss cannot be found to the detriment of a world-known trademark.

428. A rather confusing debate occurred in the Parliament between those MPs who wanted to reason in the usual terms of a time bar and those who thought it

('Globex') (the use under Art. 11 must take place within Switzerland; in this writer's view that rule is too restrictive; it should be enough if there have been contacts with clients within Switzerland, e.g., through a webpage the server of which is located abroad); for the proof of use or non-use see Fed. Trib. SIC 2018, 59. For use by being present on the Net and targeting or to the contrary geoblocking a given market see Fed. Trib., ATF 146 III 225 and cons. 4.2 printed in SIC 2020, 629, 634-635 (not published in ATF). Somewhat more restrictive, Fed. Trib. SIC 2009, 268 ('Gallup') (the sheer possibility of ordering goods on the Net would not be a sufficient use within Switzerland); *see* generally S. Antreasyan, *Biens virtuels et droit des marques* (Virtual Goods and Trademark Law), SIC 2017, 327, 337 ff.

540. ATF 116 II 463; Fed. Trib., SIC 2009, 36–37; Fed. Adm. Trib., SIC 2008, 638; Com. Ct Berne, SIC 2008, 901; Appeal Committee, SIC 2006, 37 ('Syscor'); for the former case law, as embedded in ATF 107 II 356, *see* F. Dessemontet, *Remarques à propos de l' ATF du 6 octobre 1981* (Remarks about the Fed. Trib. Decision of 6 Oct. 1981), RSPIDA 1982, 134.

541. Appeal Committee, SIC 1998, 406 (the restriction to the use of a trademark by reason of a State monopoly in Switzerland which is a fact known and foreseeable to the trademark owner is not a good defence against the loss of right stemming from the non-use of the trademark); ATF 134 III 555 (an opposition proceeding abroad is not a good reason not to use the trademark in Switzerland).

wholly inappropriate for a trademark.[542] It should be remembered that under Swiss law, as under most Continental laws, the time bar is not a procedural issue, but a question of substantive law. Basically, the time bar (*Verjährung*) is a defence which the judge cannot entertain ex officio, whereas the non-use of a trademark leads to the loss of trademark rights *ipso iure*.[543] Further, if the time bar is an absolute one (*Verwirkung*), the loss of the right is absolute, too and it cannot be recovered. On the contrary, the trademark right can be recovered when the trademark owner reuses it, if no third party litigated against the trademark owner, as we shall see now. Thus, it is better to think of a period of five years for use as a sui generis institution.

429. The trademark owner has the burden of proof to show use, as soon as the opposing party has made it likely that no use occurred in fact (Article 12(3) Trademark Act).

B. In the Absence of Litigation

430. If no litigation involves the trademark right, the non-use during five years does not prevent the trademark owner to be reinstated with a valid right having priority as from the date of the registration, through a valid use on the products or for the services that were originally claimed (Article 12(2) Trademark Act).

§9. Duration of Protection: Termination

I. Duration of Protection

A. Original Registration

431. The rights that are acquired through the original registration last for ten years (Article 10(1) Trademark Act), with the exception of the international trademarks valid for twenty years (Article 6(1) Madrid Agreement). For Swiss marks, the delay is reckoned from the filing of the application and for international trademarks from the day of the international registration.

432. Details are regulated in the Ordinance on the Protection of Trademarks, Articles 2 and 25, as well as in the Federal Law on the Administrative Procedure of 20 December 1968,[544] Article 20(3).

542. *See* Stenographic Bulletin of the Swiss Parliament 1992, 399–400.
543. ATF 62 II 60 (digest ch. 3).
544. RS 172.021.

B. Prolongation of Registration

433. The new Trademark Act allows for the prolongation of the validity of the registered trademarks as they are, without a renewed examination by the Institute for Intellectual Property. The only formality is the payment of the required fees. The fees can be paid later within a month. Of course, no modification of the trademark nor of the claimed products or services may be made on the occasion of the prolongation.

434. The former case law on the possibility for the Registrar to reject the request for renewal for material reasons[545] is no longer applicable.

II. Termination

435. If no request for prolongation has been made before the expiry date of the trademark, the termination of all trademark rights is definitive.

436. There is an extraordinary cause for termination through the cancellation of the trademark following a court order (Article 35(2) Trademark Act) or a request for cancellation either for a part of the claimed products or services (with a fee being due) or for the whole list (no fee being due then).

437. As soon as a registration is cancelled, a trademark can be registered anew, be it by the former trademark owner or by a third party. If the former owner does not register anew immediately, another person can file an application for registration, and the former owner has no priority rights that would be based on the former registration.

§10. Infringement and Remedies

I. General Presentation

A. Three Remedies

438. The new Trademark Act is based on the availability of three sets of remedies:

(1) civil actions (Articles 52 through 60 Trademark Act);
(2) criminal actions (Articles 61 through 69 Trademark Act);
(3) administrative measures (Articles 70 through 72 Trademark Act).

545. *See*, e.g., ATF 112 II 263; ATF 103 Ib 16 and 268. Under the new Trademark Act *see* Appeal Committee, SIC 2004, 932 ('Bin Ladin').

B. *Main Features of the New Legislation*

439. The intent of the legislature has been to harmonize all provisions bearing on the remedies for infringement of intangible values.[546] Thus, both the 1992 Trademark Act and the 1992 Copyright Act, as well as the Act against Unfair Competition of 1986, follow the general pattern of the 1983 revision of Articles 28 et seq. Civil Code. The 2007 revision of the Patent Act also harmonized the remedies available under the Trademark Act, especially as it concerns the intervention of customs authorities. Also, the new Federal Code of Civil Procedure of 19 December 2008 (RS 272) gives a basis for interim measures in all areas of intellectual property.

440. Further, stiffer penalties characterize the new criminal remedies, with jail up to one year or a fine and ex officio actions against the 'professional' pirates who may go to jail for up to five years.

II. Civil Actions

A. *Action for Declaratory Statement of Invalidity*

441. Article 52 Trademark Act allows any person having a legally protected interest to petition the court for an order stating that a given legal situation prevails as to a trademark.[547]

442. The most frequent statement sought after should be the statement of the invalidity of a given mark which is registered. Such a statement can be asked for by the defendant in a litigation for infringement. The petition can be filed by a consumer organization inasmuch as a certification, or collective trademark is at stake.[548]

546. *See* Message of the Federal Council, FF 1991 I 39 No. 224.

547. According to ATF 110 II 352, such an action derives from the federal law, at the exclusion of the cantonal law. *See* F. Dessemontet, *L'action en constatation de droit spécialement pour les contrats de licence (*The Declaratory Action, Especially Regarding the Licensing Agreements*)*, in *Festschrift für Roland von Büren* 253 (Basle, 2009). The Swiss courts accept the system of the centralized attack of international trademarks in the country of first filing for a period of time of 5 years under the Madrid Agreement of 1967 and the Protocol of 1989; *see* Fed. Trib., SIC 2021, 76. According to this case, the claimant need not prove competition with the respondent on the Swiss market.

548. *See* Art. 56(2) Trademark Act. Such an action could also be entertained by a consumer organization against (abusive) geographic denominations. *See* Art. 56(1)(b) Trademark Act. For geographic denominations generally, *see* hereinafter paras 467 et seq.

B. Action for Transfer

443. In case of fraudulent registration through an unauthorized party, the person or legal entity that is truly entitled to the trademark can bring an action to have the benefit of registration transferred to him.

444. There may be a better right only if the registrant has known that the trademark was used on account of the true owner.[549] No proof of fault is required.[550] For example, an agent can believe in good faith that after having secured the contractual right to put a *trade name* of a foreign manufacturer into his own trade name, he can also file that name as a trademark. Nonetheless, when the agent is no longer an authorized sales representative, the manufacturer can claim the trademark back for him (Article 52(2) Trademark Act).

445. The misappropriation has to be established by the claimant. This writer suggests that if the claimant has shown that the defendant registered the trademark with actual or constructive knowledge of the better right of the claimant, then the burden of proof reverts to the defendant, who may, for example, show that he legally used the said trademark in Switzerland before the other party. However, the fraudulent intent may derive from the fact that the trademark is a well-known one; then, there might be no possibility of rebuttal.

446. The action must be filed within two years from the publication of the registration or from the termination of the licence.

447. If the claimant is successful, the judgment stating a given right and the judgment for transfer shall be open to the Swiss Institute for Intellectual Property, and the necessary correction will be carried out by the Registrar of Trademarks (Article 54 Trademark Act). The award of arbitral tribunals could also be sent to the Institute, to the extent that their award concerns substantive claims of the parties and are not only of a preliminary nature or bearing on administrative issues.

549. In general *see* Fed. Trib., SIC 2021, 69 (*Fractal*)(an action in transfer may be filed as soon as a trademark has been filed; it is not necessary to wait for the mark to be registered, in spite of the clear wording of the law); ATF 139 III 424 (relevant considerations not reported in the Official Reporter of the Fed. Trib., which however cites them later in SIC 2017, 412 ('Reiko I') and SIC 2018, 402 ('Reiko II'); the Reiko I judgment is erroneous in our view: taking into account all facts of the case, notably the participation in the stock of the Swiss company and the exclusive marketing agreement, the mark should have been deemed to be an agent's mark. *See* already F. Dessemontet, *Remarques à propos de l'ATF du 6 octobre 1981* (Remarks about the Fed. Trib. Decision of 6 Oct. 1981), RSPIDA 1982, 132 et seq.; David, No. 5 *ad* Art. 53 Trademark Act.

550. *See* generally Fed. Trib., SIC 2008, 732 ('GMail'); Cant. Ct Fribourg, SIC 2009, 869; David, No. 5 *ad* Art. 53 Trademark Act.

C. *Injunctions*

448. The trademark owner can petition the court to obtain the following relief:

- an order to prevent an infringement which is on the verge of happening;
- an order to stop-and-desist from an infringing act;
- an order to indicate the names and addresses of the providers of infringing goods and wares.

If this order is not complied with, the defendant could be sentenced to a fine or to imprisonment for up to one year (Article 61(2) Trademark Act).

D. *Actions for Monetary Relief*

449. Three actions are given for monetary relief, whereas Article 55(2) of the Trademark Act only refers to the general provisions of the Code of Obligations for the conditions that must be fulfilled for the court to award those remedies:

(1) *Damages*, that is, the loss of some sales by the rightful owner of the trademark and the cost of preventing the trouble, or repairing it through advertisement campaigns, etc. Damages are at least equal to the royalties that have not been paid. The fault of the defendant must be established.[551]
(2) *Compensation for 'moral suffering'*, that should fix the intangible loss suffered by the trademark owner. A special seriousness of the wrongful injury shall be established by the court under Article 49 Code of Obligations. Dilution could be compensated in that way.[552] The fault of the defendant is necessary.
(3) *Disgorgement of profits*. Accounting for profits made through the infringement of intellectual property rights has been a long-standing practice under the Copyright Act[553] and the Patent Act,[554] so the legislature introduced it for all injuries to intangible assets under the Article 28 Civil Code, the Unfair Competition Law, the Copyright Act and the Trademark Act. Examples are rare in practice. A controversy has arisen about whether the fault of the defendant would be necessary, which is not the case in my view.[555]

---

551. For damages awards between CHF 200 and CHF 800'000, *see* David, No. 40 *ad* Art. 55 Trademark Act. It is rumoured that settlements out of court often exceed this latter amount. An unfortunate Fed. Trib. judgment applying the Patent Act negates the methods of the license analogy: ATF 132 III 379 (it would no longer be possible to reckon the damages on the basis of the royalty rate that is usual in the industry, contrary to the solution prevailing in the EU). However, the practice of lower courts is to accept the royalties analogy. *See* Cant. Trib. Vaud, SIC 2013, 300 c. VII ('bd').
552. *See* ATF 59 II 25; Just. Ct Geneva *in* RSPI 1985, 49.
553. *See* para. 182.
554. *See* para. 327.
555. *See* the present case law oscillates. *See* ATF 125 III 29 requiring bad faith; Fed. Trib., SIC 2013, 360 ('Pneus on line II'); *contra*, under general rules of unjust enrichment, Fed. Trib., SIC 2006,

E. Seizure of Infringing Goods and Wares

450. The wares and goods on which a trademark has been unlawfully affixed can be seized by order of the court. This is a definitive measure if it is ordered in a final judgment. Of course, interim measures *pendente lite* are also possible for a limited period of time.[556]

451. According to the text of Article 57 Trademark Act, it is only the wares and goods with the infringing trademark that can be seized. The machinery and production facilities of the defendant cannot be seized.[557]

452. If these marks can be taken away from the products, the court shall so order. Otherwise, the wares should be destroyed.[558]

F. Venue

453. For actions that would lead to a final judgment, the cantons must provide for a sole jurisdiction (with an appeal to the Federal Tribunal under the requirements of federal law). Interim measures can be requested in another court if the cantons so decide.

454. Within Switzerland, the claimant can file an action either at the domicile of the defendant, or at the place where the infringing acts take place, or at the place where the results take place. In the view of this writer, as the 'results' are usually losses to the claimant, the venue could be at the place of the main business establishment of the trademark owner, but the older case law is to the effect that the 'result' is where the infringing products or services are marketed.[559]

455. In case of counterclaims, the venue is given by the opening of the claim, to the extent only that the court that entertains the claim is also competent for the substance of the counterclaims.

---

774 ('Rohrschelle'); RSPI 1991, 198; Com. Ct Berne, SIC 1999, 657; Cant. Ct Zurich, RSPI 1991, 402; Dessemontet, *L'enrichissement illégitime dans la propriété intellectuelle* (Unjust Enrichment in Intellectual Property), *Festschrift Kummer* (1980) 191 et seq.; *id.*, *Le droit d'auteur* (Copyright) 836 et seq. with cit. (Lausanne, 1999). Courts that require so-called bad faith in order to grant an order for accounting for profits do attenuate that stringent requirement by accepting that there is a presumption of bad faith when the imported goods come from a country that is known for its loose enforcement of IP legislation; *see*, e.g., Fed. Adm. Trib., SIC 2014, 560 concerning Taiwan.

556. *See* hereinafter for 'interim measures' para. 456.

557. The question may be solved otherwise under Copyright Law, *see* para. 178.

558. *See contra* Com. Ct Zurich *in* RSJ 1968, 356.

559. ATF 68 IV 54; ATF 89 II 422; Just. Ct Geneva *in* RSPIDA 1974, 106. ATF 132 III 586 (for declaratory actions on the validity or invalidity of the trademark, venue is Berne, Switzerland if the respondent has no seat or domicile in Switzerland). *See also* ATF 124 III 509 and Fed. Trib. SIC 2017, 311 (inside Switzerland the venue to request an injunction is in a Canton in which the infringing wares have been delivered, rather than in one or several Cantons from which the orders have been placed by the customers; that differs from the larger rules on venue under EU law).

G. Interim Measures

456. Article 59 Trademark Act provides for interim measures for which the courts are very often petitioned and that, from a statistical viewpoint, very often terminate the litigation.[560]

H. Publication of the Judgment

457. The publication of the final judgment can be ordered upon request of the claimant, for example, if the litigation has been lasting a long period of time[561] or if further infringing acts are feared.[562] In fact, many judgments decide against the publication request, for example, in export cases or cases when the infringing acts did not stir trouble on the market.

I. Time Limitations

458. There are no longer particular provisions on the time bar for those civil actions. The general provision of Article 60 Code of Obligations as revised effective date 1 January 2020 applies to most actions for monetary relief:

- three-year limitation from the knowledge of the wrongful acts and the damage resulting therefrom;
- five-year extraordinary limitation if the wrongful acts are felonies within the meaning of Articles 61 through 64 Trademark Act;
- ten-year absolute limitation from the wrongful act.

459. For the accounting of profits, there is some controversy in the commentary, most writers wishing to apply – on the basis of Article 67 Code of Obligations – the quasi-delictual time limitations that were mentioned *hereabove*, some commentators, however, wishing to apply the quasi-contractual time bar of Article 127 Code of Obligations (ten years from the facts). In the opinion of this writer, most cases are clearly quasi-delictual, but a few which may be quasi-contractual (former licensee, agent, etc.) may warrant the longer time bar of Article 127 Code of Obligations.

460. Beside the ordinary time limitation (*Verjährung*), there is also an absolute time limitation (*Verwirkung*) that may not be suspended according to Article 134 Code of Obligations or interrupted according to Article 135 Code of Obligations

560. *See* Fed. Trib. SIC 2016, 536 concerning the fine for '*contempt of court*'; already generally F. Dessemontet, *Les dommages-intérêts dans la propriété intellectuelle* (Damages in Intellectual Property), JdT 1979 I 322 et seq.
561. *See* ATF 82 II 346, esp. 360; ATF 102 II 122, esp. 127; Fed. Trib. *in* RSPI 1989, 93.
562. Appel. Ct Zurich *in* RSPI 1987, 104, esp. 111.

(e.g., through summons served in bankruptcy proceedings). The absolute time limitation is nowhere expressly provided for in our laws, but derives from Article 2 Civil Code against the misuse of one's right, as has been construed by the case law. The protection of the investment of a *bona fide* defendant requires that the trademark owner should not wait too long before initiating legal proceedings. This rule entails that the absolute time limitation does not alter the position towards all competitors, but only against the one defendant who is respondent to the infringement or repossession action. In a recent copyright case, the Federal Tribunal accepted as a defence that the action was not started before eighteen months (or, at most, four years) since the time the claimant knew the cause of action, and in a trademark case, the time limit of twenty-four months has been mentioned;[563] however, this solution should not be generalized in this writer's view, as the reaction time of Swiss industry is slower than that seems to have been admitted by the Federal Tribunal.

III. Criminal Remedies

A. *Intention Required*

461. Criminal remedies are available only for intentional infringement i.e., *dolus malus*; *dolus eventualis* may be deemed to exist in the meaning that the defendant accepts the result (wrongful act) in the event that his behaviour would result in such an infringement. For example, the packager who affixes a trademark that does not belong to his customer and does not clarify the legal situation, although he entertains or should entertain doubts, may be committing a *dolus eventualis*.

B. *Complaint Required*

462. Generally speaking, a complaint by the trademark owner or his licensee is necessary for the criminal enquiry to start. The exception concerns the infringing acts that are made during the practice of a regular business.[564]

563. Fed. Trib. *in* SIC 1998, 320–322 (copyright case); for trademark cases, *see* Fed. Trib., SIC 2021, 293 (long inaction of the trademark owner during approximately 10 years); Fed. Trib. 4A_265/2020 (*Luminart*); Fed. Trib. 4A_630/2018 (*Avia*)(even where five years and a half have elapsed since the first use of the respondent's infringing trademark, there will be no time bar against the action in transfer or deletion of the infringing sign when in case of transfer the respondent would not suffer an unjustified harm because his business is based on personal relations rather than advertising); SIC 2019, 686 (*VW-Land Toggenburg*): if a warning letter has been sent, the right of the owner will not be misused when the action is filed after one year; SIC 2008, 890 c. 3; SIC 2006, 500; ATF 73 II 183, esp. 190; Ct Just. GE, SIC 2018, 405.

564. *See* for that definition in RSPI 1991, 234 (*Lacoste*). It is more restrictive than the former practice, according to David, No. 17 *ad* Art. 61 Trademark Act.

C. Felonies and Misdemeanours

463. All following acts are classified as felonies according to Article 9(2) Penal Code, with the exception of two misdemeanours:

(1) fraudulent use of a trademark by an importer, an exporter or a repository (Article 62(3) Trademark Act);
(2) violation of the rules on the producer identification, which are known in the watchmaking industry.[565]

464. The following acts or omissions are prohibited:

- the infringement against the rights of the trademark owner through misappropriation or imitation of the mark, or through use of such an infringing mark to market products, to provide services or advertise them;
- the refusal to disclose the origin of infringing goods and wares;
- the fraudulent use of the trademark belonging to a third party with the intent to deceive the consumers or the shopkeepers (who both can file a complaint);
- the passing-off of one's products or services as the products or services of the original brand owner;
- the unlawful use of a certification or collective trademark against the regulation accompanying the registration of that mark.

IV. Administrative Procedures

465. As under the Copyright Act,[566] the customs authorities may advise the trademark owner or his representative that the import or export of infringing goods is likely to take place. Then the trademark owner can request the temporary seizure of the infringing goods, for ten days at most. It is up to him to petition a court of law for interim protection *pendente lite*.

466. The Trademark Act has been adapted to the TRIPS Agreement (possibility of an extension of ten days more for the administrative detaining of the infringing wares and goods).

565. *See* Arts 51 and 65 Trademark Act, as well as Art. 53 Ordinance.
566. *See supra* para. 176. Exportation was from the beginning foreseen in Arts 70 et seq. Trademark Act, whereas an amendment to the Copyright Act was necessary to comply with the TRIPS requirements.

§11. GEOGRAPHIC DENOMINATIONS

I. Overview

A. *Federal Legislation*

467. There are four federal statutes and ordinances.

1. The Trademark Act

468. The Trademark Act, Articles 47 through 51, sets up the legal regime of the geographic denominations. Although the wording has been somewhat modified from the former Act of 1890, the general legislative framework is still the same. The Trademark Act mentions only the indications of source (*Herkunftsangaben, indications de provenance*). The indication of source is in itself devoid of connotations as to the quality or to the characteristics of the products coming from a given geographic origin, but if an indication as to the quality or characteristics is made through the use of a given word which is understood as an indication of source, it will fall under Articles 47 et seq. Trademark Act.[567]

2. The Ordinance on Wines of 14 November 2007

469. This Ordinance,[568] Articles 21 et seq., protects the Appellations of Origin, and recognizes several categories:

(1) The appellation of origin which consists of a geographic indication of source and the words *vins de pays* (country wine), or *vin de pays* together with a traditional denomination (such as Dôle, Goron, Fendant, Nostrano, Mesolcina, Dorin, Salvagnin, Païen, Heida, Johannisberg of Valais, Ermitage or Hermitage of Valais, Malvoisie of Valais).[569]
(2) The cantons no longer have the sole legislative power to determine which area may be indicated by which appellation,[570] as well as the proportion of various varieties that may be combined;[571] only the Confederation may determine the

567. Examples: *Schwyzer Qualität* for German chocolate: Appel. Ct Munich *in* GRUR Int. 1980, 668; 'Goron', where this word is used for a given Wallis wine ATF 124 II 398. For the differences between the old Trademark Act and the new one, *see* ATF 132 III 770, 774.

568. RS 916.140 as amended last on 18 Oct. 2017. This Ordinance is based on the Federal Act on Agriculture of 29 Apr. 1998 (RS 910.1), commented below para. 3. For the modifications effectuated in the Swissness legislation effective 1 Jan. 2017, *see* below fn 577.

569. This traditional denomination may in itself be reserved to wines from a given Canton. *See*, e.g., for 'Goron' indicating a source in Valais ATF 124 II 398. The list is expanded from time to time.

570. For example: former Regulation of 19 Jun. 1985 of the Canton de Vaud on the Appellation of Origin.

571. For example: Former Arts 10(3) and 11(3) of the Fribourg Regulation of 15 Sep. 1997 on the Controlled Appellations of Origin, provided that every used plant variety must be at least 30% of the

acceptable quality and traditional denominations of wines, for example, as regards the control of the production, the quantities per 100 square metres and the sugar content. However, the Cantons have an additional, limited regulatory power to decide based on local circumstances that they best know.

(3) The controlled appellation of origin, which corresponds not only to a given geographic denomination but also to a certain level of quality.

(4) Table wines, without any specific requirement of quality, cannot include on their label any geographic indication. But if a 'Swiss origin' is mentioned, then certain federal rules apply as to the location of the vineyards from which the grapes originate, which must be within Switzerland, and the minimum sugar content (Article 24 Ord. Wines).

470. As a rule, the wines of controlled appellations cannot be prepared with grapes from other locations.[572]

3. The Federal Law on Agriculture of 28 April 1998

471. Article 16 of this Law provides for the setting up of a Register of Appellations of Origin and Geographic Denominations for agricultural products other than wines.

472. The Ordinance of 28 May 1997[573] gives more precision. A Committee examines each request (so far, around six to ten each year) and the Government decides on the registration of a given indication. The definitions that are valid for wines are not for other agricultural products. The agricultural products of 'protected appellation' can bear the name of a given area if they are made with raw materials and manufactured in that area.

They have to be prepared in a traditional way. A further category is created: the 'protected geographic denomination', for products that enjoy a particular renown when originating from that area. These products can be prepared with raw materials of some other origin, but one step of manufacturing at least must take place in the area referenced.

473. For both protected appellations and protected geographic denominations, a chart agreed upon by the producers set up the characteristics of the product, the

total. If a name such as 'Clos', 'Château', 'Domaine' is used, no combination is allowed. *See* Fed. Trib. SIC 2016, 222 confirming that cantonal law is still applicable to the denomination 'Château'; the applicable law may request the existence of an old building or a building traditionally called 'château (meaning "castle" or "manor"))' on the premises of the vine grower who is desirous to use that denomination.

572. Fed. Trib. SIC 2009, 423 ('Geneva AOC' cannot be made out of grapes collected in nearby France, in spite of the exiguity of the Geneva territory).

573. RS 910.12, as amended. *See*, e.g., Fed. Trib., SIC 2011, 246 (once defined by the producers, the characteristics of the product cannot be unilaterally modified by them); Fed. Trib., SIC 2012, 727 (conditions under which a delimitation of the method of manufacturing cheese may be stricter for a given protected denomination under general rules).

methods of the production, the precise delimitation of the area, the designation of the controlling organization (that has to be recognized according to the European Norm 45011), and the detailed rules or labelling.

474. An opposition procedure is established for the registration, for example, in favour of a trademark owner whose rights would be injured by the registration of a given appellation of origin or geographic denomination.[574]

4. Ordinance of 23 December 1971 on the Use of the Indication 'Swiss Made' on Watches, as Revised

475. Article 51 Trademark Act and Article 53 Trademark Ordinance provided the necessary basis for the Ordinance of 23 December 1971 on the Use of the Indication 'Swiss made' on Watches.[575] Watches were deemed to be 'Swiss made' if the movements have been assembled, checked, regulated and tested by the manufacturer in Switzerland, and if the manufacturing steps of the movements which take place in Switzerland make up at least 60% of the value of all the parts, excluding the assembly costs.[576] The legislation called 'Swissness' *(Bundesgesetz über den Schutz des Schweizerwappens und anderer öffentichen Zeichen)* has revised this Act on 21 June 2013, and the new provisions entered into force effective 1 January 2017. A specific ordinance deals with Swiss geographic indications for cosmetics (RS 232.112.3).

476. The former Law on Food Products of 1905 and the Ordinance of 1936 implementing it used to play an important role in the protection of geographic denominations, as they aimed at preventing any labelling that would be deceptive to the public. The new Law of 1992[577] and the Ordinance of 16 December 2016[578] appear to focus on the protection of the consumers' health and the protection against

574. *See*, e.g., Fed. Trib., SIC 2010, 534 ('Damassine'); SIC 2008, 131 ('Raclette II') following ATF 131 II 753 ('Raclette I'); for the determination of the quality requirements for cheese *see*, e.g., Fed. Adm. Trib., SIC 2012, 727 ('Vacherin Mont d'Or'). For the determination of the geographic production area, *see* Fed. Adm. Trib., SIC 2014, 88 ('Raclette du Valais'); Fed. Trib. SIC 2016, 217 ('Gruyère Tradition'); Fed. Adm. Trib. SIC 2018, 66 ('Bündner Bergkäse').

575. RS 232.119. The former legal empowerment for that Ordinance is no longer valid since 31 Dec. 1991; *see* David, No. 4 *ad* Art. 51 Trademark Act.

576. Ars 1a & 2(1) of the 1971 Ordinance. Art. 2(2) gave some more details about the cost of dials and hands. *See also* the Complementary Agreement of 20 Jul. 1972 Concerning Watch Products between the Swiss Confederation and the European Economic Community (RS 0.632.290.131).

577. RS 817.0. *See* Fed. Trib., SIC 2007, 455 (mentioning that this new Act aims only at protecting consumers, while the Law on Agriculture furthers the quality of Swiss agricultural products, hence the development of their market). The Swissness project as voted into law encompasses agricultural products. The totally new Law on Food Products of 24 Jun. 2014 conforming to the European Regulation 178/2002 entered into force effective 1 May 2017. A treaty of 1999 amended from time to time governs the trade of agricultural goods with the European Union. *See* N. Guyot, *La nouvelle réglementation relative à l'utilisation de mentions du type 'Swiss design' ou 'Swiss research'* (The New Regulations relating to the use of mentions such as 'Swiss Design' or 'Swiss Research'), SIC 2016, 650; D. Stärkle, Die Rechtsdurchsetzung von Swissness durch das IGE und die Verbände im In- und Ausland, Zurich 2018, 81 p. For the situation before entering into force of the

misleading labelling in areas other than the geographic denominations, so that the administrative procedures through the cantonal authorities in charge of applying the Law on Food Products should no longer be of great help to the private parties.

477. Finally, in some cases, the provisions of the Act against Unfair Competition may play an important role in a litigation concerning false or misleading geographic denominations.[579] As – contrary to the new Act – the former Trademark Act did not cover the so-called indirect indications of source,[580] recourse was necessary to the unfair competition legislation. One should also mention an array of federal laws protecting the public Coats of Arms and other Emblems[581] and the Emblems of international organizations such as the Red Cross, the United Nations, etc.[582]

B. International Treaties

1. Multilateral Conventions

478. Switzerland is a party to the Convention of Paris of 1883 as revised most recently in Stockholm on the 14 July 1967.[583]

Swissness legislation see the 'Swiss Military' trademark case, Fed. Adm. Trib. B_850/2016, as summed up in SIC 2019, at 283 (a mark incorporating the Swiss cross is illegal, and this must be taken into account in opposition proceedings).

578. RS 817.02.

579. Art. 3(b) and (d) Unfair Competition Law: 'Shall be deemed to have committed an act of unfair competition, anyone who, in particular: (b) makes incorrect or misleading statements in respect of himself, his undertaking, his trade name, his goods, his works, his services, his prices, his stock or his business circumstances or who, by such statements, favours one party to the detriment of competitors, (d) takes steps that are such as to cause confusion with the goods, works, services or businesses of others.' *See*, e.g., Com. Ct Zurich, SIC 1996, 298 ('Swiss Chocolate Liquor'); ATF 124 II 298 ('Goron' is deceptive for wines stemming from outside Valais); Fed. Trib. 6B_873/2018, SIC 2019, 229 (summary) (declining to decide whether 'Davos sledge' is a geographical denomination or indication as to the type of sledge).

580. For example: Eiffel Tower, Big Ben, Red Square for products purporting to come from France, England, Russia.

581. The Federal Law of 5 Jun. 1931 has been abrogated and superseded by the Law of 21 Jun. 2013 (RS 232.21) following the bill known as the Swissness project. From now on the Swiss cross may be used for marks concerning service providers and manufacturers. Further, the law opens the possibility of registration of cantonal geographic denominations susceptible to be filed as geographical trademarks (e.g., Geneva for watches). For a case under the former law *see* ATF 139 III 424. A grandfathering time limitation of 2 years has expired on 1 Jan. 2019. For agricultural products and foods an Ordinance of 2 Sep. 2015 (RS 232.112.) and an accompanying Ordinance of 15 Nov. 2015 (RS 232.112.11) regulate the geographic denominations.

582. *See* the Federal Law protecting the Emblem and the Name of the Red Cross (RS 232.22) and the Federal Law protecting the Emblems and the Names of the United Nations and other Intergovernmental Organizations (SR 232.23).

583. RS 0.232.04.

479. Further, Switzerland is a party to the Madrid Arrangement Concerning the Repression of the False Indications of Source on Wares of 1891, as revised in Lisbon on 31 October 1958[584] and to the Additional Act of Stockholm of 14 July 1967. Switzerland was originally not a party to the Lisbon Arrangement on Appellations of Origin of 1958 but has adhered to the Geneva Act of the Lisbon Arrangement of 2015, as it has participated in its elaboration as an observer (effective date 1 December 2021). Articles 50c, 50d, 50e and 50f Trademark Act were introduced in 2021, as well as Chapter 6b of the Trademark Ordinance (Article 52p *et seq.*).

480. Moreover, Switzerland is a party to the Stresa Convention of 1 June 1951[585] on the Use of Denominations and Appellations of Origin for Cheese.

481. Finally, Switzerland is a party to the TRIPS Agreement, Articles 22 through 24 which deal with the indications of source generally (Article 22) and for wines and spirits (Articles 23 and 24).[586]

2. Bilateral Treaties

482. Bilateral treaties exist with the Federal Republic of Germany (7 March 1967),[587] the Spanish State (9 April 1974),[588] the French Republic (14 May 1974),[589] and the Socialist Republic of Czechoslovakia (16 November 1973),[590] as well as with Portugal (16 September 1977), Russia (29 April 2010), Jamaïca (23 September 2013) and Georgia (31 May 2018).[591] All these treaties are almost identical in their legal provisions;[592] of course, the appendix enumerating the protected denominations varies with each different party. Single articles on geographic denominations will also be found, for example, in a Convention of 25 November

584. RS 0.232.111.13.
585. RO 1954, 325 et seq. and 612; RO 1973, 1784. RS 0.817.142.1.
586. *See* for a general introduction D. Vivas-Engui & Ch. Spennemann, *The Evolving Regime for Geographical Indications in WTO and in Free Trade Agreements (1996–2015),* in C.M. Correa & A.A. Yusuf, *Intellectual Property and International Trade, The TRIPS Agreement*, (3d. ed., Kluwer, 2015).
587. RO 1969, 538 et seq. This treaty takes the place of Art. 8 of the Convention between Switzerland and Germany on the reciprocal protection of patents, models and trademarks of 13 Apr. 1892 (RO 14, 999 et seq.).
588. RO 1975, 1657; RO 1976, 515.
589. RO 1975, 1657 et seq.
590. RO 1975, 1657 and 2422 et seq. to which two States have succeeded.
591. FF 1978 I 359.
592. The Swiss-German Treaty of 1967 has served as the model for all these conventions (*see* the governmental Message for the Swiss-German Treaty, FF 1968 I 225 *et seq.* and for the three following treaties, FF 1974 II 1178). That model itself had been patterned after the French-German Treaty of 1960. *See* M. Kuhn, *Zum Schutzumfang geographischer Bezeichnungen nach den zweiseitigen Verträgen über den Schutz von Herkunftsangaben* (The Extent of the Protection of Geographic Denominations under Bilateral Contracts about the Protection of Indications of Source), GRUR Int. 1967, 268 et seq.; A. Krieger, *Der deutsch-schweizerische Vertrag über den Schutz von Herkunftsangaben und anderen geographischen Bezeichnungen* (The Swiss-German Treaty about Protection of Indications of Source and Other Geographic Denominations), GRUR Int. 1967, 334 et seq.

1957 on Commerce and Payments with Argentina;[593] a Convention of 25 April 1961, concerning the exportation of Italian wines to Switzerland;[594] and another one of 23 November 1972, on economic exchanges with Bulgaria.[595]

483. Swiss judges have to apply foreign laws and regulations if protection is sought under one of the bilateral treaties concluded with Germany, France, Spain, Czech Republic and Portugal. According to all these conventions, one must distinguish between the legal protections generally afforded to foreign denominations, which is tailored after the law of the source country, and the prohibition of deceit, which calls for exclusive application of the domestic law.[596] Furthermore, the denomination to which foreign wines are entitled in their country of origin is decisive for lawful use within Switzerland, by virtue of Article 4 of the Madrid Arrangement. For all other purposes, the foreign law will be taken into consideration at least as a circumstance of fact,[597] which might be deemed more or less relevant.[598]

II. General Protection of Geographic Denomination

484. The following observations focus on the general protection of indications of source under the Trademark Act.

A. Penal Law

485. Under Article 64 Trademark Act, it is a felony to use intentionally a false indication of source on a product, or to use a denomination which may be taken for an indication of source that would be inexact, or to create a risk of deception through the use of a name, an address or a trademark for products or services of another origin.

B. Civil Law

486. Under Article 55 Trademark Act, any person who is entitled to use an indication of a source may obtain an injunction against the wrongful use of that indication, and information about the providers of wares and goods that wrongfully bear that indication. He has further all claims for monetary damages that are open to a trademark owner.

593. RO 1958, 38, Art. 2.
594. RO 1962, 189, with protocols and amendments in RO 1963, 531; RO 1964, 475; RO 1975, 1893.
595. RO 1973, 598, Art. 5.
596. *See* FF 1968, 235–236.
597. *See* ATF 73 II 133 (State monopoly on French tobacco products).
598. For example, it is of no avail to the petitioner that other countries may have accepted registration of a geographic denomination as a trademark; ATF 89 I 297. Conversely, the validity of a Swiss trademark is decided exclusively by application of Swiss law; *see* S. Vitali, *Champagne (Vaud)*, SIC 2009, 319; F. Dessemontet, *Note under the judgment 'Schaumpagne*r', RSPI 1990, 376.

487. Furthermore, associations of producers[599] and consumers' organizations can file an action for a declaratory judgment or for an injunction.

488. It is interesting to note that the Trademark Act does not define who are the persons entitled to use an indication of source for products. According to the former Act of 1890, only the producers having their production facilities or factories in the location to which the denomination refers or in its immediate surroundings could use that denomination (Article 18(2) Trademark Act). The test was the actual location of the plant where the products are manufactured; it was not enough merely to maintain an office, a legal or fiscal domicile, a sales outlet or a post or railway address.[600]

Now, for services only, the new Trademark Act is more liberal. An indication of source will not be deemed to be inexact whenever the user has his legal seat at the place to which reference is made, or if its officers and effective managers are of the citizenship to which the indication refers, or if they are domiciled there (Article 49(1) Trademark Act).

489. For both products and services, the law sets the rule that if the indication corresponds to trade usages, it is presumed to be correct. It should be noted that the intermediaries of products that are legally marketed under a given indication are entitled to use it in their advertisements, etc., although they are not located in the area to which it refers.

490. Although the question was debated under the former Act,[601] the new Law does not provide an answer to the rather theoretical question about the nature of the right to use a given indication of the source. Is it only a right to claim protection against its wrongful use or misuse by third parties, as is the case under the Act against Unfair Competition?[602] Is it rather a property interest that is an asset of the producer? In our view, there can be no licence of an indication of source, nor a separate assignment, so that it is not really a property interest.

491. Producers who are entitled to a given denomination may insert any and all additions consistent with the truth. However, a third party cannot use an otherwise unjustified denomination with a differentiating addition such as 'type of', 'after the manner of', etc. The former Federal Office for Intellectual Property already held that

599. If their articles of incorporation or by-laws authorize them to protect the economic interests of their members.

600. ATF 89 I 49 (obiter dictum in a trademark case).

601. *See* E.M. Lustenberger, *Die geographischen Herkunftsangaben* (Geographic Indications of Source), thesis, 56–58 (Berne, 1972); Ph. Colelough, *La protection des indications de provenance et des appellations d'origine: étude de droit suisse avec référence aux droits français et allemand et au droit international* (Protection of Indications of Source and Appellations of Origin: Swiss Law Study with Reference to French, German, and International Law), thesis, 133 (Lausanne, 1988); Ph. Journot, *Les indications de provenance et les appellations d'origine des fromages suisses, en particulier le droit au nom Bagnes* (Indications of Source and Appellations of Origin of Swiss Cheeses, especially the Right to the Name 'Bagnes'), thesis, 54 (Lausanne, 1979).

602. *See* F. Dessemontet, *Théorie fonctionnaliste de la concurrence et droits subjectifs* (Functionalist Theory of Concurrence and Subjective Rights), RSDA 1994, 117–119.

view thirty years ago,[603] and the Administration still shares it;[604] some explicit provisions also lay down the same rule.[605] Nevertheless, obiter dicta in old precedents indicate that an addition which is truthful may suffice to evade the repression that is directed towards false geographic denominations.[606] Furthermore, some modern professional codes of conduct allow for such additions.[607] Finally, even the TRIPS Agreement does not prohibit such additions in the most general manner, but only for the wines and spirits, that are subject to a more stringent regulation than usual indications of source.[608]

In this writer's view, the question should be examined from case to case, and the answer may vary according to the more or less general use in the trade of a given denomination in order to indicate a specific type of product. In other words, is the process known as the 'Degeneration into a generic name' already taking place? If yes, the consumers will perfectly understand the addition 'type', and they will not be deceived.

492. According to Article 47(2) Trademark Act, the geographic denominations or signs that are not deemed to indicate the source of a product are not 'indications of source' within the meaning of the law. One of the main cases is whenever a product is designated after the name of a place or country which has become generic, that is indicative of the nature rather than the origin of the product.

The difficulty is to ascertain whether a given denomination has become generic. The burden of proof lies with the person who contends that degeneration has occurred. The test will be the opinion of the average consumer and that of the merchants. Even the existence of a minority opinion among the consuming public is sufficient to prevent degeneration.

For example, in an unpublished case concerning Vaud sausages,[609] between 19% and 26.9% of all polled consumers thought that a given sausage was manufactured only in the Canton of Vaud; this was deemed enough for the court to protect the Vaud manufacturers.

---

603. *See* Informative Note, PMM Bl 1970 I 8, reprinted *in* GRUR Int. 1970, 325.
604. *See* Fed. Department of Public Economy, *Le cycle d'Uruguay du GATT* (The GATT Uruguay Round) No. 2.4.8.3. 223 (French ed., Berne, 24 May 1994); Federal Department of Agriculture, Report on AOC Wines, (Berne, May 2008), Ch. 3.4 (b).
605. Art. 23(1) TRIPS; Art. 3(2) of the Ordinance of 23 Dec. 1971 regulating the use of the mention 'Swiss made' for watches; bilateral treaties with Germany, France, the former Czechoslovakia and Spain. The Swissness legislation has outlawed the use of 'type' etc.
606. ATF 33 I 196; ATF 40 I 298; in both cases that defence was not accepted.
607. *See*, e.g., the Guidelines published by the Swiss Association of Carpet Retailers (RSJ 1970, 367–368), permitting such denominations as 'Swiss Berber', 'Bulgarian Tabriz', 'Rumanian Serabend', 'Macedonian Afghan'.
608. Compare Arts 22 and 23 TRIPS.
609. Just. Ct Geneva, 31 Oct. 1983, Case No. 265, 23, as cited in F. Dessemontet, *'Etude de cas: Le saucisson vaudois'* (Case Study: 'Vaud State Sausage'), *Colloque 'Signes de reconnaissance des produits agricoles et des denrées alimentaires'* (Symposium 'Recognition Signs of Agricultural and Food Products') (Sion, 1995), 42 et seq. The whole legal regime has evolved since the adoption of Ordinances on Appellations of Origins and Geographic Denominations in 2015; *see* RS 232.112.2 and 232.112.21. The main difference between Appellations of Origins (AOP) and Protected Geographic Denominations (IGP) is that for IGP, it is enough that one step in the process of producing the product takes place in the location to which the denomination refers. For AOP the human and

The opinion of the local producers and of the merchants of similar wares will be taken into account only with the utmost caution because they are thought to be prone to use geographic denominations excessively and too broadly, in order to combine the benefit of the locally fabricated products with the fame of the genuine foreign wares.[610] Yet, even when consumers take for granted that a name is a generic one, the court will still look at the evidence on the opinion of the circles of merchants who know better, for example, because they are aware of litigations concerning the denomination.[611] As a rule, Swiss courts are much more cautious in admitting degeneration than foreign courts. The Federal Tribunal protected *Pils,* emphasizing that a geographic denomination must have been used for decades to describe a material quality to be deemed generic; further, the degeneration must be so complete that no regeneration may even be achieved, whatever the advertising endeavours to this end.[612] Such a condition is hard to meet, considering that even the *Havana* cigars, at the turn of the century undoubtedly a generic denomination, were found later by a Zurich court to have to be made out of Havana tobaccos.[613] Some other examples of regeneration may be found in the literature[614] and some

geographic factors of production are mainly responsible for the quality or characteristics of the product, while for IGP the location connotes a quality or a reputation through the use of the traditional denomination. Those two regimes parallel the different norms of Art. 47 *et seq.* Trademark Act that tend to protect the truthfulness of the reference to a specific geographic denomination. One of the main legal safeguards relates to the proportion of the constitutive elements coming from the location to which the denomination refers, directly or indirectly. For food products those proportions are regulated in the Ordinance of 2 Sep. 2015 (RS 232.112.1). For example, water is usually excluded from the requirement that most elements of the product stem from the location referenced (Art. 3 (3) Ord.). For milk and milk products 100% of the milk must come from Switzerland. For other food products the usual rule is 80%, with specific rules for meat, venison, fish etc. For industrial products the proportion is 60% of the elements as assessed by their share in the costs of manufacturing.

610. *See* Fed. Trib. *in re* Holiday Pils, *in* PMM Bl 1970 I 8, *in* GRUR Int. 1971, 26, *in* RSPIDA 1974, 142, esp. 148, and *in* PMM Bl 1974 I 11.
611. ATF 40 I 298; ATF 60 II 249 (*'Bel Paese'*, a trademark case); Fed. Trib. *in* RSPIDA 1974, 142, esp. 147. For a recent trademark degeneration into public domain, *see* ATF 131 II 121 (*'Eile mit Weile'*).
612. Fed. Trib. *in* RSPIDA 1974, 142, ATF 114 II 171; *see also* ATF 96 II 243 and ATF 93 II 260. *See* ATF 125 III 193: the American brewer Anheuser-Busch is not allowed to sell its bier '*Budweiser*' into Switzerland, because his name is similar to the Czech bier 'Budweiser Budvar' and 'Budbräu'. Other European courts decided in favour of the American producer.
613. Com. Ct Zurich *in* ZR 1924, 235; *see before* Berker, *GRUR* (1922), 127 for the change of mind of the consumers.
614. *See Propriété industrielle* 150 (Indus. Prop. 1937); Com. Ct Zurich in ZR 1937, 175 (Old Cologne). For example, the Convention with Germany excluded the denomination *Kölnisch Wasser* from the public domain where it belonged for decades in Switzerland – in order to keep it for use by the German producers only. The Convention has had the same questionable effect on the denomination *Steinhäger*, for which, however, an extended transition period of twelve years has been foreseen, so as to allow the legitimate users of that then free denomination to continue using it.

others resulted from the signature of bilateral treaties.[615] Even within the last few years, an effort has been made to regenerate such names as 'Gruyère' and 'Bagnes' for cheese.[616]

C. Relation to the Registration of Trademarks

1. Registration of a Trademark Containing Geographic Elements

493. As a rule, Swiss geographic names pertain to the public domain; hence, they may not be registered as trademarks.[617] The same applies to foreign geographic denominations under the Paris Convention.[618] There are, however, important exceptions to the rule. First of all, a geographic name may be registered whenever it is obvious that no allusion is made thereby to the place of production or manufacture.[619] Furthermore, the Federal Tribunal admits the registration of geographic names even if, within the locality referred to, it is not absolutely impossible to establish a factory, so long as it is believed by the judges that most customers either ignore the name of the village or town, or know the location well enough to brush aside the idea that such production facilities would be found there.[620] It would even be possible to register as a trademark the name of a town of some importance, provided that this name was not reputed for the manufacture of the items on which

615. Under the Convention with Germany, *eau de Cologne* and *Acqua di Colonia* are not considered a protected denomination but a generic denomination. This exception to protection is to be strictly construed; *in re* Parfumerie Gal SA (*Colonia aneja* is not a registrable mark), Fed. Trib. *in* RSPIDA 1977, 65: *Frankfurter Würstchen* is protected, but not *Frankfurterli, saucisse de Francfort, salsiccia di Francoforte; Selters* is protected, but not *Selterswasser. See* FF 1968 I 234. Under the Convention with Spain, the denomination *Gruyère* for cheese is protected in Spain (Ch. 10 of the Protocol to the Convention), RO 1976, 524; however, only until the ratification by Spain of the Stresa Convention of 1951.

616. *See* the Colloque of Sion here above n. 1 and the steps taken with the Federal Government for the protection of Gruyère under Art. 18c Law on Agriculture (hereabove Nos 482–484). For recent cases with many citations *see* Fed. Trib., SIC 2011, 176 ('*Försterkäse III*'); Fed. Trib. SIC 2012, 399 ('*Alpenkäse*), ATF 138 II 134 (where the cheese producers use a Protected Geographic Denomination under the aegis of the Intercantonal Authority for Certification, public law regulates their relationship); Fed. Trib. SIC 2016, 217 (no milk from the Canton of Berne is allowed to enter into the manufacturing of the *Gruyere* cheese).

617. Art. 2 Trademark Act; David, 31, *ad* Art. 2 Trademark Act; Matter, *Kommentar zum Bundesgesetz betreffend den Schutz der Fabrik- und Handelsmarken, der Herkunftsbezeichnungen von Waren und der gewerblichen Auszeichnungen* (Commentary of the Federal Law Concerning the Protection of Trademarks, Geographic Denominations and Mentions of Industrial Awards) 175 (Zurich, 1939). *See* ATF 117 II 327.

618. Art. 6 *quinquies* (B).

619. *See* David, 32, *ad* Art. 2 Trademark Act; A. Troller, 333. Examples: 'Diablerets' for bitters, 'Greenland' for wool, 'Congo' for shoe polish, 'North Pole' for ice cream, 'Bernina' for sewing machines, 'Mont Blanc' (ATF 91 I 50) and 'Mont Cervin' for fountain pens, 'Pilatus' and 'Rigi' for cheese. ATF 128 III 454 (Yukon) (commented by Appel. Ct, SIC 2007, 211, 213). Another example is the geographic name that will be understood as reference to a legend rather than to an existing location (Argos), e.g., Phoenix understood as a mythical bird rather than the city of the same name in Arizona; Fed. Adm Trib. SIC 2014, 707 at 710; 'Rilke' understood as a reference to Valais.

620. ATF 79 II 98.

the trademark would be affixed.[621] The practice of the Registrar had been more severe than the Federal Tribunal's recent jurisprudence; the Registrar allowed until January 2022 the registration of a geographic denomination as a trademark only when the products for which the mark is filed, actually came from the location described.[622] The prior ruling of our Supreme Court had attracted deserved criticism.[623] First, who is apt to decide if even a Swiss locality is really unknown to the Swiss public? Moreover, the tests set out in the decided cases are rather fuzzy. Finally, the unsatisfactory consequences of the registration would be that no other person would be able to use that name for similar products, even if his production facilities were located in the town or hamlet concerned.[624] Hence, it would be better altogether not to register the names of Swiss localities in which a plant or other production facilities may be thought to exist, even if only by a few Swiss residents.[625] It remains to be seen how the newly-announced liberal practice of the Registrar will really affect the registration of geographic trademarks and the ensuing case law.

494. For geographic names already registered abroad, it has been submitted that they should be registered in Switzerland under an extended construction of the *telle-quelle* requirement of the Paris Convention. The opinion of the Swiss retailers and consumers would henceforth be irrelevant,[626] except if the trademark were deceptive as to the source of the products.[627] However, this opinion on an extended *telle-quelle* registration is now contrary to the view of the Federal Tribunal.[628] If such

621. ATF 81 I 298 ('Bernex'). This decision draws no distinction between Swiss and foreign geographic names when registration is applied for under Art. 6 *quinquies* (B) Paris Convention. *See* for 'Reno' Fed. Adm. Trib. SIC 2017, 383 (a location that is not known by most people in Switzerland may be registered as mark).
622. *See* Swiss Institute of Intellectual, Newsletter 5/2021 of 21 Sep. 2021 announcing the liberalization of the registration practice, commented by A. Stanisavljevic & S. Keehnen, SIC 2022, 3 et seq.
623. *See* A. Troller, 331 et seq. (for the looser conceptions of old, *see* Bretscher, *Der Schutz geographischer Herkunftsbezeichnungen* (Protection of Geographic Indications of Source), thesis (Zurich, 1931), 100 et seq.).
624. ATF 55 I 262 (Tunbridge Wells); ATF 59 II 207 (Tavannes); ATF 77 II 321 ('Sihl' and 'Lonza'); ATF 82 II 346 ('Weissenburg'); ATF 100 Ib 351 ('Haacht'). In the event that use of the trademark gives, down the years, some renown to the location of such products, A. Troller, 335–336 appeared to consider that if a producer (other than the trademark owner) started manufacturing at the location referred to by the mark, use of the trademark would remain permissible; except, in the event that the mark be confusing or misleading, would it become invalid. However accurate in equity, these observations do seem to be at odds with the cases *cited above*. In favour of Troller's opinion, *see* an older case: ATF 38 II 693. *See also* Jaton, *La répression des fausses indications de provenance et les conventions internationales* (The Repression of False Indications of Source and International Conventions), thesis, 17–18 (Berne, 1926), who thinks that no producer located elsewhere may lawfully use a geographic denomination as soon as a local manufacturer starts production.
625. A. Troller, 334–335.
626. ATF 100 Ib 351 ('Haacht'); A. Troller 331–332.
627. ATF 89 I 298 ('Florida'); ATF 91 I 50 ('Monte Bianco'); ATF 95 I 472 ('Slivowitz Herzegovina'); ATF 96 I 251 ('Pussta Senf'). The same opinion prevails under the new Swissness legislation, *see* N. Guyot/S. Khalès, *La conformité des indications de provenance étrangères* … (Conformity of foreign denominations of origin …), SIC 2018, 3.
628. Fed. Trib. *in* RSPIDA 1977, 65 ('Colonia Aneja').

foreign denominations are not registered as trademarks abroad, the Swiss authorities may more freely examine if registration is feasible. Notably, for tobacco products, they have to take into account the fact that geographic marks will often be understood as indications of source.[629] The mere possibility of a misleading reference to a definite country, through the association of ideas, is enough to bar registration.[630] For both Swiss and foreign denominations, registration may be allowed if, after long and constant use, a name has come to distinguish a sole producer so as to give distinctive value to the name when utilized in connection with the products or wares of that producer.[631] The same holds true if the locality referred to is wholly owned by the producer who applies for registration,[632] or if he enjoys a statutory monopoly on given products stemming therefrom.[633] Finally, apparent geographic denominations which actually are contrived by the registrant (e.g., *Vineta*) are valid trademarks when not misleading about the source of the product.[634]

2. Geographic Denominations as Collective Trademarks

495. It is possible to protect geographic denominations as part of collective trademarks, according to an old practice[635] and the rare literature on that topic.[636] The protection will be subject to the requirements that have been expounded above for individual trademarks containing geographic elements. For example, it would be illegal to monopolize general geographic terms in favour of the sole producers entitled to use collective trademarks, to the extent that other producers who were also located in this area or might be later located in this area, would not be able to use that name. The practice doubtlessly favours collective marks which consist of

629. ATF 89 I 290 ('Dorset' and 'La Guardia'); ATF 93 I 570 ('Trafalgar'); Fed. Trib. *in* RSPIDA 1964, 122 ('Matterhorn').
630. ATF 56 I 469 ('Kremlin'), for oil not imported from Russia; ATF 72 I 238 ('Fifth Avenue' ATF 79 I 252 ('Schweizer Gruss') for German roses; ATF 89 I 298 ('Florida'), registered only for fruit juices from the US; ATF 97 I 79 ('Cusco'); Fed. Trib. *in* RSPIDA 1977, 65 ('Colonia Aneja'). For a further exception *see* e.g., Fed. Trib. SIC 2016, 212 ('Indian Motorcycle').
631. ATF 55 I 262 ('Tunbridge Wells'); ATF 59 II 207 ('Tavannes'); ATF 77 II 321 ('Sihl' and 'Lonza'); ATF 82 II 346 ('Weissenburg'); ATF 100 Ib 351 ('Haacht').
632. ATF 72 I 238; ATF 73 II 126; *See* Geisser, *Die Weinbezeichnungen* (The Denomination of Wines), thesis (Freiburg, 1968), 74; A. Troller, 332.
633. '*Cigarettes françaises*' is a valid trademark when the registrant is the company entitled to the tobacco monopoly in France. ATF 73 II 126. A factual monopoly may suffice; Fed. Trib. SIC 2017, 282 ('Meissen').
634. David, 32 *ad* Art. 2 Trademark Act.
635. For example: a collective trademark of March 1935, figuring a rose with the words '*quinzaine genevoise*'; a collective trademark of May 1935, '*Maison genevoise*'; a collective trademark with the Lausanne castle and the words '*produits du sol vaudois, société coopérative*'. *See* J-D Pahud, *La Marque Collective* (Collective Trademark) 88–89 (Lausanne, 1940).
636. Pahud, *La marque collective* (Collective Trademark) 40 (Lausanne, 1940). *See also* C. Maradan, *La marque de garantie au secours des indications de provenance suisses (*The certification mark to help Swiss geographic denominations), SIC 2005, 4; V. Piaget, *Les signes dotés d'un effet 'presque distinctif' (*Marks that are 'almost distinctive'), SIC 2007, 255.

original figurative or verbal elements, such as the collective mark *Viti* for good Tessin wines,[637] or the crossbow for Swiss-manufactured wares.[638]

§12. Domain Names

I. Definition

496. The domain names on Internet are both identifications of the computer hooked to the Net and addresses to which a person or a legal entity may be reached.

497. Domain names are for mnemotechnical reasons expressed in words, although the actual identification of the computer is made through a series of numbers.

498. The identification is not arbitrary, to the extent that the registrant of a domain name intends to be recognized by everyone already doing business or having contacts with him under his or her usual business name.

499. Further, the identification may give information (clear or computer-readable only) on the area of business.[639] It is obvious that advertising considerations are never far away when choosing a domain name, would it be only to ensure a uniform image of the business among its consumers.

II. Source

500. The Swiss law contains no specific provision about Internet domain names (or Internet commerce generally), except for an Ordinance of 2014.[640] Therefore, two general provisions of the Act against Unfair Competition shall apply:

---

637. 'Viti' is really an abbreviation for Vini Ticinesi, but probably does not convey that generic meaning to most consumers outside Tessin.
638. Collective trademark of May 1931.
639. For hidden indication legible by research engines only, *see* the US cases *Playboy v. Calvin Design Label* and the case 'Estelle Lauder' as cited in Yasmine Kaplun, *Marques et noms de domaine* (Trademarks and Domain Names), www.club-internet.fr/cyberlexnet/COM/A971205.htm and E. Wery, *Marques protégées et metatags* (Protected Trademarks and Metatags), www.droittechnologie.org. A case alludes to ad words on Google but mainly holds that some descriptive elements must remain in the public domain and cannot be made the subject matter of an exclusionary right under the guise of the protection of domain names; Cant. Ct Zurich, SIC 2013, 612, '*www.Comparis.ch*' *v.* '*www.Comparez.ch*'.
640. The Confederation has delegated the role of central registrar of Swiss domain names to SWITCH, a Company based in Zurich. Now other registrars are also certified to accept Swiss domain names. A specific variant of the URDP, with partly different rules, applies since 2004 to the cybersquatting of domain names ending in .ch and .li. (Rules of procedure for Dispute Resolution Proceedings for .ch and .li Domain Names, as revised in 2020 in accordance with the Swiss Ordinance on Internet Domains of 2014/ RS 784.104.2). The Disputes are first settled by the WIPO Centre for Arbitration and Mediation, and civil proceedings may be filed with the Zurich courts. For public law concerning the registration of domain names, *see* also Arts 28–30 Act on Telecommunications of 30 Apr.

(1) Article 3(d) UCA prohibits any and all measures that are apt to give rise to a confusion with the wares and goods, works, services or business of another person. Thus, any passing-off in any regard whatsoever is unlawful, under this provision. Of course, domain name grabbing (cybersquatting) is wrongful under Article 3(d) Unfair Competition Law.[641] Other conflicts may be harder to solve.[642] Since 1986, the Act against Unfair Competition does not require that the claimant and the defendant be competitors. It still requires that there be a market for goods and services and that the market be somehow impacted by the behaviour of the defendant. This prerequisite should be met in most cases of domain name piracy. If not, a second legislation will apply, to wit:

(2) Articles 29 and 28 Civil Code, which protect the name and the personal interests of the rightful user of a given name. Legal entities might benefit from that protection as well as human beings.[643]

1997, as amended (RS 784.10); for the private law of contracting on the Internet, which is not entirely codified yet, *see* e.g., F. Dessemontet, *Licensing and Contracting on the Net*, in *Festskrift Gunnar Karnell* 111 et seq. (Stockholm, 1999); *see also* F. Dessemontet, *La dématérialisation des conventions* (The Dematerialization of Conventions), PJA 1996, 939. *See* now the new Art. 3(s) UCA, FF 2011, 4575 requiring among others a clear identification of the name and address of the seller in e-commerce, as well clear explanations concerning the process of concluding a e-contract and of verifying the order for purchase, finally an immediate confirmation of the order.

641. Domain name grabbing is the registration by a third party of a name which is well-known as trade name or trademark, often in order to sell it to the true holder of the name or mark against consideration. *See* R. Weber, *Schutz von Domänennamen in Internet* (Protection of Domain Names on Internet), RSJ 1996, 408 (UCA applicable). *See* now for the application of Art. 3d of the Act against Unfair Competition ATF 126 III 239 ('berneroberland.ch'). In this regard, it has not been possible to follow I. Cherpillod, *Droit des marques et Internet* (Trademark Law and Internet), SIC 1997, 123, when he argued that any and everything which is possible under the Trademark Act cannot be prohibited under the Law against Unfair Competition. *See contra* Fed. Trib. SIC 2009, 793 cons. 4.1 ('Maltesers'); ATF 92 II 257; ATF 95 II 191 and 461; ATF 96 II 400; ATF 107 II 356. I. Cherpillod, *Le droit suisse des marques* (Swiss Law on Trademarks) 258 (Lausanne, 2007), presently admits the application of the UCA in cybersquatting cases. *See also* Sup. Ct Thurgau, SIC 2002, 612 and 683; ATF 135 III 446 (c. 4 unpublished, but referenced in Fed. Trib. SIC 2018, 162 at 164) (cases on the unlimited application of special legislation and UCA).

642. Further in an exceptional case, Art. 2 UCA might apply (general prohibition of unfair competition). The costs of the URDP proceedings are a financial harm inflicted on the rightful trademark owner, who can claim them back from the respondent under Art. 41 CO; see Dist. Ct. Baden, SIC 2019, 448 ('*migros.blog*').

643. ATF 128 III 401 ('*Luzern.ch*'); ATF 128 III 250 '(*Montana.ch*'); Fed. Trib., SIC 2003, 438; 2006, 481. For the possibility of legal entities to invoke the protection of Arts 28 and 29 Civ. Code, *see* F. Dessemontet, *La presse et les sociétés commerciales* (Press and Business Companies), in *Die Verantwortlichkeit im Recht* (Liability in Law), 186 et seq. (Zurich, 1981); for cases, *see*, e.g., ATF 72 II 380; ATF 77 II 321; ATF 80 II 281; ATF 91 II 17; Appel. Ct Lucerne, *in* RSPI 1988, 100 (Art. 29 Civil Code and the UCA are cumulatively applicable); Com. Ct Berne, *in* RSPI 1988, 238; Just. Ct Geneva, *in* RSPI 1988, 151; Com. Ct St-Gall, *in* RSPI 1988, 223; Just. Ct Geneva, *in* RSPI 1988, 97.

III. Protection of Domain Names

501. Obviously, domain names are not trademarks and cannot be protected as such if they are not registered as trademarks.[644] If they are, the use of similar names for similar services or products may be an infringement under the Trademark Act.

502. Domain names are not necessarily registered trade names, and they will not be protected as trade names under Article 956 Code of Obligations without registration.[645]

503. The use of a domain name is a use in 'business life' according to the Federal Tribunal.[646]

504. Domain names are, in my view, business names; that is, identifications of their user in the course of ordinary business transactions, and as such, they are protected under the Act against Unfair Competition and/or Articles 29 and 28 Civil Code.

505. Between domain names, the priority of the first registrant is technically ensured by the registration system to the extent that the names are absolutely identical, since they are the identification of one computer only (or an internetwork of computers).

However, as soon as there is a slight modification (e.g., concerning the Top Level Domain Names),[647] there is no automatic protection. Hence, the legal protection may take place on the basis of territoriality and priority in time – and to some extent of the speciality principle. In other words, the first to register a domain name in a given country with the Top level of that country, for example, ch for Switzerland, will be able to protect it against a second applicant. There is no possible conflict between the first registration and the first use within the same territory for identical addresses. For slightly modified addresses (say: 'amazon.ch'), there may be a difficult question to solve: was the use in Switzerland of the domain name registered elsewhere (say: 'amazon.com') sufficient to afford protection to the foreign registrant?

506. There are some cases defining what is 'use within Switzerland' for the purpose of the protection of foreign trade names, and they apply to foreign domain names.[648] It is possible that foreign public entities could not claim rights under the

644. ATF 125 III 91 (*Rytz*); Fed. Trib., SIC 2005, 200; SIC 2005, 390 (*maggi.com*); *see further* F. Thomann, *Kennzeichnungs- und Wettbewerbsrechtliche Aspekte der Internet-Domänennamen* (Aspects of Mark and Competition Law for Internet Domain Names), in *Le droit au défi d'Internet* (Law Challenged by Internet) 46, 48 (Genève, 1997).

645. *See* paras. 543 *et seq.*

646. SIC 2005, 200; *see also* Sup. Ct BL, SIC 2000, 26 (*hotmail.ch*).

647. Top Level Domain Names indicate a country or a type of organization, such as '.ch' or '.com'.

648. For Internet in particular, *see* Fed. Trib., 4A_510/2018 ('dekton')(use of trade names on a webpage that introduces the enterprise is 'use' as trade names); Fed. Trib. SIC 2007, 543 (*la-suisse.com*); ATF 76 II 77; ATF 90 II 192; ATF 98 II 57 and 67; ATF 109 II 483 (*Computerland*); Fed. Trib. *in*

Paris Convention.[649] It is this writer's view that the mere possibility of connecting to a foreign address is not a 'use' within these cases. However, if there is a geo-targeting towards Switzerland, or if effective connections to an extent commensurate with the sort of business made on the Internet can be proved (and technically, it is mostly possible to prove them), then there is a 'use' sufficient to justify the protection of foreign domain names. The need for protection is not only to be appraised in view of the private interests at issue but also with regard to the consumers or dealers who could be misled by a deceptively close domain name (e.g., 'amazone.com').

507. For very well-known domain names, the use in Switzerland may not be necessary, according to several cases that are applicable *per analogiam.*[650] The well-known character of a domain name may derive from its identity or similarity with a trademark. World-known trademarks are therefore protected against a Swiss national or Swiss resident who would register them.[651]

IV. Protection of Trademarks and Trade Names Against Domain Names

508. The general principle regulating the exclusive rights of owners of trademarks, trade names, logos, shop signs, etc., as regards the signs of another category infringing on their business values is the priority in time.

509. It is settled law that it is an act of unfair competition to use a distinctive sign, for example, a trade name, against the better rights of a prior trademark owner,[652] even when the Trademark Act offers no remedy. The same principle would seem to apply to someone who would use a posterior domain name against the better rights of a prior trademark owner, or trade name prior user.[653]

510. The main exception to that principle derives from the limited ambit of the priority principle: it covers only the area in which the prior registrant or prior user has been actually active. If the persons or legal entities prior in time extend their activities to new business, they will not be protected as of right; they may even have to prevent confusion and passing-off in those new areas through modification of

RSPI 1990, 327 (*Cebit*); cf. also Just. Ct Geneva *in* RSPIDA 1983, 120; Fed. Trib. and Com. Ct St-Gall *in* RSPIDA 1984, 189; Cant. Ct Vaud *in* RSPI 1987, 246, and *in* RSPI 1987, 259; Just. Ct Geneva *in* RSPI 1988, 104.

649. *See* Cant. Ct Neuchâtel in RSJ 1960, 174 (at least where foreign public entities claim under the rights of local foreign producers).

650. ATF 109 II 483 ('Computerland'); Fed. Trib. *in* RSPI 1990, 327 ('Cebit').

651. *See* I. Cherpillod, '*Droit des marques et Internet*' (Trademark Law and the Internet), SIC 1997, 122.

652. ATF 107 II 356. *See also* Fed. Trib. SIC 2013, 360 (*Pneus-Online II*), awarding an important disgorgement of profits for a very small percentage of effective confusions among clients.

653. *See* ATF 125 III 91 (*e contrario*).

their trade name.[654] Nevertheless, in itself, the use of Internet is not a new area within the meaning of case law, if the goods sold or the services offered are the same as those were sold or offered through the traditional channels.

654. ATF 85 II 323; Fed. Trib. SIC 2016, 207 ('*Von Roll Hydro*').

Chapter 5. Trade Names

§1. Source of Legislation

I. The Code of Obligations

511. Articles 944–956 Code of Obligations regulate the registration and protection of trade names. The revision of 25 September 2015 has considerably changed the former rules on the formation of trade names, especially for companies limited by shares, as well as the protection of all trade names (RO 2015, 3631). Prior literature should be consulted with caution.

II. Articles 26–28 of the Ordinance on the Register of Commerce

512. Article 28 of the Ordinance on the Register of Commerce, as revised on 17 October 2007,[655] sets out the precise framework for the administrative examination to be conducted before registering a trade name or a company name. As the Ordinance considerably modifies the existing law to adopt a more liberal practice, literature and cases that are anterior to 2008 should also be consulted with caution.

III. The Act Against Unfair Competition and the Civil Code

513. The Act against Unfair Competition may protect trade names if the Code of Obligations does not apply. In exceptional cases, the protection of personal interests under Articles 28 and 29 of the Civil Code may also find application, as these provisions extend the legal protection to legal entities as well as to physical persons.

§2. The Selection of Trade Names

514. Two sets of rules apply: the general principles that are laid down for all trade names, and the specific rules that apply only to given partnerships and companies.

I. Area of Application

515. The rules applicable to the trade names are not as such applicable to the associations of the Civil Code or to the foundations, even if they have to be registered in the Register of Commerce.[656] The associations and foundations may only benefit from the protection of Article 29 Swiss Civil Code (or from that of Article

655. RS 221.411, hereinafter 'ORC'.
656. For example, ATF 102 II 161; ATF 103 Ib 6.

28 Civil Code). Nonetheless, if they are applying for registration, their name and the other details of their registration must conform to the basic requirement of Article 28 ORC.[657]

516. The Swiss legislation does not directly bear on trade names as they are used in practice, for example, under a shorter form, to characterize an economic entity. Rather, the Code of Obligations and the Ordinance aim at regulating the registered business name of an individual firm or company. The protection of commercially used names that are not registered or that are used under an abbreviated form depends mainly on the Act against Unfair Competition. Under the new Article 954*a* (Code of Obligations), the registered business name shall be used in full and without modification in business papers, such as invoices, letters, ordering forms and communications by the company. Logos, shop signs, abbreviations may be added there.

II. Truthfulness

517. Although a business may freely select the fantasy or descriptive part of their trade name, they have to give indications that are true and in no way misleading, nor otherwise contrary to the public interest (Article 944(1) Code of Obligations).

518. The truthfulness requirement implies that the business name has to mention *important facts*. For example, the sole owner of a business has to take as the main element of the registered business name his or her family name, with or without a first name, with or without indications as to his or her products or services (Article 945(1) and (2) Code of Obligations).[658]

Formerly, all companies that used the names of persons and only those companies had to indicate which incorporation they chose ('Company limited by shares' ('S.A.'; 'AG'), 'company with limited responsibility' ('Sàrl'; 'GmbH'), or 'Coopérative'), etc. This rule was extended to all commercial companies and cooperatives in 2015 (Article 950 (1)).

657. *See* hereinafter 'para. 518'; for cases, *see* ATF 116 II 605; Fed. Trib. *in* RSPI 1986, 299 (deceptive name of an association).

658. If law firms that are not incorporated are deemed to be individual entities within the meaning of Art. 945 Code of Obligations, these rules apply also to law firms. Therefore, the name of a former lawyer should be left out when he retires, but it could, however, still be used if this name has been registered as a trademark. Law firms that are incorporated (usually now as a commercial Company limited by shares or otherwise) follow the rules applicable to the type of company, that is they are free to select their name, be it even that of a defunct partner or a letter, a figure etc. This name will remain as long as it wished by the entity.

519. Those facts that are required may be expressed in any of the national languages, and in a foreign language to the extent that the Registrar can verify the accurateness of the meaning on the basis of a notary public's document, even if the phonetic transcription from a foreign language is necessary, as is the case with Arabic, Hebrew, Japanese, Russian, etc.[659]

520. The business name should avoid everything which may be *deceptive*. It would, for example, be misleading for the public if someone used the name of another person which is at the same time a well-known trademark, although his or her business has no ties with the trademark owner.[660]

521. Formerly, the courts derived from that requirement that no puffing element should be admitted in a business name.[661] To the extent that deceptive indications are concerned, those cases are still good law.[662] However, first the practice of registration had been modified,[663] then the Law in 2015 as well as the Ordinance in 1997, 2007 and 2015, so that some elements will now be admitted, such as 'Excellence', etc. However, such elements may not be claimed to the exclusion of third parties, who may also introduce them in their business names.[664]

III. Public Interests

522. Beside the requirement to be truthful, Article 944 Code of Obligations enhances the public interest to protect consumers, business partners and authorities against any difficulty due to a misleading or a too clever selection of a registered business name. It is, for example, not allowed to choose a trade name which connotes that the business is active in an area in which diplomas and federal or cantonal authorizations are necessary to carry on business, where no such diploma or authorization exists in the particular case.[665] Further, no connotation should arise

659. ATF 106 II 58.

660. For example, 'Daimler' for an automotive spare parts dealer; Com. Ct Berne *in* RSPIDA 1981, 67. *See*, however, for the rule that no shareholder can be barred from using his name in his company's name: Com. Ct St-Gall *in* RSPI 1990, 331 and Com. Ct Zurich *in* RSPI 1990, 49 (but an addition shall ensure that the public is not misled). For the general rule that no trade name may be used in a deceptive way, *see also* Art. 326*ter* Swiss Penal Code in force since 1 Jan. 2008 (RO 2007, 4838), abrogating the Federal Law of 6 Oct. 1923 on the criminal repression of the misleading use of trade names and other denominations registered in the Register of Commerce.

661. Were not authorized, *e.g.*: 'American Automobile Service', ATF 91 I 212; 'International Bank of Berne', ATF 95 I 276; 'Centre romand du leasing', ATF 96 I 606; 'Pars-Oriental AG Zürich', ATF 104 Ib 264; 'Eur-Control Industries S.A.' for a trading company, Fed. Trib. *in* RSPI 1986, 288; 'Registered Trust Co' where the company does not own an authorization to practise as fiduciary, necessary under the Liechtenstein Law, Supreme Court Liechtenstein *in* RSPI 1988, 85; 'Liquidationsposten AG' for a company that does not organize special close-out sales, Fred. Trib. *in* RSPI 1986, 290.

662. ATF 117 II 192.

663. *See* M.K. Eckert, *Jahrbuch Handelsregister,* 212 (Y.B. Reg. Com.1994).

664. *See* Fed. Trib. *in* SIC 1998, 41, esp. 45.

665. *See* ATF 65 I 269; ATF 100 Ib 345; ATF 102 IV 263; *per analogiam* ATF 113 II 280 ('Dr h.c.' for an academic grade).

with an international organization,[666] or a national and cantonal public administration or authority, or a religious community.[667] The impression that raises a possibly misleading business name might, however, be mitigated by the fact that any interested person will have to know the address of the business in order to reach it, as is the case in distance-selling.[668]

523. During some twenty years, the case law was to the effect that the generic terms should not form the main element of a registered business name.[669] Even during that period, some combinations of two or several descriptive elements were acceptable to the courts.[670] The recent practice has come back to the point where more freedom is allowed in that regard.[671] Nevertheless, some bizarre limitations may subsist.[672]

524. If a business name has been wrongly registered, although it should have been deemed contrary to the public interest, then it can be stricken out by the order of the competent authority.[673]

IV. Interest of Third Parties

525. At the stage of selecting a business name, the rights of third parties should be ascertained through an enquiry at the Federal Register of Commerce. The rule is that the Registrar will not reject an application for registration unless it is absolutely identical to another registered business name.[674] Nevertheless, Article 951 Code of Obligations provides that the business name of a company limited by shares must be different from any other registered business name, which is not such an easy task since there were 686,856 firms in Switzerland that were registered in the Register of Commerce on 22 September 2021. Another 471,875 entities were registered under the Identification Schemes of enterprises. The procedure for the opponent to prevent the registration of too similar a business name is by way of a petition for an

666. ATF 105 II 135.
667. ATF 77 I 158.
668. ATF 108 II 130; no indication of place should be accepted if not true: ATF 113 II 73.
669. *See* ATF 101 Ib 361; (*contra*: ATF 100 II 224); further *see* Just. Ct Geneva *in* RSPIDA 1980, 185 ('Transcontainer' not allowed); Supreme Court Liechtenstein *in* RSPIDA 1981, 104 ('Bauchemie' is too generic); Com. Ct Zurich *in* RSPIDA 1982, 168 ('Justitia' is allowed [a curious decision]).
670. ATF 107 II 246 ('Index Management'); ATF 109 II 483 ('Computerland'); Com. Ct Zurich *in* RSPIDA 1984, 114 et seq. ('Interhotel').
671. The case law and the Federal Office have changed the practice from 1991 onwards. *See* Fed. Trib. SIC 1998, 415.
672. *See* ATF 118 II 319 ('MacCooperative' not permissible [a doubtful decision]).
673. ATF 105 II 135, esp. 141–142. For the observation that many very similar trade names are to be found in the real world, *see* ATF 125 III 91, 94. The courts do not hesitate to admit of a risk of confusion when two company names are extremely similar even where they are active in two different areas; e.g., Fed. Trib. SIC 2019, 436 ('Riverlake' active in oil transportation vs. 'RiverLake Capital AG' active in the financial sector).
674. *See* A. Meier-Hayoz & P. Forstmoser, *Schweizerisches Gesellschaftsrecht*, s. 7 120 (10th ed., Berne, 2007).

interim order of the court that will then have cognizance of the litigation – the said interim order barring the registration up to the judgment.

If there is prima facie no likelihood of confusion, the interim order will most probably not be issued, so that the second business name will be registered; nevertheless, the final judgment may still order the losing second registrant to request the striking-out of the registered name, and/or the registration of a modified name, for example, with additions that prevent all risks of passing-off.[675]

526. The substantive rights of third parties are now to be expounded in more detail.

§3. The Protection of Trade Names

I. Protection of Registered Business Names

A. *Specific Protection*

527. Under Article 956 Code of Obligations, the registered business name of an individual business owner, and that of a partnership or a company of any kind is for the exclusive use of the registered owner, partnership or company as soon as the registration has been published.

528. Various trade names are therefore not protected under Article 956 Code of Obligations:

- names of associations, foundations and public organizations;
- names of foreign business owners or companies that are not registered in Switzerland;
- shop signs and abbreviated logos, acronyms, etc.;
- domain names on the Internet.

The Act against Unfair Competition and the Civil Code may provide for the protection of those names.[676]

675. According to Com. Ct Zurich (unique judge) *in* RSPI 1986, 105; Com. Ct Zurich *in* RSPI 1988, 170; Fed. Trib. *in* RSPIDA 1973, 187, esp. 192: the court should not address its order for striking-out to the Office of the Register of Commerce, but should order the defendant to request himself the striking-out.

676. *See* Art. 3(b) and (d) UCA as cited *supra* n. 548 and Arts 28 and 29 Civil Code.

B. Exclusive Use

529. The territorial exclusivity of use extends to the whole of Switzerland for the registered name of companies limited by shares and cooperatives, as well as for the companies with limited liability (and only those) that do not include the name of a person in their registered name.[677]

530. Article 956 Code of Obligations protects against the use by a third party using the same name, or a confusingly similar name, *as a trade name*, in business transactions, advertising, etc.[678] The use of a delivery truck has been judged, however, not to be such use as a trade name.[679]

C. Distinctive Elements

531. The risk of passing-off is adjudicated only on the basis of the distinctive elements of the registered trade name. A distinction in the indications concerning the legal form (partnership, company, cooperative) is not relevant,[680] nor is the distinction due to different locations for the seat of the two interested entities.[681]

532. The relevant elements are compared to each other. If they are identical, the risk of confusion is certain. If not, a comparison will take place:

- a grammatical analysis will determine how many syllables are involved, the visual impression remaining in the memory of the addressees being decisive;[682]

677. The German text of Art. 951(2) Code of Obligations is clearer than the French text, which may explain why the Federal Tribunal delivered ambiguous opinions in ATF 95 II 456; ATF 95 II 568; Fed. Trib. *in* RSPIDA 1973, 187 (these cases state that the name of a company of limited liability that does not include the name of a person is to be distinguished from any other registered business name throughout Switzerland). *See* ATF 131 III 572 (when the protection of a single person entity is limited to a township, the name of the town may refer to the entire metropolitan area, like Geneva and its suburbs).

678. *See* ATF 34 II 114, esp. 120 and all following cases, e.g., ATF 92 II 270, esp. 278; ATF 77 II 321, esp. 327, criticized, e.g., by P. Troller, *Kollisionen zwischen Firmen, Handelsnamen und Marken* (Conflicts between Firms, Trade Names and Trademarks), thesis, 72 (Freiburg, Basle, 1980).

679. ATF 107 II 356, esp. 362. According to the president of the Tribunal of the Arrondissement of Lausanne (SIC 2002, 55), the use of a trade name as Internet domain name would not necessarily be a 'use as a trade name'.

680. ATF 90 II 192; *see also* the Direction of Justice of Zurich *in* RSJ 1969, 28; Supreme Court Liechtenstein *in* RSPIDA 1981, 104.

681. Fed. Trib., SIC 2010, 101; SIC 2000, 397, 399–400; ATF 92 II 95; Cant. Ct Graubünden *in* RSPIDA 1981, 64.

682. *See* ATF 130 III 478 (unpublished c. 5.3); ATF 127 III 160, 168; Fed. Trib., SIC 2000, 399. Supreme Court Liechtenstein *in* RSPIDA 1981, 104 (with cit. of Swiss cases).

- a phonetical analysis will determine whether the succession of vowels and consonants – each category being taken separately – is likely to provoke a risk of confusion, especially over the phone;[683]
- a semantic analysis may finally settle the point, especially when the distinctive elements have a precise meaning.[684] Such an analysis requires to take into account who are the consumers and other interested circles to be protected. It is enough that the distinctive elements have an identical or similar meaning in one of the national languages.[685] A passing-off is less likely for a business name than for a trademark since the business name will be seen on letterheads where there exists a clear link with the company, while a trademark is often seen alone.[686]

D. Prevention of the Risk of Confusion

533. The confusion between the two businesses should be prevented by the second registrant or second user. He must do it if he is free to select any name as the name of his company. If the law requests him or her to use his or her name, however, he or she must add the necessary first name or other addition that may help prevent confusion.[687] The Act against Unfair Competition may also prevent someone from using only his name if this leads to a passing-off.[688]

534. The distinction should be all the more manifest when both names are imaginative rather than descriptive. The diverse letters preceding a similar wording may, however, sufficiently help the public to make the distinction.[689]

535. When the two businesses are geographically near each other, the distinction between their names should be made easier.

536. When the two businesses are competing, the distinction should also be made easier.

683. *See* Fed. Trib., SIC 2019, 692 ('*Altrimo*'): it is not contrary to federal law for a trial court to give a great importance to the phonetic aspect and to possible idea associations; see also ATF 92 II 95; ATF 93 II 40; ATF 97 II 234; Just. Ct Geneva *in* RSPI 1992, 191.
684. *See* Dist. Ct Appenzell *in* RSPIDA 1973, 186 (*'Trank AG' v. 'Drink AG'*); Fed. Trib. *in* RSPI 1990, 66 (*'Finorsud SA' v. 'Finotrust'*).
685. *See* Cant. Ct Graubünden *in* RSPIDA 1981, 64.
686. ATF 102 II 161. ATF 131 III 572 & ATF 128 III 401 (what remains in the memory is determinative).
687. *See* ATF 73 II 119, unpublished part of the opinion reproduced *in* Troller, 219, fn. 59; *See also* ATF 47 II 64; ATF 61 II 121; ATF 85 II 323; ATF 88 II 371; ATF 91 I 504; Fed. Trib. *in* RSPI 1994, 53 et seq.; ATF 116 II 614 (Gucci).
688. ATF 79 II 182, esp. 189; ATF 85 II 323, esp. 330; ATF 88 II 371, esp. 374; Fed. Trib. *in* RSPIDA 1971, 188, esp. 195 et seq. The risk of confusion will be adjudicated under the same principles applicable under trademark law, law of corporations, protection of names and unfair competition law; *see* Com. Ct. Zurich, SIC 2019, 429 et sq. ('Zurich').
689. ATF 124 III 363, esp. 369. ATF 131 III 572; Fed. Trib., JdT 2007 I 206; Fed. Trib. SIC 2017, 475 ('Centro Funerario' – the adjonction of 'ti' is not sufficient to prevent confusion).

The Federal Tribunal did not accept yet that the exclusivity of use be asserted only vis-à-vis competitors.[690] In practice, there are often parallel registrations for similar names of companies that are active in different areas, especially if one of them is managing one house or apartment house (so-called Real Estate Co, Immobilien AG, Société immobilière). Nonetheless, the risk of confusion is greater for competitors.

537. In order to win his case, the prior registrant of a business name does not have to show that confusion or passing-off occurred, in fact. It is enough to convince the court that the 'abstract' risk of confusion exists.[691] Of course, if a mail was wrongly directed, or customers mistook one business for the other, this will be a relevant indication that the risk of confusion exists.[692] Further, the fact that real *quiproquos* happened without the second user doing something to prevent them may lead to a finding of fault against him, so opening the way for an action for damages.

E. Remedies

538. Article 956(2) Code of Obligations provides for two actions:

(1) an injunction or stop-and-desist order;
(2) an action for damages, that is subject to the general conditions of Article 41 Code of Obligations.

539. If a prior registrant waits for too long before bringing a suit against the use of the second business name, his claims may be dismissed.[693] However, it is not a bar to have tolerated the use of similar elements in third parties' names.[694]

540. The registered business name has to be used as registered, with the exception of ads, packages of wares (if no specific regulation requests otherwise), delivery trucks, shop signs, etc. Penal repression is provided under Article 326*ter* Penal Code.[695]

690. *See* ATF 100 II 230; Cant. Ct Graubünden *in* RSPIDA 1981, 64; Fed. Trib. SIC 2012, 816 ('Keytrade Bank' protected against all other Swiss corporations – not only competitors).
691. ATF 100 II 230. *See* Fed. Trib., SIC 2016, 207, following up on Fed. Trib. SIC 2015, 386; *see also* Ct Just. Geneva, SIC 2018, 25 ('Octo'): if the parties are competing in a service industry that assumes a higher degree of trust towards the service provider, such as a family office in banking, the public will less easily be confused even if there is a great similarity between the trade names.
692. ATF 91 II 17.
693. 'Absolute time bar' (*Verwirkung*). *See* ATF 109 II 338.
694. Cant. Ct Zug *in* RSPI 1993, 87; Civ. Ct Basle-Countryside *in* BJM 1968, 39; claimant may be estopped because he did not select his own business name in conformity with the law: Fed. Trib. *in* RSPI 1990, 77.
695. Abrogating the former Federal Law of 6 Oct. 1923.

541. The venue follows the general rules. It has been established that the courts of the location of a subsidiary are competent to adjudicate claims concerning the subsidiary's name, even if the suit must be filed against the main party, that is, the company itself.[696]

542. Further, the legal protection can be claimed even by a domicile company,[697] that is not active as such in Switzerland, under Article 956 Code of Obligations (or Article 29 Civil Code). However, in our view, the same rule is not applicable under the Act against Unfair Competition, which requests a real effect of the infringing acts on the market.[698]

II. Protection of Unregistered Names and Foreign Names

A. Names of Entities That Are Not Registered

543. Protection for the names of entities that are not registered in the Register of Commerce is possible under the Civil Code and under the Act against Unfair Competition. This holds true even for names that are made up of generic words, as long as they have been used long enough to acquire a secondary meaning of the reference to the legal entity.[699] Even if an entity is registered, Article 956 Code of Obligations will not apply as long as this entity is not a commercial company, a cooperative or a privately owned business within the meaning of Article 945 Code of Obligations.

B. Foreign Names

544. The protection of foreign business names in Switzerland raises various issues on conflicts of law.[700] Those questions are not theoretical, especially when a foreign company is subject to expropriation proceedings that do not encompass a Swiss subsidiary, as happened after 1981 with some French industries. It is, however, impossible here to delve into those difficult issues.

---

696. Com. Ct Berne *in* RSPI 1991, 379.
697. Fed. Trib. *in* RSPI 1989, 38.
698. *See* Art. 2 UCA and comments in F. Dessemontet, *La nouvelle Loi contre la concurrence déloyale* (The New Law against Unfair Competition) JdT 1993 I 370 & 374–375.
699. Fed. Trib., SIC 2007, 115.
700. *See* generally F. Dessemontet, *Le nom commercial des entreprises étrangères en Suisse* (Trade Names of Foreign Companies in Switzerland), in *Les étrangers en Suisse, Recueil de travaux publié par la Faculté de droit pour la Société suisse des juristes* (Compilation of Articles published by the Faculty of Law for the Swiss Lawyers' Association) esp. 175 et seq. (Lausanne, 1982). For the names of banking companies, *see* F. Dessemontet, *La raison sociale des banques en droit international privé* (The Banks' Firms in International Private Law), in *Festschrift Beat Kleiner* 145 et seq. (Zurich, 1993).

545. As a rule, the protection of foreign names in Switzerland is subject to Swiss Law.[701] Switzerland is a party to the Paris Convention, Article 8 of which provides that the trade name will be protected in all countries of the Paris Union without a duty to file it or to register it, be it part of a trademark or not. Therefore, Switzerland has an obligation to protect foreign trade names. The Federal Tribunal has decided that the protection will derive from the Act against Unfair Competition, or in an exceptional case, from Article 29 or 28 Civil Code, but not from Article 956 Code of Obligations, when the foreign trade names are not registered in the Swiss Register of Commerce.[702]

546. The passing-off or the risk of confusion are found to exist on the basis of the same method of comparison which is valid also for registered business names.[703] There is, however, a further requirement when applying the Act against Unfair Competition: the trade name of the foreign entity must be used within Switzerland,[704] or at least be well-known among the Swiss public.[705] The protection of a foreign well-known trade name is not automatic, but if there is no reason to believe that this business will not extend its activities in Switzerland in the near future, it shall be protected.[706] Of course, if a sales representative uses the name for the products or services of a foreign entity, such use will benefit the foreign entity.[707]

547. There is a further difference between the protection which is afforded to commercial companies and cooperatives under Article 956 Code of Obligations and under the Act against Unfair Competition. The geographic extension of the protection under the unfair competition legislation is not automatically congruent with the Swiss territory, but it can be limited to a given zone, for example, where the consumers are aware that the foreign trade names exist because they cross the border for their shopping.[708] Under Articles 28–29 Civil Code, however, the same limitation should not apply.[709]

---

701. Since ATF 79 II 305, before the principle of universality led to the application of the law of the seat or of the main place of business. *See* ATF 37 II 370. For trade names used on Internet, Swiss law also applies, and it has been decided that a foreign trade name deserves protection against misappropriation as soon as it may be accessed from Switzerland: Fed. Trib., SIC 2011, 727 ('Jetfly').

702. Fed. Trib., SIC 2002, 162, 165.

703. Com. Ct Zurich *in* RSPI 1985, 74; for that method, *see* hereabove paras 531 et seq.

704. ATF 79 II 305, esp. 314; ATF 90 II 192, esp. 199–200.

705. ATF 109 II 483 (advertisements in transborder magazines are enough to make a trade name well-known in Switzerland).

706. ATF 109 II 483; if the extension is unlikely, no protection is granted, *see* ATF 76 II 77, esp. 90–91.

707. ATF 107 II 356.

708. *See* F. Dessemontet, *Le nom commercial des entreprises étrangères en Suisse* (Trade Names of Foreign Companies in Switzerland), in *Les étrangers en Suisse, Recueil de travaux publié par la Faculté de droit pour la Société suisse des juristes* (Compilation of Articles published by the Faculty of Law for the Swiss Lawyers' Association) 194–195 (Lausanne, 1982).

709. *See* ATF 100 II 224; ATF 102 II 161, esp. 168; *see*, however, ATF 90 II 315, esp. 320; ATF 88 II 28.

548. The Swiss regime for foreign trade names so appears to be in conformity with Article 8 of the Paris Convention, but less generous towards foreign entities than, say, the German law.[710]

710. Compare Supreme Court Liechtenstein *in* RSPIDA 1981, 90 and *Entscheidungen des Reichsgerichts in Zivilsachen* (Judgments of the *Reichsgericht* in Civil Law) 117, 215 et seq.

Chapter 6. Industrial Designs

§1. Sources of Legislation

549. The Act on Designs and Models of 30 March 1900 was the oldest intellectual property statute still in force in Switzerland in 2000 when the first edition of this book was published.[711] It was replaced on 1 September 2001 by a new Act which entered into force on 1 July 2002 (RS 232.12) and conformed to the European Directive No. 98/71/CE of 13 October 1998 on the Legal Protection of Designs and Models, as well to current Swiss case law. Therefore, there is no more requirement for industrial use, and the notion of originality is described in the Act: this criterion is less demanding than in the Copyright Act. The new Act provides twenty-five years of protection. Designs that have been registered before entry into force of the new Act enjoy a longer period of protection of the new Act.[712]

550. For international priority, there was an Act of Parliament of 3 April 1914 that (since 1954) no longer concerned patents for inventions and was still valid for designs and models. It gave priority rights for Paris Union prior applications and Paris Union recognized exhibitions (*see* Articles 4 and 11 Paris Convention). This Act was abrogated on 16 December 1994 (RO 1995 1784).

551. The law is completed by the Ordinance of 8 March 2002 as amended.[713]

552. Switzerland is a party to the Hague Arrangement Concerning the International Deposit of Industrial Designs of 6 November 1925, as revised on 28 November 1960 and 2 July 1999.[714] Switzerland is also party to the Arrangement of Locarno on the international classification of designs.

§2. Subject Matter

I. Designs and Models

A. *Designs*

553. Designs are ornamental lines that may be combined with colours to be used as patterns for the industrial production of a given product. The design will be an ornament, either on the whole surface of the product or on a part thereof.

711. RS 232.12, hereinafter 'LDM'.
712. ATF 129 III 545.
713. RS 232.121; *see also* RS 232.148 (Ordinance of the Swiss Institute of Intellectual Property of 2 Dec. 2016 on taxes).
714. RS 0.232.121.2.

554. Cases have decided that ornamental designs must be viewed by the public,[715] but this does not mean that underwear could not be protected.[716]

555. Only the combination of two or more colours can be protected as a design, since a colour should remain free for all competitors to use.[717]

B. Models

556. Models are ornamental shapes, which either decorate products (e.g., by being affixed to a label or a package) or are the form of the product itself (furniture)[718] or of its package (perfume bottle).

557. Models are ornamental and not utility models, so-called small patents. Although the question was raised a long time ago whether Switzerland should not follow the German system of utility model protection,[719] the Swiss government decided in 2021 to take no step towards such a protection.

558. Models being ornamental, they have to be seen by the consumers.[720] They also have to be used on products or as products. A two-dimensional (design) or three-dimensional (model) logo cannot be registered as a design or model, to the extent that it does not serve as a pattern or mould for an industrial product.[721]

C. Relationship with Copyright Law

559. Switzerland never followed the system under which either model or design protection or copyright protection could be claimed. In this regard, Swiss law was based on the French system of '*l'unité de l'art*'. In spite of theoretical objections,[722] the French system is simpler in practice, and more equitable for the authors of designs and models who do not comply with the finicky registration system of designs and models.

---

715. *See* recently Fed. Adm. Trib. SIC 2016, 401; compare also hereinafter 'paras 555 and 577'.
716. Civ. Ct Lucerne *in* RSPI 1988, 216.
717. ATF 95 II 470, esp. 474. This opinion has been reversed for trademarks (*see* hereabove para. 337), so that a distinction could be made in the future between basic colours (that remain free for all) and rare colours (like lilac), that can be a trademark and could be claimed as a design.
718. *See* ATF 83 II 475.
719. *See*, e.g., A. Martin-Achard, *Y a-t-il lieu d'étendre la protection légale aux modèles d'utilité?* (Is it Necessary to Extend the Legal Protection to Utility Models?) RDS 1934 II 214–255a.
720. *See* ATF 113 II 77; Com. Ct Zurich *in* ZR 1935, 259. *See also* Fed. Trib., SIC 2008, 445, 447 (when a design differs from a prior one only by details that are not visible, it lacks *novelty*) (emphasis added).
721. *See* ATF 99 Ib 343.
722. *See* F. Perret, *L'autonomie du régime de protection des dessins et modèles* (The Independence of the System of Designs and Models' Protection), thesis, esp. 243–246 (Geneva, 1974).

560. Nevertheless, there is in Swiss courts and commentary a strong undercurrent of discrimination against the protection of industrial objects as works of art, and case law at times has requested under the Copyright Act more originality from designs and models than from ordinary works of art.[723]

This was all the more erroneous since designs and models under the special legislation enjoy a special regime protecting them from parallel creations by third parties, but have to comply with strict novelty requirements and formalities, whereas the copyright protection does not extend to parallel creations and does not require either novelty or formalities. As the new Act requires 'originality' besides 'novelty', it may be hoped that 'originality' might be understood by the courts as somewhat less stringent a requirement than the 'accrued originality' that was the test for designs before 2002. The result should be that a design that is 'original' under the new Act but lacks some other specific compliance with the formalities of the Design Act could be protected as a work of art if it fulfils the test of the Copyright Act, such as the 'individuality' of the creation. The recent modification of the German case law that used to put more stringent requirements for the originality of designs than other works of art and just abandoned that view might contribute to changing the Swiss jurisprudence in the years to come.

II. Novelty Requirement

561. The protection of a registered design or model is subject to the requirement that the design or model be *novel*. The registration will be deemed to be null and void, if the design or model was not new at the time of the deposit or of the priority abroad. The novelty is the state of something that is not known (so-called *formal novelty*) rather than the characteristic of something which did not exist before (so-called *substantive novelty*). In Switzerland, the public and the interested circles must therefore ignore it,[724] but it may have existed elsewhere in the world (or even in Switzerland if it was under a cloak of secrecy).

562. There is no examination by the Swiss Institute of Intellectual Property about the novelty, but it will be a defence in the courts if the owner of the design or model files a suit for infringement. Even a disclosure by the owner before the deposit or the priority date abroad will destroy the novelty.[725] There is no grace period save for disclosure by a third party in breach of a confidentiality agreement or of another agreement implying non-disclosure, or by the designer himself or herself within the last twelve months.

723. *See* above paras 47 et seq. and the Fed. Trib. Decision in the Max Bill case, SIC 2017 723 c. 2.6.1 which alludes to an alignment with the recent German case law.

724. *See* ATF 134 III 205, 208 (the Claimant to a declaration of invalidity of a design may win his case by producing items with an identical design and establishing that these items were marketed in Switzerland before the filing of the design); Fed. Trib., SIC 2012, 644 (it is enough to destroy novelty to produce a prior Swiss registration of an identical or similar design, ART. 6 LDes); *see* already ATF 54 II 56; ATF 56 II 66; ATF 59 II 195.

725. *See* ATF 104 II 322, esp. 326.

563. As under the Patent Act, but with less exacting a standard, there must not be an obvious variation or combination of what was formerly known,[726] but a slight show of originality should suffice.[727] However, a recipe to combine various forms and shapes (as in given lines of furniture) is not protectable per se being an idea.[728]

564. The novelty is assumed to exist for registered designs and models, but it is a rebuttable presumption. The burden of proof rests with the party claiming nullity of the design.

565. Protectable models are, for example: confectionery cones broader than they are tall[729] and decorated boots.[730] A record player's sound head,[731] a product combining a mailbox and a milk box,[732] or a laundry bag[733] were not protected.[734] The very best shape for a given product cannot be monopolized by the effect of the Design Act.[735]

III. Requirement of Originality

566. The new Act on Designs has introduced a requirement of originality that is additional to the requirement of novelty.[736] The test is not whether there was a creative methodology to obtain the design,[737] but only if the result is original, that is, if there is a gap between the new design and the prior designs.[738]

726. *See* David, No. 12 *ad* Art. 2 LDM; *see*, e.g., ATF 134 III 205, 210; ATF 84 II 653, esp. 661; Fed. Trib. *in* RSPI 1991, 153.
727. ATF 77 II 372.
728. Fed. Trib. *in* RSPI 1991, 145.
729. ATF 87 II 49.
730. ATF 104 II 322 (no protection granted *in casu*).
731. ATF 113 II 77.
732. ATF 95 II 470.
733. ATF 92 II 202.
734. *See also* Com. Ct Zurich *in* RSPI 1993, 309; Appel. Ct Ticino *in* RSPI 1994, 231; Civ. Ct Appenzell-AR *in* RSPI 1996, 155; Just. Ct Geneva *in* RSPI 1996, 378. For other examples, *see* David, No. 15 *ad* Art. 2 LDM.
735. Fed. Trib., SIC 2007, 550 ('jewelcase'). *See also* SIC 2017, 633 (App. Ct BS) (jewellery).
736. ATF 130 III 636, 641; ATF 133 III 189. It will be noted that Art. 25 TRIPS does not allow the States party to WTO to choose between novelty 'or' originality in their national legislation, in spite of its wording. *See* A. Kur, *TRIPS und der Designschutz* (TRIPS and the Protection of Designs), 185, 189 GRUR Int. (1995).
737. ATF 134 III 205, 211 (the comparison is not limited to prior items of the very same sort, but may include other similar items, such as necklaces for designs of rings); ATF 133 III 189, 191–192 and Fed. Trib., SIC 2008, 445, 448; the comparison should try to focus on the similarities between the design at issue and the prior designs that are opposed to prove that the design is not original. *See also* Fed. Trib. SIC 2016, 526 for the onus of proof. The standards for protecting a design and for avoiding confusion under the Law against unfair Competition (LCD) are not identical; Art. 3 (1)(d) LCD encompasses a risk of indirect confusion through a mistaken connotation that two products, different in themselves, originate with the same producer, while Art. 8 LDes only prohibits the direct confusion between the products themselves; see Fed. Trib., SIC 2017, 566 at 570.
738. For example, a bath tub has been protected because it was not banal (Dist. Ct Signau, SIC 1999, 47, 48). The prize that has been granted to the design at issue may be an indication that it is original (*contra* Sup. Ct Luzern, SIC 2003, 731, 739 (under Copyright Act)); *see also* Sup. Ct

§3. Conditions of Protection

567. Two conditions of protection must be fulfilled:

(1) the subject matter must comply with the legal requisites as indicated above;
(2) the formalities must have been fulfilled, as indicated here below.

§4. Formalities

I. Procedure of Registration

568. The application for registration is to be filed with the Swiss Institute for Intellectual Property in one of the three official languages, and the fees for the first period of five years must be paid at once.

569. The designs or models can be filed with the Swiss Institute for Intellectual Property as bundles of several designs or models, which is less expensive than one at a time.

570. However, the bundle must contain either designs (two-dimensional) or models (three-dimensional), but not both designs and models. Besides, there are no requirements that the bundle of designs or models covers only one industry.

571. There is a summary examination by the Institute to ascertain that the subject matter is a design or model, and that no law or *boni mores* [739] are violated.

II. Open or Sealed Deposit

572. The publication of the file may be postponed for the first thirty months.

573. The fees are extremely low, so it may be interesting as a policy to file many a design or model to obtain all-round protection for a new shape or a new ornament.

Appenzell-AR, SIC 2013, 49 ('Blumenkistenhalter') (Swiss design N° 129'389 is not original because there are only minor differences, that can be explained by technical reasons, between that design and prior art). *Contra* SIC 2016, 158 (App. Ct BS): hinges for a movable wall are protectable; Fed. Trib. SIC 2016, 526: sauna wall supports are protectable.

739. *See* ATF 71 I 134: a deceptive device (purporting to protect against radiation without any scientific basis) is not protectable.

§5. OWNERSHIP AND TRANSFER

I. Ownership

574. The name of the registrant is always mentioned in the Register of Designs and Models, as well as his or her domicile. If the registrant is abroad, a Swiss address for serving notices must be mentioned (Article 9(2)(a) Ordinance on Designs of 8 March 2002 as revised in 2011).

575. There are rules in Article 332 of the Code of Obligations on the ownership of designs and models when they are created under an employment contract. The same old-fashioned regime that still prevails for inventions is, since 2002, applicable to designs.

Basically, the rights accrue to the designer, as they cannot originally belong to the employer (so-called *principle of the creator*, *Schöpferprinzip*). However, the employer has a 'shop right', and will own the design if the designer has been hired to design. In that case, no further indemnity is due. For other cases, the employer may receive the property of a design against due compensation if the contract provides for a shop's right towards any design created within the course of employment but not by a designer hired to design, to the extent that the necessary formalities have been fulfilled. On the contrary, in the case of an independent contractor who has been commissioned to create a design, it will not be assumed that he has transferred his title onto the registration to the other party (*see* Articles 7 and 34 LDes, as applied by Com.Ct; Berne, 2021, 325). This regulation applies even if the design or model is not registered or not registerable.

Third parties having already worked on a similar or identical design may continue working on it, as is also the case under the Patent Act for inventions.

II. Licences and Assignment

576. The cases applicable to the licence of other intellectual property rights, especially patents,[740] will also apply to the licence of designs or models.

577. Only the registered owner has the right to assign the registered design or model.

There can be a registration of the assignment or of the licence. The licence agreement shall be deemed to be null and void *ab ovo* if the design or model was invalid.[741] As under the Patent Act, royalties are due, however, as long as there is an effective hindrance to competition, a 'quasi-monopoly' justifying a consideration.[742] The exclusive licensee may file a suit against infringement, as the case law already admitted with some hesitations.[743]

740. *See* paras 256 et seq.
741. ATF 116 II 191, esp. 195.
742. ATF 116 II 191, esp. 196.
743. Com. Ct Aargau, SIC 2006, 187, 190–191.

§6. SCOPE OF EXCLUSIVE RIGHTS

I. Right to Use

578. The registered owner of designs or models receives the exclusive right to use them in the industry within Switzerland.

579. As the design or model owner would anyhow have the right to use them, the law really states that he or she enjoys the right to prevent other manufacturers from using the registered design or model.

580. The first prohibition is against counterfeiting and imitating the model or design as both would be infringing upon the registered owner's right, to the extent that counterfeiting is 'illegal', that is 'unauthorized',[744] and that the imitation leaves such a thin difference that only careful scrutiny would disclose the diversity between the registered design or model and the defendant's one.

There is thus a difference between sheer counterfeiting and imitation, since the imitation must lead to a risk of confusion among the buyers or the public.[745] The courts do not mainly have to look for differences when comparing the two designs or models at issue, but they rather have to consider the overall impression, which is often derived from the similarities between them.[746] The similarities must be apparent to the laymen, the buyers and the consumers.[747] They will be relevant, however, only when they exist between protected elements of the registered design or model.[748] Further, there is a difference between the risk of confusion as found to exist for trademarks and the risk of confusion between designs and models because for designs and models, the comparison is made under the assumption that the consumer sees both objects at the same time.[749]

581. According to an obiter dictum, there could even be sometimes an imitation without a risk of confusion.[750]

744. *See* David, No. 3 *ad* Art. 24 LDM.

745. *See* K. Troller, 884–885.

746. Fed. Trib. SIC 2017, 566; ATF 130 III 636, 641 (jewels); ATF 130 III 645, 647–648 (watches); ATF 129 III 545, 547 ff; *see* already under the former Act ATF 83 II 475, esp. 480; ATF 104 II 322, esp. 328.

747. ATF 77 II 372.

748. ATF 129 III 545, 551; *see* already ATF 113 II 77. One case points out that when the respondent has not filed a different design, he may rely on the product as it is marketed (Com. Ct Aargau, SIC 2006, 186). Note that there exists no right to cite a part or an excerpt of a design under Swiss law; however, a two-dimensional photographic reproduction of a design does not infringe on the rights accruing from the registration of the design. *See* F. Wigger/M. Handke, *EuGH: Zuständigkeit, anwendbares Recht und Zitatrecht in internationalen Designrechtskonflikten* (Jurisdiction, applicable law and right of citation in international design law conflicts), SIC 2018, 350, 356–357.

749. ATF 83 II 475, esp. 480; ATF 104 II 322, esp. 328; for trademarks, however, the consumer is not supposed to see both brand products at the same time, and the risk of confusion might be often higher because the consumer has kept only vague memories of the features of the trademark seen in the first instance.

750. ATF 83 II 475, esp. 480.

582. Just a modification of colours does not suffice to prevent a risk of confusion. The same has been asserted by cases for a change of material,[751] or for not using a trademark on a watch.[752]

583. Finally, an interesting test has been used by commercial courts;[753] if the overall impression is different, this means that the consumers have a real choice between two products, a choice that is based on taste. In such a case, there is no imitation.

II. Right to Sell

584. The registered owner enjoys the exclusive right to sell, offer for sale, market or import the registered design or product.

585. The most striking feature of that definition is that there is no application of the first-sale doctrine when unauthorized products are sold or marketed for the first time abroad. Hence, the Law of Designs and Models follows the former pattern of the Patent Act, rather than that of the trademark and copyright cases.[754]

586. The accomplice is subject to an independent criminal action.

III. Right to Receive Information

587. Through a request addressed to the defendant by a court or another 'competent authority', which is necessarily a judge, be he a civil or a criminal judge,[755] the claimant has the right to receive information about the providers of counterfeiting or imitating wares.

588. However, it is forbidden to let the public believe that a design or model is registered when such is not the case.

§7. Limitations of the Scope of Protection

589. A design or model has to be registered in order to be protected. This is a formal requirement, but there are also substantive requirements, as have been mentioned above.[756]

751. Com. Ct St-Gall *in* RSPIDA 1968, 58.
752. Sup. Ct Obwald *in* RSPI 1991, 397.
753. Com. Ct Zurich, Com. Ct St-Gall, Civ. Ct Lucerne, altogether four decisions *in* RSPI 1988, 205.
754. *See supra* para. 415 (trademark), and para. 35 (copyright).
755. *See* David, No. 16 *ad* Art. 24 LDM.
756. Novelty and originality: *see* paras 561 et seq.

590. Further, there is no protection against the method of fabrication, the functional end and the technical effects of the objects made after the registered design or model. This limitation is due to the system of the intellectual property laws, that protect technical improvements mainly through the Patent Act, the rules of trade secrets being ancillary to this end. For its part, the legislation on designs and models protects only the ornamental innovations, the design, the look of the products.

591. Many cases have rejected the protection of designs[757] or models.[758] For example, the protection of a car body part was rejected because the new shape was a mere technically oriented adjustment of the unprotected older part.[759] However, rectangular trousers have been protected,[760] as well as shades for lamps with stripes,[761] or packages for sweets that were wider than tall.[762]

§8. Duration of Protection

592. The legal protection of designs and models extends for five periods of five years, running without interruption from the date of filing the application – which means the date on which the Swiss Institute for Intellectual Property receives the complete application together with the first five years' fees.

593. The Institute has to serve notice of the nearing termination of the rights after each period, but no liability is provided by law for failure to do so.

594. A prolongation for the second or further period is possible for all or part of the designs or models deposited in the bundle.

595. Hence, Swiss law provides for protection for up to twenty-five years.

§9. Infringement and Remedies

596. There are criminal and civil remedies, akin to the remedies that are afforded under the other intellectual property laws.[763] Criminal sanctions require that the connected pirates have acted with intention, be it with *dolus eventualis*.[764] Without intention, there are only civil remedies. There may be interim measures, for

757. *See* Fed. Trib. *in* RSPIDA 1955, 71; Federal Office of Intellectual Property *in* RSPIDA 1968, 58; Federal Office of Intellectual Property *in* PMM Bl 1985 I 12.
758. ATF 69 II 421, esp. 429; ATF 92 II 202; Federal Office of Intellectual Property *in* RSPIDA 1964, 98; ATF 95 II 470, esp. 475; Federal Office of Intellectual Property *in* PMM Bl 1985 I 47; Fed. Trib. *in* RSPI 1991, 145.
759. Fed. Trib. *in* RSPI 1991, 153.
760. Com. Ct Zurich *in* ZR 1976, 93 and *in* RSPIDA 1976, 43.
761. Fed. Trib. *in* RSPIDA 1976, 41.
762. ATF 87 II 49.
763. For accounting of profits, *see* Fed. Trib. *in* RSPI 1989, 105, esp. 111. For a judgment of 25 Jun. 2019 by the Fed. Trib. denying a request for interim measures see 1B_65/2019 (www.bger.ch).
764. *See* ATF 84 IV 127. For developments *see* hereabove para. 461.

example, with a view to know where the products already sold come from, or with a petition to seize the infringing products (against a bond to be filed by the petitioner with the court). Publication of the final judgment is also possible.[765]

765. *See* ATF 47 II 360, esp. 364; ATF 62 II 317, esp. 330; Civ. Ct Zurich *in* RSPI 1987, 104.

Chapter 7. Plant Variety Protection

§1. Sources of Legislation

I. Swiss Law and Ordinances

A. *The Federal Law of 20 March 1975*

597. The Act of 20 March 1975 on the Protection of Plant Varieties[766] is the first Swiss law that has been enacted for the protection of vegetal organisms. It has been modified from time to time, the last substantive revision being on 5 October 2007, entering into force on 1 September 2008.

B. *The Ordinance of 25 June 2008*

598. The Ordinance organizes the Office for Plant Variety Protection, a division of the Federal Office for Agriculture.

II. International Conventions

599. Switzerland is a party to the Paris Convention of 2 December 1961 on the Protection of Plant Variety, as revised at Geneva on 10 November 1972, 23 October 1978 and 19 March 1991.[767]

§2. Subject Matter

600. Plant varieties are defined under Article 2 LPPV as under the original Paris Convention of 1961. It is an exceptional legislative technique that embodies within Swiss law the Paris Convention (Article 1(1)), so that this Convention is self-executing before our courts, and that no provision of Swiss law may be at variance with the Paris Convention definition.

601. Not only hybrids but also all-new varieties are protected, even if their origin is artificial (e.g., for clones or asexually reproduced plants) (Article 1(2) LPPV).

602. The new varieties must be stabilized and homogenous (Article 8b LPPV). They have to be part of a known botanical genus or species as under a list that is prepared by the Government.

766. RS 232.16, hereinafter 'LPPV'.
767. RS 0.232.162.

§3. Conditions of Protection

I. Novelty

603. A plant variety is deemed to be novel if it significantly differs, for one or more important features, from any other variety which is generally known to exist at the time of filing the application (Article 8b LPPV).

There is a grace period of four years for the breeder to market his variety without destroying the novelty; the Government can extend that grace period for up to six years altogether (Article 5(3) LPPV). Under the Paris Convention, the grace period of six years applies to grapevines and trees, including rootstocks. An interim grace period was granted between 1 July 2008 and 1 July 2009 (Article 53 LPPV).

There is the protection of discovery (contrary to what happens under the Patent Act).[768]

The legal protection extends to all commercial uses of the plant variety, but an experimental use or the use to breed a new variety is possible. There is international exhaustion (Article 8a LPPV).

II. Denomination

604. The denomination which is already registered abroad should, as a rule, be used in Switzerland. The denomination shall not be a number only, and it shall not be misleading or deceptive, or contrary to the public order or against *bonos mores*, nor otherwise contrary to Federal law and treaties.

605. A trademark can be used for marketing the variety, but if the trademark is the same as the usual denomination, no trademark protection can later be claimed (Article 13b LPPV).

606. The use of the selected denomination is compulsory for whoever sells seeds or other reproductive material.

§4. Formalities

I. Registration

607. Swiss citizens and persons or legal entities having their domicile or seat in Switzerland, as well as nationals of the Paris Union for the Protection of Plant Varieties, have the right to benefit from the legal system of protection; for nationals of the Paris Union, the variety must figure within the list of Article 4(2) and (3) Paris Convention, or the country of that nation must protect varieties of the same species.

768. *See* hereabove para. 190.

608. For nationals of other countries and persons or legal entities with domicile or seats in those countries, protection is granted if Swiss citizens and residents are granted the reciprocity.

609. The person entitled to the protection is either the breeder or his successor in title.[769]

II. Application

A. Filing of the Application

610. The application is to be filed with the prescribed form, in one of the three official languages, and fees have to be paid.

611. Corrections may be requested by the Office.

B. Publication of the Application

612. The application shall be published with specific information as required under Article 28 LPPV.

C. Opposition Procedure

613. For three months from the date of publication, there is an opposition procedure open to everyone, by means of a written deed, with plants or documents as an appendix. The courts may be petitioned later to state that the deposit is invalid (Article 16 LPPV).

III. Examination

614. The Federal Research Facilities for Agricultural Products will examine the variety and the oppositions. Tests can be made by the Research Facilities, and the applicant can follow their progress and comment on them.

It will be remembered that the Paris Union has adopted 'Guidelines for the Conduct of Tests for Distinctiveness Homogeneity and Stability', a separate test for each species drafted by government experts. Such tests are not conducted in Switzerland, where no centre for research is deemed to be appropriate for it. However, tests that are made abroad are recognized in Switzerland under Article 30 LPPV.

769. *See* hereinafter para. 616. *See also* Art. 4 of the LPPV.

IV. Grant

615. The protection is formally granted by the registration of the variety. The law explicitly states that '*there is no guarantee of the Confederation*' (Article 31(2) LPPV). The registrant receives an extract from the Register. In certain cases, the Office may cancel the registration (Article 17 LPPV).

§5. Ownership and Transfer

I. Initial Ownership

616. The breeder or his successor in title is entitled to the protection. There is a rebuttable presumption that the registrant is entitled to it.

617. For employees of breeders, the system is the same as has been explained above for employed inventors under Article 332 Code of Obligations, be they public servants or not.[770]

618. The system of first-to-file is followed rather than the system of first-to-breed, so that the priority of right belongs to the first registrant.

619. There is an international priority of twelve months deriving from the registration in a Member State of the Paris Union. Any application for the same variety that would be filed by another person within the period between the breeder's first and later applications is of no consequence to the rights of the breeder. Further, any use of the plant variety occurring within the said period will not affect his rights either.

II. Transfer

620. The right to the registration as well as the rights deriving from the registration may be assigned in whole or in part to third parties and may be inherited by the heirs of the breeder.

621. In case of transfer, the rights of third parties may be opposed to the assignee only if they are registered.

622. The Law provides for two cases of licences:

(1) The *contractual licence* (Article 21 LPPV). If there are several persons having a joint ownership of the plant variety, they all have to agree.

770. For a comment on the formerly applicable particular regime of the public servants' inventions, *see* F. Dessemontet, *Inventions in Swiss Universities*, 1982 Indus. Prop. 338 et seq., esp. 343 et seq.

(2) The *compulsory licence* (Article 22 LPPV, in case of a public interest). The public interest may consist in ensuring the widespread distribution of the new variety. The licensee has to pay an 'indemnity' which is equivalent to fair royalties ('an equitable remuneration' under the Paris Convention, Article 9(2)). A non-exclusive licence may also be requested by the patentee for an invention concerning biological material where his invention embodies an important progress with a definite addition of economic value (Article 22a LPPV). In that case, the owner of the plant variety will get a cross-licence from the patentee.

The compulsory licence is not transferable and non-exclusive. A bond is to be filed by the claimant to guarantee the payment of royalties.

§6. Scope of Exclusive Rights

623. No one can professionally, without the authorization of the registered breeder, produce propagating material of the plant variety, offer it for sale, market such material, or repeatedly use the new plant variety for the production of another variety.

624. Propagating materials are seeds, fruits, etc. and plants or parts of plants, like roots, rhizomes, etc.

625. There is a specific provision for the protection of ornamental plants (Article 13 LPPV).

§7. Limitations of the Scope of Protection

626. The use of a new variety as the initial source of variation for creating other new varieties and marketing them does not require the breeder's authorization, as long as it does not qualify as a 'repeated use'.

627. Compulsory licences are granted, as seen above.[771]

628. There can be cancellation of the registration upon request of the breeder, or if the annual fees are not paid. The Swiss Confederation may expropriate the plant variety certificate if supplying the Swiss market requires that measure. The Federal Tribunal will, in the last instance, determine an equitable compensation (Article 20 LPPV).

771. Para. 622.

§8. Duration of Protection

629. The protection is granted for thirty years, with the exception of grapevines and trees (including rootstocks), for which the protection is twenty-five years (Article 4(2) Ordinance). The owner may file a written statement relinquishing his rights (Article 15 LPPV).

§9. Infringement and Remedies

630. There are the same actions for infringement as in the other areas of intellectual property. An injunction may be delivered by the court even if there is no fault, but the fault is necessary for damages. Damages can be claimed for the period immediately following the filing as well as for the period after the grand of the protection, but the action in damages cannot be filed before the grant; this solution is not identical to the European regulation. The Law does not provide for the accounting for profits, but there appears to be no reason not to apply the patent case law relating to Article 423 Code of Obligations in the event of an infringement.

631. Interim injunctions are possible starting from the date of publication of the application. The Federal Code of Civil Procedure of 2008 will apply. Damages may be had from that date, but the action cannot be filed before the registration.

632. A specific provision relates to the protection of trade secrets in the case of litigation (Article 40 LPPV).

Chapter 8. Chip Protection

§1. Sources of Legislation

I. Federal Legislation

A. *The Law of 1992*

633. The Federal Law on the Protection of Topographies of SemiConductor Products of 9 October 1992 as amended[772] was first prepared in 1986–1987 by the Third-Expert Committee on the Revision of the Copyright Act (chaired by this writer).[773]

634. There had been some opinions to the effect that the Act against Unfair Competition, especially Article 5(c),[774] might suffice to fulfil the reciprocity requirement of the US.[775] The Government seems to have been of that opinion.[776] Nonetheless, this provision fights only the outright piracy, the copying rather than the imitations.[777] Further, the existence of an action in Unfair Competition does not allow for registration of the rights, nor does it specify which level of non-obviousness should attain the original products.

Therefore, the Expert Committee, then the legislature, decided to enact a complete law and, later on, to make it a separate act, different from the Copyright Law of the same date. As it is a separate act, no provision of the Copyright Act is applicable in and of itself. Nevertheless, by way of simplification, there are references to some articles of the Copyright Act.[778]

B. *The Ordinance of 1993*

635. The extremely concise statute is supplemented by the Ordinance of 26 April 1993 as amended for the last time on 1 October 2021, which also makes a reference to the Copyright Act.[779]

---

772. RS 231.2. Minor modifications have been introduced in 2004, 2006, 2008, 2016 and 2021.
773. *See* T. Dreier, *Der Schutz von Mikrochips* (Chip Protection), RSPI 1988, 37 et seq., esp. 43–51.
774. Art. 5(c) UCA: 'Exploitation of the Achievements of others: Shall be deemed to have committed an act of unfair competition, anyone who, in particular, (c) by means of technical reproduction processes and without a corresponding effort of his own, takes the marketable results of work of another person and exploits them as such.'
775. *See* SemiConductor Chip Protection Act, 17 U.S.C s. 902 (a) (2).
776. *See* Message, FF 1989 III 494–495.
777. *See* N. von Werdt, 122–123 with cit.
778. *See* Art. 10 Topographies Law referring to Arts 61 through 66 of the Copyright Act; Art. 12 Topographies Law referring to Arts 75 through 77 thereof; Art. 10(2) Topographies Law distinguishing from the provision on seizure under Art. 63 Copyright Act; Art. 21 Topographies Law on the simultaneous entry into force of both Acts.
779. *See* Art. 18(3) Ordinance providing for the Customs seizure, supplemented by Art. 18a through 18c since 1 Jul. 2008 (RO 2008, 2543). Further minor amendments have been adopted in 2014, 2016 and 2021.

II. International Treaty

636. Switzerland is not a party to the Washington Treaty on Intellectual property in Respect of Integrated Circuits of 1989.

637. Nonetheless, Switzerland is a party to the TRIPS Agreement and therefore has to apply the substantive rules of the Washington Treaty on the protection of semiconductor chips, save for the exception of compulsory licensing which was embedded in the 1989 Treaty but disavowed in the TRIPS (Article 37).

§2. Subject Matter of Protection

I. Three-Dimensional Structures of Semiconductor Chips

638. Under Article 1(1) Topographies Law are protected the '*topographies*', that is, the three-dimensional structures of semiconductor chips, whatever their modalities of engraving or coding.

It is less restrictive than the 'mask work', which is protected under section 17 U.S.C. section 902. It is also less restrictive than the 'micro-electronical' semiconductor chip under section 1 of the German Semi-Conductor Protection Act of 22 October 1987.

639. Parts of structures may also be protectable,[780] as well as projects of structures.[781]

II. Originality

640. The requirement of novelty as under the Patent Act plays no role in the protection of semiconductor chips because it is thought to be impossible that topography could be substantially identical to an already existing one, in view of the complexity of the structures at issue.[782]

780. For example, 'isolated transistors', or 'masters of gate array'.

781. For critical observations *see* von Werdt, 184.

782. However, according to Th. Dreier, *supra*, 45 and N. van Werdt, 106 et seq. respectively under the Third-Expert Committee proposed draft bill and the Federal Council Bill, the structure must not have been known by professionals at the time of its creation. A different opinion was later to be read in the Message 1989, 96: *'a structure is not common place when it is not known among professionals'*. This idea is obviously wrong. The reciprocal statement only is admissible: if a structure is not known, then it can be common place or not. In the result, the Act does not require novelty.

641. The only legal requirement is the requirement that the structure be not commonplace. This level of 'originality' is supposed to be lower than the 'individuality' under the Copyright Act.[783] There appears to be no case law in this regard, as in the whole area of semiconductor chips.

§3. Condition of Protection

642. The law requires the registration of semiconductor chips,[784] their originality as defined, and the fulfilment of given criteria as to the registrant.

643. Swiss producers, residents of Switzerland, and legal entities having their main place of business in Switzerland are protected as of right under Article 2(1)(a) Topographies Law. Semiconductor chips that have been put onto the market for the first time in Switzerland are protected as well.

644. Further, the Government extended the benefits of the law to nationals of various countries granting reciprocity to Swiss residents.[785]

§4. Formalities

I. Register

645. The Swiss Institute for Intellectual Property keeps the register for semiconductor topographies. Altogether there have been less than fifteen registrations since 1 July 1993 and for the first six years since the entry into force of the new system. Nowadays, there are a few registrations every year. An analysis of the cost/benefit ratio might uncover that this has been the most expensive and least useful piece of legislation of the last century, but of course, it was necessary to please the US and Europe. Nevertheless, other countries such as the United Kingdom, Sweden, Belgium and Australia did not feel obliged to set up a full-fledged registration system for nothing.

II. Protection

646. The full legal protection is granted upon marketing the semiconductor chip, even if the registration is posterior, but it has to be registered within two years from marketing in order for the protection to last ten years.

Otherwise, the protection stops after two years.

---

783. *See* I. Cherpillod, *Originalité et banalité à propos de la protection des programmes d'ordinateur* (Originality and Banality in Connection with Computer Programs), in *Mélanges J. Voyame* 48 et seq. (Lausanne, 1989); Dreier, *supra*, 45.

784. *See* para. 654.

785. *See* GRUR Int. 1994, 182: Europe, Japan, Australia, US, Canada.

§5. OWNERSHIP AND TRANSFER

I. Initial Ownership

647. The law grants the entitlement to the rights on semiconductor chips to the 'original producer', that is, the person or legal entity which developed the structure at his own costs and risks (Article 3(1) Topographies Law).

648. Employees' rights are not mentioned. As for the software,[786] in the absence of a contractual provision to the contrary, no compensation is due to the employee other than his or her wages.[787]

II. Transfer

649. The transfer of rights is possible, and they can be inherited (Article 4 Topographies Law).

§6. SCOPE OF EXCLUSIVE RIGHTS

650. The producer has the exclusive right to copy the semiconductor structure with whatever means and on whatever material, as well as the exclusive right to offer to the public, sell, lease, distribute or import the chips or copies thereof.

651. The first-sale doctrine applies. It is suggested that international exhaustion is applicable in this area as well; of course, for two years since marketing began, the protection exists irrespective of any registration, which is more akin to the Copyright Act than to the Patent Act. Economic interests are similar to those under the Patent Act, which used to provide for national exhaustion but now foresees international exhaustion with the exception of medicines and possibly other items that are subject to an official price control.[788] Further, while the law itself grants the right to import to the producer, the matter would not thereby appear to be settled since this right too is susceptible to be exhausted by a first use abroad.[789]

786. *See* para. 80.
787. There is some controversy for the original entitlement under Art. 17 Copyright Act, but there should not be for semiconductor chips: the employer is immediately entitled to the rights. *See* Message, FF 1989 III 557–558; von Werdt, 158.
788. *See* hereabove para. 286 with the exception of one court decision, reported in ZR 1998, 259 et seq.
789. *See* however G. Lück, *Halbleiter-Topographieschutz* (Protection of Topographies of SemiConductor Products), *in* SIWR II/2, 368, who does not seem to assess the full impact of the exclusive 'right to import' on the first-sale doctrine. One could argue, of course, that the TRIPS do recognize a right to import for patents on inventions, and still do not purport to regulate the international *v.* national exhaustion issue (*see* TRIPS' fn 6). Therefore, the right to import could, in theory, be exhausted by the first sale abroad with the consent of the patent owner.

§7. LIMITATIONS OF THE SCOPE OF PROTECTION

652. In any event, the first-sale doctrine is less important in that area, due to the rule that Article 8 Topographies Law lays down: It is lawful to put again onto the market semiconductor chips that have been bought in good faith, even if they embody wrongful copies of registered structures. However, the producer is entitled to a fair remuneration.

653. There is a legal exception for the reverse engineering done in research and teaching (Article 7(1) Topographies Law). The commentary is to the effect that reverses engineering in order to professionally derive profits from research and teaching would be excluded.[790] According to our view, the legislature did not wish to limit lawful 'research' to public-owned or public-operated research facilities but extended that exception to all research activities, the end result of which may very well be to put onto the market a new, improved semiconductor chip. Besides, the legal text expressly provides for the right to use new structures that are not commonplace.[791]

§8. DURATION OF PROTECTION

654. As has been noted, the protection without registration lasts two years, and the registration extends to ten years from the first distribution. There appears to be no exception for the distribution taking place under a 'black-box' agreement, that is, under a confidentiality clause that would prevent the recipient from proceeding with reverse engineering.[792]

655. In any event, the duration of the protection may not exceed fifteen years from the creation of the structure.

656. All years are reckoned from 31 December of the year in which the event happened.[793]

790. Lück, *Halbleiter-Topographieschutz* (Protection of Topographies of SemiConductor Products), *in* SIWR II/2, 368.
791. Art. 7(2) Topographies Law; according to N. von Werdt, 139, such a provision only makes sense to the extent that it refers to the patent legislation – which is for him the sole source of protection for the technical ideas, the building of the structures. However, there would be technically a wrongful act in the copying of structures for research and development if Art. 7(1) Topographies Law did not legitimize it.
792. *See*, however, Art. 4 European Directive on the Chip Protection, OJ No. L 24/36 of 27 Jan. 1987.
793. Art. 9(4) Topographies Law.

§9. INFRINGEMENT AND REMEDIES

I. Civil Remedies

657. Civil actions are those of the Copyright Act.[794]

II. Criminal Remedies

658. Upon complaint of the injured producer, imprisonment of up to one year or a fine under the general provisions of the Penal Code may be inflicted upon any person having intentionally and wrongfully used the structure or refused to indicate the providers of infringing goods.

659. For professional counterfeiting, the fine and imprisonment follow the general provisions of the Penal Code.[795]

660. Articles 75 through 77h of the Copyright Act are applicable to the seizure of goods at Customs.

794. Art. 10 Topographies Law referring to Arts 61 through 66 of the Copyright Act. *See* hereabove paras 177 et seq.
795. *See* hereabove para. 183.

Chapter 9. Trade Secrets and Confidential Information

§1. Sources of Legislation

I. Penal Law

A. Article 162 Penal Code

661. Article 162 Penal Code is the main provision in the area of the protection of trade secrets. It makes it a felony for someone to disclose a trade secret which he should keep confidential under a legal or contractual duty. It is a separate count to use such a disclosure to one's benefit or to the benefit of a third party. If convicted, the punishment will be imprisonment or a fine.

B. Article 161 Penal Code

662. Article 161 Penal Code makes insider dealings a felony for officers and managers of a corporation. The same punishment is foreseen, but to this writer's knowledge, there have been few convictions yet, after more than two decades since the entry into force on 1 July 1988, although several enquiries have been launched.[796]

C. Article 273 Penal Code

663. Under Article 273 Penal Code, it is a felony or a crime in serious cases to try and uncover a trade secret, and to make it accessible to official or private foreign organizations.

664. This provision was introduced before World War II in order to protect refugees from Nazi Germany against the spies who wanted to find out what the refugees owned in Switzerland.[797]

796. *See* generally, M. Giovanoli, *La répression des opérations d'initiés et l'évolution du droit du marché financier en Suisse* (Insider Trading Repression and Evolution of Financial Market's Law in Switzerland), in *La répression des opérations d'initiés* (Insider Trading Repression), CEDIDAC No. 15, at 11 et seq. (Lausanne, 1990).

797. *See* V. Hafter, *Wirtschaftsspionage und Wirtschaftsverrat* (Economic Spying and Economic Informing), in *Festgabe Fritz Fleiner* 203 (Zurich, 1937). This achievement of the Swiss legislature during the dark years of the Nazi regime has been contested of late without historical basis, as is shown by this 1937 study. *See* another contemporaneous study: E. Thilo, *Contre les espions, les mouchards et les agents provocateurs* (Against Spies, Informants and the Agents Provocateurs) (Lausanne, 1936). Art. 273 Penal Code enacts a formal notion of trade secret, *see* Fed. Trib. SIC 2017, 128 (a reporter cannot publish confidential parliamentary committee's draft report before its official disclosure to the public).

D. Article 47 Law on Banking Institutions

665. This article makes it a felony for an officer, employee, agent, liquidator or auditor of a bank, or for an observer of the Federal Bank Commission to disclose a secret confided to him or known to him through his function and for any third party to entice him to do so.[798] This is a rare case of a provision punishing also the disclosure that takes place after the official or employer-employee relationship has been severed.[799] Any third party who discloses or takes a financial advantage of a secret that has been entrusted to him can also be fined or jailed for three years. To the extent that newspapers would be making money out of revealing banking accounts of clients of Swiss banking institutions, such as in the Credit Suisse leak case of early 2022, the legal entities or persons responsible for that leak could also be punished. This should help prevent extortion, blackmailing or other wrongful use of the information on the clients' accounts.

The punishment is imprisonment for up to five years or a fine, limited to up to CHF 250,000 in case of negligence rather than intent. For the time being, Switzerland does not know in this area of an exception in favour of the whistle-blower, such as in the case of UBS in France or the Credit Suisse leak in February 2022.

E. Articles 4(c) and 23 Unfair Competition Law

666. Article 4(c) Unfair Competition Law makes it a civil tort and Article 23 Unfair Competition Law a felony to entice workers, agents or ancillary persons to disclose or to uncover trade secrets of their employer or principal. Punishment is imprisonment or a fine.

F. Articles 6 and 23 Unfair Competition Law

667. Article 6 Unfair Competition Law makes it a civil tort and Article 23 Unfair Competition Law a felony for someone to use or to disclose trade secrets that he uncovered or otherwise got to know in a wrongful manner. Punishment is imprisonment or a fine.

668. It has been decided that the Act against Unfair Competition is a special legislation, which regulates the entire area in which trade secrets are enticed away for

---

798. Law of 8 Nov. 1934 as amended from time to time, lastly in 2009, 2015 and 2018 (RS 952.0) (*see also* RS 956.1 Ch. 15 of the Appendix).

799. *See* Fed. Trib., 6B_247/2019 c. 2.2; M. Aubert, *Le secret bancaire* (The Banking Secrecy) 4 (2d ed., Geneva, 1997). In 6B_247/2019 the Fed. Trib. found that a lawyer filing with a court a document with names of clients in order to assist his own client in his defence will violate Art. 47 Banking Law as soon as the filing of this document, or the entire document, is not to be deemed *necessary.* In judgment 6B_45/2021of 27 Apr. 2022 the Fed. Trib. affirmed a lower court decision sentencing a bank employee under Art. 273 (and 305bis regarding money laundering) Penal Code for having collected data pertaining to bank clients and sold them to German tax authorities, then put the payment of the German authorities in foreign accounts.

competitive purposes, with the effect that the provisions of the Swiss Penal Code, most notably Article 162 Penal Code, would not be applicable.[800] In our view, this is not true as regards Article 273 Penal Code, which is a specific provision protecting the interests of the Swiss industry against spying, *inter alia,* on behalf of their foreign competitors.[801]

There may be other provisions protecting trade secrets as entrusted to professionals, such as Article 321 Penal Code or to the Administration.[802] Further, Article 143 and 143*bis* Swiss Penal Code punish those who misappropriate data in electronic files and intrude into an electronic retrieval system.

II. Civil Law

A. Articles 4(c) and 6 Unfair Competition Act

669. Those provisions make it a tort to misappropriate trade secrets.

B. Article 2 Unfair Competition Law

670. If the precise wording of the specific Unfair Competition Law provisions is not met, it is possible to apply the general provision of Article 2 Unfair Competition Law to the disclosure of trade secrets entrusted, for example, during the course of contracting works.[803]

C. Article 38 of the Former Federal Civil Procedure Law

671. Under this provision, the Federal Tribunal might hold a trial about a trade secret *on camera.*[804] [805] The Federal Code of Civil Procedure of 2008, entered into

---

800. *See* Appel. Ct Lucerne *in* RSJ 1965, 66; Dist Ct Zurich, SIC 2006, 112, 115. *See also* Fed. Trib., SIC 1999, 300 (in order for this provision to apply, the work product must have been 'entrusted' to the respondent); Fed. Trib., SIC 2007, 462 (notion of 'entrusted work product').

801. *See* Bindschedler, *Der Strafrechtliche Schutz wirtschaftlichen Geheimnisse* (The Penal Protection of Trade Secrets), thesis, 66–67 (Zurich, 1981).

802. Art. 27 of the Law on the Officials' Regulation (RS 172.221.10). Fed. Trib. SIC 2016, 607 c. 5.2.1 mentions different provisions protecting trade secrets, such as Art. 25 (4) of the Law against Anti-competitive Practices. Fed. Trib. SIC 2016, 671 notes that the name of experts consulting with a view to authorize the marketing of medications is not a protected secret. In ATF 147 II 137 the Fed. Trib. found that the name of an expert working for the selection of projects of scientific research to be supported by public funding is not a secret deserving of protection *in casu.*

803. *See* ATF 88 II 319; Fed. Trib. *in* SJ 1962, 55; Com. Ct St-Gall *in* RSPIDA 1983, 137.

804. Law of 4 Dec. 1947 on the Federal Civil Procedure (RS 273). This provision was applicable to international arbitration in Switzerland according at least to this writer. *See* F. Dessemontet, *Arbitrage et confidentialité* (Arbitration and Confidentiality), in Le droit en action (Law in Action) 61 (Lausanne, 1996) (Faculté de droit de l'Université de Lausanne).

805. *See* ATF 79 I 84; ATF 90 II 467; ATF 92 I 185; ATF 95 I 103 and 439; ATF 100 Ia 97, esp. 103; Appel. Ct Zurich *in* RSJ 1985, 269. In the same sense, based on Art. 77 (3) LBI, *see* now Fed. Pat.

force on 1 January 2011, provides in Article 156 that the court may issue orders aiming at the protection of justified interests of the parties during the instruction on the proofs.

672. This provision has been repeated in many laws dealing with sensitive information during the course of civil or administrative proceedings, for example, Article 15 Unfair Competition Law, Article 16 Law on Cartels of 6 October 1995,[806] Article 40 of the Law on Plant Varieties, etc.[807]

§2. Protection

I. Definition of Trade Secrets

673. Switzerland being party to the TRIPS Agreement, Article 39 TRIPS on the protection of trade secrets and confidential information is binding for Swiss courts, so that any statutory definition under one of the aforementioned pieces of legislation should be read in the light of Article 39 TRIPS. Now, even if the heading of section 7 TRIPS is 'Protection of Undisclosed Information', it is this writer's assumption that *trade secrets* are what is really protected under Article 39 TRIPS.[808] Article 39 TRIPS reunites the US definition of trade secrets and the European concepts of unfair competition and honest commercial practices. Nevertheless, the subject matter of protection under the TRIPS and the Swiss statutory law is substantially the same. In order to get legal protection,[809] a piece of technical or commercial information must be objectively secret; its owner must keep it as proprietary information, and it shall evidence some economic value.

A. Objective Secrecy

674. The *secrecy* is the status of information which is not readily accessible to the persons who normally deal with this category of information. It is not absolute

---

Trib., S2012_007: a respondent may be barred to have access to the precise technical description of an invention, but not its Counsel nor its Patent Attorney (status usually summed up as *Confidential: Counsel's Eyes Only* (available at www.patentgericht.ch/fr/). For trade secrets under the Code of Civil Procedure applicable in all courts see e.g., Art. 166.2 CPC. Art. 26 of the Law on Administrative Procedure applies when infringing wares are seized at the Swiss borders, *see* Fed. Adm. Trib. SIC 2017, 749.

806. RS 251.

807. *See* Cant. Ct Neuchâtel *in* RSPIDA 1975, 115; for the protection of a source code of software, *see* Cant. Ct Nidwalden *in* RSPI 1989, 271.

808. *See* F. Dessemontet, *Protection of Undisclosed Information*, in *Intellectual Property and International Trade, the TRIPS Agreement* 337 et seq. (C.M. Correa & A.A. Yusuf eds.), (3d edn., 2016).

809. In order to benefit from a contractual protection, confidential information must fall within the ambit of the contractual definitions that may be broader or narrower. *See* F. Dessemontet, *Les accords de confidentialité* (Confidentiality Agreements), in *Mélanges Pierre Engel* esp. 34. (Lausanne, 1989).

secrecy in the meaning that only one person or legal entity in the world would partake of it.[810] However, the market is the master: if another producer puts onto the market a similar product which embodies the same technology, there is no longer a trade secret when the competitors are so put in the position to know the manufacturing secret.[811] To define what is readily accessible, it is not compulsory to remain within the Swiss boundaries. A court has observed that technical information published in official registers in Germany can no longer be a secret in the German part of Switzerland.[812]

675. Of course, if a licensee, a supplier[813] or employees[814] partake of the knowledge, there may still be enough secrecy to warrant the legal protection, as long as they are placed under a duty not to disclose it.

676. Swiss commentary[815] is also to the effect that secrecy is both objective and relative.

677. Of course, the novelty of patentable inventions is of no relevance for trade secrets that are not protected by a monopoly.[816]

B. Reasonable Steps

678. The Swiss Courts require that the owner of trade secrets takes positive steps to prevent their misappropriation. The requirement is less the efficiency of these measures, that were obviously unable to prevent the litigation before the court, but rather the intent to keep the information secret.[817] Those steps can be of a commercial nature – for example, a letter to a contractor[818] – or of a technical nature, for example, restricting the visits to production facilities.[819] A court will note when no measures have been taken.[820] In our view, this could be envisioned as a relinquishment of any and all claims on the formerly proprietary information.

---

810. *See* ATF 64 II 162, esp. 170–171; ATF 117 II 480, 482. For the protection of trade secrets in the case of public tenders, *see* Fed. Trib., 2G_890/2008 of 22 Apr. 2009.
811. *See* ATF 93 II 272 and JdT 1952 I 200 (not published in this regard in ATF 77 II 263). Addresses of suppliers are not secret (*see* Com. Ct St-Gall *in* RSPIDA 1983, 137). However, customers are among the trade secrets of a business, as well as price calculations, sources of products and possibilities of sale. *See* Fed. Trib., 6B_179/2016, c. 1.4; Appel. Ct Zurich *in* RSPI 1989, 139; more restrictive, Appel. Ct Liechtenstein *in* RSPI 1982, 217.
812. Com. Ct Zurich *in* RSPIDA 1982, 228.
813. Appel. Ct Basel-Countryside *in* RSPIDA 1981, 155. For an example of confidentiality agreement and the jurisdictional issue relating to it *see* Fed. Trib. SIC 2018, 162.
814. ATF 60 II 467 esp. 471–472; ATF 35 II 631 esp. 642.
815. *See* Fed. Trib. SIC 2018, 419 (protection requires an '*objective interest to protection; only asserting an interest is not sufficient*'); O. Weniger, 146–147 with cit.; F. Dessemontet, Le savoir-faire *(Know-how)*, SIWR IV, 2006, 829–840.
816. ATF 77 II 263, esp. 269.
817. ATF 64 II 162, 170; ATF 77 II 263, esp. 270; ATF 142 II 268 ('intent to keep secrecy').
818. ATF 80 IV 22.
819. Com. Ct Zurich *in* ZR 1971, 157, esp. 161 et seq.
820. ATF 88 II 319.

C. Economic Value

679. There would be no risk of litigation if the trade secrets at issue were not of some economic value. It is, however, interesting to note that the TRIPS require the economic value of the information. It is the proof that the trade secret pertains to the business sphere of the owner, that it is an asset in trade. It is also the indication of an idea put forward some thirty-five years ago, according to which *scarcity* in the economic meaning of the word is really what the law requires when speaking of secrecy.[821]

In Switzerland, the requirement of value does not appear to play an important role. It just helps define the subject matter of secrets that deserve to be protected.[822]

II. Protection

680. There are two areas in which the protection of trade secrets is of utmost importance: the protection against eavesdropping or other unlawful methods of collecting information, and the protection against misuse of information by former employees.

A. Unfair Methods of Acquisition

681. The reverse engineering has been judged not to be an unfair method of lifting the cloak of secrecy that surrounds a technical secret.[823] However, it is unlawful for the new employer to use a trade secret that his employee acquired in his former employment and disclosed in spite of a covenant not to compete.[824]

682. As all claims under intellectual property laws, trade secret claims are subject to the defence of estoppel by conduct, if the trade secret owner did not act swiftly enough to protect his rights and so let the other party build a valuable investment.[825]

---

821. *See* F. Dessemontet, *The Legal Protection of Know-how in the United States of America, Geneva/ South Hackensack*, 189–191 (NJ, 1976); M. Schneider, *Schutz des Unternehmensgeheimnisses vor unbefügter Verwertung* (Protection of Business Secrets against Unauthorized Use), Thesis (St-Gall, 1989). The Fed. Trib. expressly recognized that know-how or goodwill, that are usually untransferable and cannot be attached, still have a value as asset of a company that goes bankrupt; *see* C. de Salis, commenting the Nespresso case in www.lawinside.ch/1099/.

822. *See* ATF 103 IV 283 (are trade secrets 'informations that may affect the profits of a business'); ATF 109 Ib 47, esp. 56; ATF 118 Ib 547.

823. Appel. Ct Basle-Countryside *in* RSPIDA 1981, 155.

824. *See* Appel. Ct Zurich *in* RSPI 1989, 139. *See also* Sup. Ct Aargau, SIC 2007, 458 (case of an employee returning to the workshop to extract secrets after the termination of the employment contract); Ct. Just. Geneva, SIC 2018, 89 (no violation of Art; 5(b) UCA *in casu*).

825. Appel. Ct Zurich *in* RSPI 1989, 139, esp. 143. In a litigation concerning patents for invention the trade secret owner must require from the court the necessary measures of protection under Art. 68 Patent Act and comparable provisions of the Federal Civil Procedure Act of 2008 (Art. 156) or special legislations on unfair competition etc.; *see*, e.g., Fed. Pat. Trib., SIC 2013, 772–773.

683. A company which has been formed by the former employee to work the trade secrets may be considered to have acquired the trade secrets in a wrongful manner.[826]

B. Use by a Third Party

1. General Rule

684. Unlike the other rights of intellectual property,[827] a trade secret is not protected against all third parties. On the contrary, the general rule is that absent a justified criminal indictment, a trade secret may be put to use by everyone but the persons who are under a specific obligation not to use it, such as employees or agents, because of their general obligation of faithfulness to the employer[828] or principal, or because of Article 321a (4) Code of Obligations protecting trade secrets vis-à-vis the employees during the relationship of employment and after its termination.

2. Exceptions

685. Nevertheless, a third party deriving his knowledge of the trade secrets from a licensee may be under an obligation to neither use nor disclose the trade secrets in some cases.

686. Together with a licence under a patent for invention or without such a patent, a licensee can receive the right to use a certain confidential technology, or a contractor can receive communication of necessary technical information.

Any use outside the scope of the contract can be a breach of the agreement. Equally, the use after termination can be considered, in many cases, as wrongful.[829] There are two exceptions at least:

(1) if the know-how is no longer secret at the time of the termination of the contract, it can be used by the licensee without royalties,[830] at least where the termination is not due mainly to the licensee's negligence;[831]

---

826. Fed. Trib. *in* RSPI 1985, 108; ATF 88 II 319.
827. Save in an exceptional case for the rights of authors of parallel works under Copyright Law; *see* hereabove, e.g., para. 59 (copyright).
828. *See* para. 244.
829. *See* F. Dessemontet, *Le contrat de savoir-faire en droit suisse* (The Know-how Contract in Swiss Law), in *LES /SSIC, Contrat de know-how, journée d'information* (The Know-how Contract, Information Day) 1 et seq. (Genève, 1981); ATF 77 II 263 (case of a contractor).
830. ATF 93 II 272, esp. 279–280.
831. ATF 88 II 319 (if the secret falls into the public domain due to the licensee's negligence, then he cannot argue that it belongs to the public domain).

(2) if the know-how that had been originally transferred to the licensee has been substantially improved or modified by the licensee in view of his own industrial background and experimentation, there is probably no action for specific performance preventing the licensee further from putting such technological package to use; nevertheless, royalties, possibly at a diminished rate, may then be due to the former licensor for the continued use of the part of the technology which was his – and which is still deemed to be confidential.[832]

C. Wrongful Disclosure by an Employee

687. The competitor who knowingly[833] uses trade secrets that were disclosed to him by an employee of the owner may be held liable for misappropriation. Under Penal Law, it is not necessary that the main perpetrator be punished in order for the accomplice to be punished. Under Civil Law, it has been judged that even where the employee was not under a duty of confidentiality, the competitor benefiting from the employee's disclosure of confidential information is liable under the general provision of the Act against Unfair Competition.[834]

688. Under Article 6 of the present Unfair Competition Law, differing from the former law of 1943, some authors hold the view that any knowledge which is 'unduly' obtained (i.e., disclosure of which is tainted by spying, wrongful inducement to disclose, breach of contractual duties, etc.) must not be put to use by the recipient, even if he himself is unaware of the faulty disclosure.[835] Some doubts have been voiced against that opinion because the legislature, so goes the argument,[836] would not have wished to change the legal rule while slightly changing its wording. In our view, the increasing recognition of trade secrets as proprietary data, especially under Article 39 TRIPS and recent EU and US legislative enactments, have a direct bearing on that question: if it is proprietary data, then all third parties may be assumed to know that that information cannot circulate without someone having violated his duty of confidentiality. In other words, there is a *constructive notice* valid against all third parties for technical and commercial sensitive information, and the third party has the burden to enquire whether the disclosure has been really lawful before putting that information to use.

689. The conclusive remark of that chapter on trade secrets is, therefore, that intellectual property is now encompassing a new area, confidential information, in

832. *See per analogiam* Art. 36 Patent Law on the so-called Dependent Invention, commented upon in F. Dessemontet, *La notion d'invention dépendante en droit des brevets* (The Notion of Dependant Invention in Patent Law), in *Mélanges Piotet* 231 et seq. (Lausanne, 1990).
833. *See* Message for the new Unfair Competition Law, Art. 5(b), FF 1983 II 1037, esp. 1103; Fed. Trib., SIC 2020, 382, c. 3.3.
834. *See* Appel. Ct Zurich and Fed. Trib. *in* ZR 1958, 25.
835. *See* A. Troller, 959–960; G. Galli, *Die Bedeutung der Absicht bei Wettbewerbsvertössen und der Verletzung von Immaterialgüterrechten* (The Import of Intent by Breach of Competition Rules and Infringement of Intellectual Property Rights) 59 (Basle and Francfort-on-the Main, 1991).
836. O. Weniger, 211–212.

which legal research was for decades rather less active in comparison with other fields of intellectual property. The trade secrets law was earlier based on fiduciary relationships and breach of confidentiality: it was contractual in essence. Now it will be more and more based on the misappropriation theory and honest trade practices under Article 10*bis* Paris Convention. The misappropriation theory aptly encompasses trade secrets as assets of the business, property interests. Hence, trade secrets develop into an independent category of their own.

The move away from a personal or contractual understanding of the intangible values that regulate social and economic life towards a mercantile conception of every innovation, every song, every performance, every mark being owned by a private entity thus proves to be incoercible, even if it is deplored by those who would like information to be freely flowing at no charge throughout the society.

Selected Bibliography

§1. INTELLECTUAL PROPERTY IN GENERAL.

Cherpillod, I. Propriété intellectuelle, Bâle, 2021.

David, L. & R. von Büren (eds). 'Grundlagen' (Basis). In *Schweizerisches Immaterialgüter- und Wettbewerbsrecht* (SIWR) (*Swiss Intellectual Property and Competition Law*), vol. I/1. 3nd edn. Basle and Francfort-on-the-Main, 2011 (cited: SIWR I/1).

David, L. & R. von Büren (eds). 'Rechtsschutz' (Legal Proceedings). In *Schweizerisches Immaterialgüter- und Wettbewerbsrecht* (SIWR), vol. I/2. 2nd edn. Basle and Francfort-on-the-Main, 1998 (cited: SIWR I/2); 2d ed. By David *et al.*, 2011.

Dessemontet, F. *La Propriété Intellectuelle et les Contrats de Licence* (Intellectual Property and Licensing Agreements), 2nd edn. Lausanne, 2011.

Kasser, A., M. Novier & R. Schlosser. *Propriété Intellectuelle: Recueil de Textes Nationaux et Internationaux* (Intellectual Property: Collection of National Laws and International Conventions), 2nd edn. Zurich, 2009.

Marbach E., Ducrey P. & Wild G. *Immaterialgüter- und Wettbewerbsrecht* (Intellectual Property and Competition Law), 4th edn. Berne, 2017.

Steiger, M., A. Gerszt & N. Birkhäuser (eds). *Immaterialgüterrecht, Textausgabe* (Intellectual Property, Text Edition), Basle, 2009.

Fl. Thouvenin, M. Bircher & R. Fischer. *Immaterialgüterrecht* (Intellectual Property), 3rd edn. Zurich, 2016.

Troller, A. *Immaterialgüterrecht* (Intellectual Property), 2 vol. 3rd edn. Basle and Francfort-on-the-Main, 1983/1985 (cited: A. Troller).

Troller, A. *Précis du droit de la propriété immatérielle* (Summary of Intellectual Property), Basle and Stuttgart, 1978.

Troller, K. *Manuel du droit suisse des biens immatériels* (Handbook of Swiss Immaterial Goods' Law), 2 vol. 2nd edn. Basle and Francfort-on-the-Main, 1996 (cited: K. Troller).

Troller, K. *Précis du droit Suisse des biens immatériels*, 2ème éd. (Summary of Intellectual Property). Bâle, Genève, Munich, 2006 (cited K. Troller).

§2. COPYRIGHT ACT

Barrelet, D. & W. Egloff. *Le nouveau droit d'auteur* (The New Copyright Law), 4rd edn. Berne, 2020 (by W. Egloff) (cited: Barrelet & Egloff).

Cherpillod, I. *L'objet du droit d'auteur* (The Subject of Copyright Law), CEDIDAC No. 1. Lausanne, 1985.

Cherpillod, I. *Le droit d'auteur en Suisse* (Copyright Law in Switzerland), *Précis et guide pratique*. CEDIDAC No. 3. Lausanne, 1986.

Cherpillod, I., et al. *La nouvelle loi fédérale sur le droit d'auteur et les droits voisins* (The New Federal Law on Copyright and Neighbouring Rights), CEDIDAC No. 26. Lausanne, 1994.

David, L. & R. von Büren (eds). 'Urheberrecht und verwandte Schutzrechte' (Copyright Law, Neighbouring Rights). In *Schweizerisches Immaterialgüter- und Wettbewerbsrecht* (SIWR), vol. II/1. 3nd edn. Basle and Francfort-on-the-Main, 2014 (cited: SIWR II/1).

David, L. & R. von Büren (eds). 'Urheberrecht im EDV-Bereich' (Copyright in Electronic Data Processing). In *Schweizerisches Immaterialgüter- und Wettbewerbsrecht* (SIWR), vol. II/2. Basle, Geneva and Munich, 1998 (cited: SIWR II/2).

Dessemontet, F. *Le droit d'auteur* (Copyright Law), CEDIDAC No. 39. Lausanne, 1999.

Dessemontet, F. 'Switzerland'. In *International Encyclopaedia of Copyright Law and Practice* (P. Geller ed.), Newark/San Francisco, Annual Suppl.

Hilty, R. *Urheberrecht*, 2d ed., Berne, 2020.

Kummer, M. *Das Urheberrechtlich Schützbare Werk* (Protectable Work by Copyright), Berne, 1968.

Müller, B.K. & R. Oertli (eds). *Urheberrechtsgesetz* (Copyright Act), 2nd edn. Berne, 2012.

Rehbinder, M. *Schweizerisches Urheberrecht* (Swiss Copyright Law), 2nd edn. Berne, 1996.

Rehbinder, M. & R. Grossenbacher. *Schweizerisches Urhebervertragsrecht* (Swiss Copyright's Contract Law), Berne, 1979.

Rehbinder, M. & A. Vigano. *Urheberrechtgesetz. Kommentar* (Copyright and Neighboring Rights), 3rd edn. Zurich, 2008.

Rouvinez, J. La licence des droits de la personnalité, Étude de droit privé suisse (The Licensing of Personality Rights, Study of Swiss Law), Ph.D. thesis Lausanne, Geneva, 2011.

Schweizer, M. *Recht am Wort /Right to Words*, Berne, 2011.

§3. PATENT ACT

Betschinger, Ch., P. Münch & Th. Geiser (eds). *Schweizerisches und europäisches Patentrecht* (Swiss and European Patent Act), Geneva, Basle, Munich, 2002.

Blum, R. & M.M. Pedrazzini. *Das schweizerische Patentrecht* (Swiss Patent Act), vol. 3. 2nd edn. Berne, 1975 (cited: Blum/Pedrazzini).

Calame Th., Hess-Blumer A., Stieger W. (eds). *Patentgerichtgesetz* (Law on the Patent Court), Basle, 2013.

David, L. & R. von Büren (eds). 'Erfindungsschutz' (Patentrecht, Sortenschutz, Schutz des Know-how) (Protection of inventions (Patent Act, Species' Protection, Protection of Know-how)). In *Schweizerisches Immaterialgüter- und Wettbewerbsrecht* (SIWR), vol. IV. 2nd edn. Basle and Francfort-on-the-Main, 2006 (cited: SIWR IV).

Dessemontet, F. (ed.). *Biotechnology and Patent Act*. CEDIDAC No. 31. Lausanne, 1996.

Gillard, N., et al. *Brevets d'invention: quarante ans de jurisprudence fédérale* (Inventions' Patents: 40 years of Federal case law). CEDIDAC No. 32. Lausanne, 1996.

Modiano, G. *Le contrat de licence de brevet* (Licence and Patent Agreement). Thesis. Geneva, 1979.

Pedrazzini, M.M. *Europäisches und Schweizerisches Patent- und Patentprozessrecht* (European and Swiss Patent Substantive and Procedural Law), 3rd edn. Berne 2008 (with Hilti) (cited: Pedrazzini).

Schweizer, M. & Zech, H.Patentgezetz, Berne, 2019, 1288 p.

§4. TRADEMARK ACT

Aschmann, Bundi, Meissen, Schmidt & Simon. *Herkunsftangaben und andere geographische Bezeichnungen* (Indications of origin and other geographic denominations), Basle 2019.

David, L. & R. von Büren (eds). *'Kennzeichenrecht' (Markenrecht, Firmenrecht, Herkunftsbezeichnung)* (Trademark Law (Trademark Act, Trade names Law, Indication of origin)). In *Schweizerisches Immaterialgüter- und Wettbewerbsrecht* (SIWR), vol. III. 2nd edn. Basle and Francfort-on-the-Main, 2009 (cited: SIWR III); 3rd ed. by E. Marbach, 2017.

David, L. & Frick, M. (eds) *Markenschutzgesetz, Muster und Modellgesetz* (Trademark and Designs and Models Law), 3rd edn. Basle, Geneva and Munich, 2017 (cited: David).

Gilliéron, Ph. *Les divers régimes de protection des signes distinctifs et leurs rapports avec le droit des marques* (The Protection of Distinctive Signs and their Relationship with Trademark Law), PhD Thesis. Lausanne, 2000.

Marchetto, F. (ed.). *La nouvelle loi fédérale sur la protection des marques* (The New Federal Trademark Act). CEDIDAC No. 27. Lausanne, 1994.

Noth, M., G. Bühler & F. Thouvenin, *Markenschutzgesetz* (Trademark Law). 2nd ed. Berne, 2017.

Streuli-Youssef, M. & Aschmann, D. Herkunfstangaben und andere geografische Bezeichnungen, SIWR III/1, Basle, 3rd ed. 2019.

Streuli-Youssef, M., Firmenrecht und Schutz nicht registrierter Kennzeichen, SIWR III/2, 3rd ed. Basle 2019.

Willi, Ch. *Markenschutzgesetz, Systematische Darstellung und Kommentierung* (Law on the Protection of Trademarks, Commentary). Zurich, 2002.

§5. INDUSTRIAL DESIGNS

David, L. *Markenschutzgesetz, Muster und Modellgesetz* (Trademark and Designs and Models Law), 2nd edn. Basle and Francfort-on-the-Main, 1999 (cited: David).

Staub, R. & A.L. Celli (eds). *Designrecht: Kommentar zum Bundesgesetz über den Schutz von Design* (Commentary on the Law for the Protection of Design), Basle, 2003.

Wang, M. 'Designrecht' (Design Law). In *Schweizerisches Immaterialgüter- und Wettbewerbsrecht* (Swiss Intellectual Property Law), edited by Von Büren & David. vol. VI. Basle, 2007.

§6. Plant Variety Protection

Flury-Jeker, A.M. *La protection juridique des obtentions végétales sous le régime de la Convention de Paris du 2 décembre 1961 et de la loi fédérale du 20 mars 1975* (The Legal Protection of Plant Variety under the scope of the Paris Convention of 2 December 1961 and the Federal Law of 20 March 1975), Delémont, 1987.

§7. Chip Protection

von Werdt, N. *Ausgewählte Probleme zum Topographienschutz von mikroelektronischen Halbleitererzeugnissen* (Selected Problems of Chip Protection for Micro-Electronic SemiConductor products), Thesis. Berne, Zurich, 1991 (cited: von Werdt).

Lück, G. 'Halbleiter-Topographieschutz' (Chip Protection). In *Schweizerisches Immaterialgüter- und Wettbewerbsrecht* (SIWR), vol. II/2. Basle and Francfort-on-the-Main, 1995 (cited: SIWR II/2).

§8. Trade Secrets

Dessemontet, F. *Le savoir-faire* (Know-how), in L. David & R. von Büren (eds.) *Erfindungsschutz (Patentrecht, Sortenschutz, Schutz des Know-how)* (Protection of inventions [Patent Act, Species' Protection, Protection of Know-how]), *in Schweizerisches Immaterialgüter- und Wettbewerbsrecht* (SIWR), vol. IV, Basle and Francfort-on-the-Main, 2nd edn. 2006 (cited: SIWR IV), 805–864.

Dessemontet, F. Protection of Undisclosed Information, in Intellectual Property and International Trade: The TRIPS Agreement (C. Correa & A. Yussuf eds., 3rd edn, 2016), 337–358.

Schlosser, R. *Le contrat de savoir-faire* (know-how Licences), Thesis. Lausanne, 1996.

Weniger, O. *La protection des secrets économiques et du savoir-faire (Know-how)* (Trade Secrets' and Know-how's Protection), Thesis. Lausanne, 1994 (cited: Weniger).

Index

The numbers here refer to paragraph numbers.

Index

Index

www.ingramcontent.com/pod-product-compliance
Lightning Source LLC
LaVergne TN
LVHW011126300926
849160LV00008B/524